Network Maintenance and Troubleshooting Guide

First Edition

**A Fluke Networks Press Publication
by Neal Allen
Fluke Networks Division**

Fluke Networks, Inc.
P.O. Box 9090
Everett, WA 98206-9090 USA

Fluke Networks Press, an imprint of Pearson PTR.

Fifth Printing

ISBN 1-58713-800-X

Printed in the United States of America

Permission to reproduce selected portions of this
book may be granted upon written request to:

Fluke Networks, Inc.
Legal Department
P.O. Box 9090
Everett, WA 98206-9090 USA

Fluke Networks, Inc., asserts that the information in this book is complete and accurate to the best of its knowledge, information, and belief. Every reasonable effort has been made to confirm the accuracy and reliability of the information and methods described in this book. Fluke Networks, Inc., does not, however, warrant that the same results will be obtained in every test performed and makes no warranty of any kind, expressed or implied, with regard to the documentation contained in this book. Fluke Networks, Inc., shall not be liable in any event for incidental or consequential damages in connection with, or arising out of, the furnishing, performance, or use
of the procedures outlined in this book.

All product names mentioned in this document are trademarks of their respective manufacturers. While Fluke has made a reasonable effort to identify trademarks and trademark owners, we may have missed some, and our failure to identify them is unintentional. Those that we have indentified are as follows: ARCNET is a trademark of Datapoint Corporation; AppleTalk, LocalTalk, EtherTalk and TokenTalk are trademarks of Apple Corporation; LattisNet is a trademark of Bay Networks; IBM® and NetBIOS® are registered trademarks of International Business Machines Corporation; NetWare® is a registered trademark of Novell,® Inc.; Microsoft,® Excel and Windows® are trademarks of Microsoft Corporation; StarLAN-10 is a trademark of AT&T; VINES® is a registered trademark of Banyan;® OpenView is a trademark of Hewlett-Packard Corporation, Inc.; SunNet Manager is a trademark of Sun Microsystems, Inc.; Spectrum is a registered trademark of Cabletron Systems, Inc.; LANMeter,® HealthScan and OneTouch are trademarks of Fluke Networks, Inc.,. All other product names mentioned are the trademarks of their repective owners.

Technical contributors: Frank Actis, Dave Fish, Henreicus Koeman, Dennis Lambert, Mark Mullins, David Skingley, Paul Stone and the Interop tradeshow NOC team (thanks for regularly scheduling network emergencies)
Project Manager: Jan Masonholder
Editor: Joan Good
Other contributors: Ruth McKnight, Tom Noe, David Hyman
Designer: Diane Chaudiere
Illustrator: Bill Shane
Page Layout: Dea Monette
Production Manager: Doug Tracy

FLUKE.

Overview

Preface

Today's rapidly changing technology offers increasingly complex challenges to the network administrator, MIS director and others who are responsible for the overall health of the network. This Network Maintenance and Troubleshooting Guide is intended to pick up where other network manuals and texts leave off. It addresses the areas of how to anticipate and prevent problems, how to solve problems, how to operate a healthy network and how to troubleshoot. The guide is written as a reference for use by professionals as well as an introduction for those who are learning about network operation.

The OSI 7-Layer Model

This guide, and most other things related to networking, are best understood when compared with the Open Systems Interconnect (OSI) the 7-Layer basic reference model. (See Figure V-1.) This model was originally created by the International Organization for Standardization (ISO) as the framework for a network protocol, but the actual protocol was not widely adopted. It has since become the single common reference point used when discussing network protocols, features, and hardware.

To aid in understanding various concepts and relationships within this guide, the following charts are offered. As much information as possible has been condensed into these two charts in order to provide a visual reference. As you read through this guide, refer back to these charts as often as necessary.

As shown in Figure V-2, the cable tester and handheld network analyzer categories offer the best value for each dollar spent since they solve the most common network problems. The handheld network analyzer category, including the LANMeter test tool, is optimized for solving OSI Layer 1 through 3 problems, and requires little training. Using a protocol analyzer or network management system requires considerable training, and is optimized for solving OSI Layer 2 and higher problems.

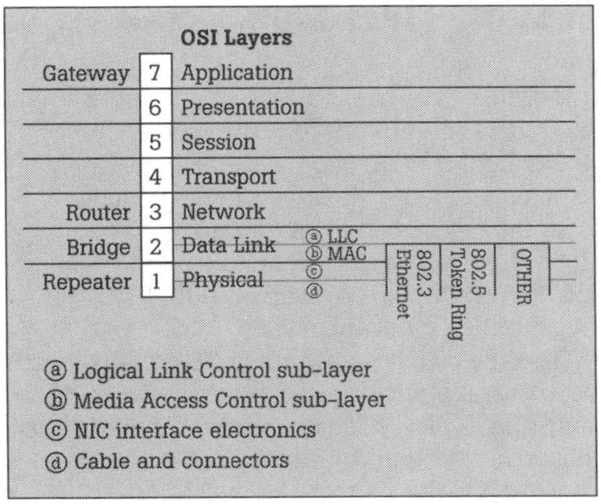

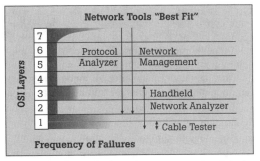

Figure V-1. *OSI 7-Layer model compared to various interconnect device functions and to several media access protocols.*

Figure V-2. *Chart of where the common network tools fit "best" in the OSI 7-Layer model, and a graph showing where the majority of network problems occur.*

How to Use This Book

Terms

Throughout most of this text, the words *workstation, station, node,* etc., have generally the same meaning, which is simply an active electronic device connecting to the network segment. An active device could be a PC, printer, modem, workstation, file server, hub, MAU, bridge, router, gateway, etc.

The only pseudo-convention that differs from this is that any device attaching to the network using TCP/IP protocols is generally referred to as a *host*. Thus, within Appendix D, all active devices connecting to the network are called *hosts*.

Organization

The text is organized into three basic chapters: how to avoid problems (Chapter 1), how to solve problems (Chapter 2), and how to form a network maintenance strategy (Chapter 3). The appendices that follow Chapter 3 are intended as both references for the network professional and as a primer for the network novice.

Thus, the suggested order for reading this text depends on your knowledge and skill level.

- If you are in panic mode, go directly to Chapter 2.

- If you are designing a new network, start with Chapter 1 and the appropriate appendix.

- If you are new to networking, start with Appendix B.

- If you need to form a network maintenance strategy, go to Chapter 3.

Author's note: While considerable research and verification have been invested in this guide, the author is the first to acknowledge Guidelines 2 and 3 on page VII. Therefore, he would appreciate your comments, changes and corrections to errors or omissions by fax at 425-356-5116 or by electronic mail at fluke-info@tc.fluke.com. For each correction or suggestion, please cite the appropriate paragraph in a published standard, RFC, or other official technical document that supports your statement and can be used to research the issue. Future editions will reflect updates and changes.

Guidelines for Safe Networking

The only constant is change

1. Because every network is different, there are almost no "straight answers." And, because networking itself is in a state of constant evolution, standards often change to reflect new technologies and approaches. Therefore, *virtually all* specific answers require a qualification to account for the inevitable exception.

Published does not mean accurate

2. Published material nearly always contains *at least* one technical error. It's always a good idea to verify everything from the source standard if possible, or multiple sources if not. These errors can often be traced back to errors in the author's reference material, or carelessly over-simplified statements.

Beware of "expert" advice

3. *Nobody* knows everything about networking. If someone makes that claim, or seems to be knowledgeable in *too many* areas, then listen with caution, and verify all facts from additional sources. It will be difficult to distinguish fact from opinion.

Guidelines for Productive Research

It's a good idea to develop consistency in your own research and notes right from the beginning. Be careful to group your studies and notes by protocol and topology when researching networking information. Similar concepts, acronyms, and terms are often used in different ways by different network system and product vendors as well as different authors. This is more likely to confuse than inform if terms are not identified by what they are related to, or clearly defined in context.

As an example, the acronym MAU is sometimes used to mean:

- **M**edium **A**ccess **U**nit—a 10BASE5 Ethernet transceiver attached between a thick coax cable and an AUI cable, that provides a physical interface between a CSMA/CD bus and a network device. A MAU is an OSI Layer 1 device.

- **M**ulti-Station **A**ccess **U**nit—a device used for allowing stations in an 802.5 Token Ring star topology to mechanically, electrically, and logically gain access to a network segment. A MAU can offer OSI Layer 1 and 2 services.

- Hub—a device used in many network star topologies (including 802.3 Ethernet, 802.5 Token Ring, ARCNET, FDDI, etc.) to allow stations to gain access to the local network segment. Other generic terms that could be substituted for hub include: concentrator, **MAU**, MSAU, multi-port repeater, multi-port bridge and switch. Depending on features, a hub can offer services from OSI Layers 1 to 3—including VLAN routing functions.

One-Minute Check-up for Ethernet

Even if you don't have the time to conduct a complete network audit you can get a quick indication of your network's condition using the Fluke LANMeter. Run the **Network Stats** test to look for warning signs of problems before they can impact network productivity. Here's how to interpret this display:

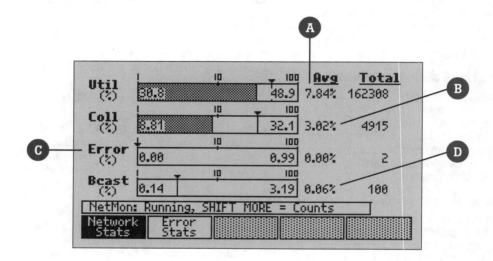

A. Utilization should average less than 40%.
Watch out for long bursts of traffic greater than 60%. If the average utilization rises above 40%, the network administrator/engineer should begin planning for expansion, such as installing switches or routers to isolate traffic.

B. Average collision counts should not exceed 5%. If average counts are consistently high, or if collision bursts can be traced back to when a specific station transmits, it usually indicates a physical layer problem or too many stations within the collision domain.

C. Errors (which include jabber, FCS, short frames, and late collisions) should never be present. If the detected number of errors is small, the problem does not constitute an emergency—but it should be investigated soon. A large number of errors typically indicates an impending disaster or a failed segment. Use the zoom function in **Error Stats** to help locate the problem station(s).

D. Excessive **broadcast** traffic adversely affects all stations on the network. Unless utilization levels are very low, investigate situations where average broadcast levels exceed 5-10% of the available bandwidth. (See section on Slow or Poor Performance on page 2-8.)

One-Minute Check-up for Token Ring

Even if you don't have the time to conduct a complete network audit you can get a quick indication of your network's condition using the Fluke LANMeter. Run the **Network Stats** test to look for warning signs of problems before they can impact network productivity. Here's how to interpret this display:

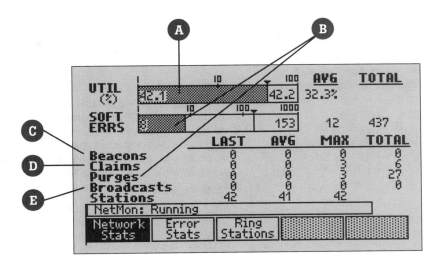

A. Utilization should average less than 60%.
Watch out for long bursts of traffic greater than 75%. If the average utilization rises above 60%, the network administrator/engineer should begin planning for expansion, such as splitting busy rings into two or more smaller rings, or installing switches, bridges or routers to isolate traffic.

B. Some **ring purges** and **soft errors** are normal during station insertion and deinsertion. If these errors occur when the ring is stable, they usually indicate a physical layer problem.

C. Beacons are the result of a hard error condition. The network can recover from some hard faults automatically. If the ring does not recover in 30 seconds, you must manually intervene.

D. Claim tokens are caused by a problem with, or change of, the *active monitor*, or a hard fault condition. Turning off the current active monitor will also result in claim tokening.

E. Excessive **broadcast** traffic adversely affects all stations on the network. Be suspicious of stations that send all-routes broadcasts. (See section on Slow or Poor Performance, Is it a software problem? on page 2-16.)

One-Minute Check-up for TCP/IP

Even if you don't have the time to conduct a complete network audit you can get a quick indication of your network's condition using the Fluke Enterprise LANMeter test tool. After running **IP Auto Configure**, run the **Segment Discovery** screen to look for warning signs of problems before they can impact network productivity. Be sure to allow the test to run for at least 20 seconds, because problem reporting is suppressed until the instrument has time to verify them. Here's how to interpret the display to the right:

Problems

There should be **NO** problems. The "Problems" category includes such errors as duplicate IP address, incorrect subnet mask, and DHCP configuration problems (supplied router address not found, etc.).

Routers

Review the list of devices acting as routers. It is quite easy to accidentally enable some workstations, servers, hubs, and switches to offer routing services. Improperly offering routing services can easily cause intermittent or interrupted network service. Also, check the offered routing protocols to ensure that only the desired protocols are in use.

Switches/bridges

Review the list of devices either detected as sending spanning tree protocol frames, or indicating via SNMP that they are configured (on some port—not necessarily the local port) to support Spanning Tree. Spanning Tree negotiated designated bridge reconfigurations tend to indicate path or machine problems, and will appear in the **Problems** category above.

Subnet info

For most networks there should be only one subnet found. Instances of using multiple subnets on a single segment are rare, and the support staff is always aware of where they should be found. Multiple subnets found usually indicates that there are unconfigured or misconfigured IP devices attached to the segment.

```
          Segment Discovery
 •Problems:          (11) Found
 •Routers:            (8) Found
 •Switches/Bridges:   (1) Found
 •Subnet Info:        (7) Found
 •IP Servers:         (2) Found
 •SNMP Agents:       (16) Found
 •Local Hosts:       (72) Found

 Inet: Elapsed 04:25:22, MENU Merges    SYM
   Run    |||||||    Address   |||||||    Zoom
  Again   |||||||     Mode     |||||||     In
```

IP servers

Review the list of devices offering DNS, BOOTP, or DHCP services. Verify that any offered DHCP configuration information is appropriate or desired. If key configuration parameters cannot be verified on the local segment, they will appear in the **Problems** category above.

SNMP agents

A list of devices that are responding to the currently configured SNMP community string, the *public* community string, or have been observed to be responding to SNMP. These devices may answer queries from the **Toolkit** test suite if you know the correct community string (password), and if security features permit the target to answer to your current IP address.

Local hosts

Review the list of devices attached to the local segment (this side of any routed connections). Look for misconfigured stations (IP addresses outside the expected subnet), too many stations for good performance, and stations that DNS is unable to resolve (either unknown new stations, or stations lacking DNS entries). After stopping the test, use the **MENU, Merge Stations** selection to create stored station lists of IP and MAC addresses bearing the DNS name. Also, use the **MENU, Print All** selection to create near-instant network documentation.

Chapter 1 — Preventing Problems

Develop a Reference Point with a Network Audit

Network administrators need to know what is normal behavior for their networks. Otherwise, they will be unaware of early tell-tale indicators and minor symptoms that warn of impending problems. The metaphor of a medical checkup for people is useful in understanding what is normal for a given network. Every person is different, yet there are certain norms that apply to healthy people in general. The same holds true for networks. The best way to become familiar with what normal operation looks like is to perform a complete and careful evaluation, or network audit. Once a reference point is established, results from regular monitoring of the network can be compared with that reference point to develop a trend analysis and alert you to any significant deviations.

In addition to day-to-day monitoring of network health during maintenance, a regular schedule of checkups should be instituted that repeats most or all of the tests in the network audit. Depending on network size and complexity, these regular checkups should be done weekly or monthly. By comparing the results with those from previous checkups and the complete audit, the network administrator can verify whether the day-to-day interpretations of test results are accurate.

Conduct a thorough audit before making any major change to the network—such as new hardware or software modifications—and at least a quick check following the change, though a complete repetition of all traffic monitoring tests is recommended. Without this pre-change audit, it is difficult (if not impossible) to interpret the meaning of test results obtained after the change. This could lead to improperly attributing performance problems to a change that had either a neutral or positive impact. Afterwards, the new results serve as a reference point against which subsequent checkups are measured.

Healthcare tip: Always audit before making changes to your network

Changes that should be monitored include:

- The addition of any new high-use software on the network.
- Structural changes, such as a new switch, bridge or router, or division of a large network segment into smaller segments.
- The addition or elimination of a new WAN pathway.
- Any moderate-to-large changes in the number of stations/users on the network.
- Changes in work shifts for users, such as moving one group to an early shift.
- Installation of a new server.
- The addition of a new protocol to the network.

This information will help guide you in exploring avenues of performance improvement, and help to quickly isolate the source of problems when they occur.

How to perform a network audit
An overview

This section explains the basics of how to perform a *network audit*. You will notice that many of the specific tests are found in what is often referred to as a network *baseline report*, but, for the network audit, the emphasis is different. A network audit covers more than just measurements of network usage and traffic patterns. Like a physical exam, it gives you a clear picture of where your network is today, and has the added advantage of establishing a framework and creating a methodology for isolating problems later.

The structure of an audit parallels the OSI 7-Layer model. By starting at the physical layer, you greatly improve the probability that a failing test result is accurate—and not just a symptom of a more basic problem.

Step 1. Document your network

- First, create a complete list of what hardware and software is in use, where each cable is routed and what numbering scheme is used to label it, as well as notes on any special non-standard wiring or configuration.

- Find out which manufacturer's NIC cards are being used and where each is installed. (Baseline Test.)

- For Ethernet, run **Top Senders** for a period of time on each segment to obtain a list of MAC addresses detected. For Token Ring, run the **Ring Stations** test on each ring to find the MAC address of each station, and what ring position each occupies. (Baseline Test.)

Step 2. Evaluate the physical layer infrastructure

- Measure cable lengths and compare results with IEEE 802 or TIA/EIA-568-A maximum-length limits for your topology.

- Count the number of stations installed on each segment and compare results with IEEE 802 maximum-station limits for your topology.

- Run **Network Stats** and **Error Stats** and look for errors that might suggest a media problem.

For Ethernet

- Stress-test each segment by transmitting high levels of traffic onto the segment (Traffic Generator) while at least one other station is moving a large amount of data (monitor **Error Stats** at the same time). (Baseline Test.)

- Run **Collision Analysis** or **Error Stats** to discover if ghosts (random energy, unformed data frames, and signal echoes) are reducing your available bandwidth by causing stations to believe the cable is already in use.

For Token Ring

- Use **Token Rotation Time** to calculate the effective cable length on each ring while all stations are active. (Baseline Test.)

- Monitor for intermittent beacon frames that might suggest a physical problem.

- Verify backup ring path operation.

- Run **Phase Jitter** to check the cumulative amount of uncorrelated jitter on each ring.

- Transmit high traffic levels with various jitter patterns (**Traffic Gen**) while monitoring for soft errors (**Error Stats**) to test for correlated jitter sensitivity on each ring.

Step 3. Evaluate data link layer health

- Run **Network Stats** and look at utilization percentage and frames per second. (Baseline Test.)

- Look for excessive broadcast traffic. (Baseline Test.)

- Run "top" tests (**Top Senders, Top Receivers, Top Broadcasters**). (Baseline Test.)

- Zero in on critical stations by setting the configuration filter address for the "top" tests to examine servers, bridges, routers and gateways, and watch for signs of trouble. (Baseline Test.)

- Check traffic patterns on the ring, comparing percentages of local and remote traffic. (Baseline Test.)

For Ethernet

- Run **Error Stats** and look for FCS errors, jabber, short frames and late collisions. (Baseline Test.)

For Token Ring

- Run **Error Stats** and look for congested receivers and frame copied errors. (Baseline Test.)

- Measure the **Token Rotation Time**, verifying that it is within the normal range. (Baseline Test.)

- Use **Station Ping** to learn the average response time to network resources from various points around the network. (Baseline Test.)

Healthcare tip:

A smart network administrator learns from his or her own mistakes. A wise one learns from the mistakes of others.

Step 4. Evaluate network layer health

- Run the appropriate "ping" test(s) (**ICMP Ping, NetWare Ping, NetBIOS Ping**) continuously to verify LAN and WAN connection paths, to learn average response times, and to ensure reliable connectivity to network resources. [Baseline Test]

- Run **Protocol Mix** to identify which protocols are present on your network, and which stations are sending how much of each protocol. This will also help identify servers and other stations that are supporting multiple protocols. [Baseline Test]

- Run **ICMP Monitor** and look for errors that indicate problems with the delivery and routing of IP traffic.

- On Novell networks, run **Packet Stats** and monitor for file server configuration and performance problems indicated by delay packets. Run **Routing Analysis** to check for abnormal or unusual amounts of routed traffic that indicates non-optimal paths between stations and network resources.

Prevent headaches by documenting your network

A well-documented network greatly simplifies troubleshooting. This is particularly important when applications running on the network are considered mission-critical or when a problem prevents numerous users from doing their jobs. Searching for unlabeled cables, missing software driver files, and vendor support telephone numbers consumes valuable time and patience during a crisis. A good way to determine the completeness and accuracy of your documentation is to ask the question, "Could someone else reconstruct or troubleshoot any portion of the network from just this set of notes?"

When sufficient care is taken during initial installation, future maintenance and troubleshooting jobs will be considerably easier. Documentation is most easily created during installation. However, it may be produced for an existing network. Assuming that cables are properly and carefully terminated, all cable runs avoid sources of electrical noise, and maximum segment lengths have not been exceeded, the next task is to prepare the documentation.

Documentation procedures

Suggested documentation and precautions include:

- Create a file server log.

  The log should include the following:

  A list of how the file server network software was configured, including any optional modules or special add-on software.

  A list of all cards installed in the file server, and how each was jumpered or configured.

  A list of all users, and a matrix showing their respective security and access privileges.

  A list of serial numbers and technical support phone numbers for all network components, cards and software vendors.

  A log of all configuration changes made to the file server.

  A log of all major problems encountered, including symptoms, and what was required to resolve those problems.

Next steps:

- Create a subdirectory on the file server—accessible by only the network administrator and support staff—that contains copies of all network adapter card driver files and other configuration files in use anywhere on the network.

- Create and store a set of duplicate diskettes that hold the boot image or configuration files for your intelligent hubs, switches, bridges and routers. It's a good idea to create a printed copy of the configuration too, although it will take longer to bring the network back online using the printed configuration.

- Label each individual piece of cable at both ends, especially if punchdown blocks or patch panels are used. Obtain a floor plan or blueprint and draw the route, location and name of each cable on each floor. For star topologies, especially note the location of all punchdown blocks and patch panels. For bus topologies, especially note the location of any cable junction or tap. For all topologies, take particular care to note the location of all repeaters, since their presence and locations are often forgotten. Users should be able to provide cable ID information to the network maintenance staff, so the ID must be clearly marked either on the cable or the wall jack in each office. (See Figure 1-1.)

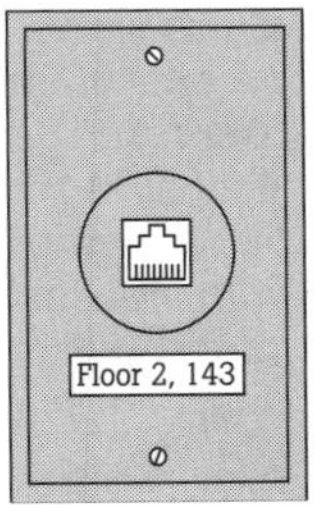

- If cables do not conform exactly to published standards, such as TIA/EIA-568-A or USOC, draw a diagram of the exact pin-out or wire-map for each cable type used. Drawing the correct wire connection order for punchdown blocks and patch panels is also highly recommended. For the "official" method of documenting a cable plant, see TIA/EIA-606. (See Figure 1-2.)

- Draw a functional block diagram showing how each major network component or segment is attached to, and functions with, the rest of the network (stations, repeaters, hubs, MAUs, bridges, routers, etc.). (See Figure 1-3.)

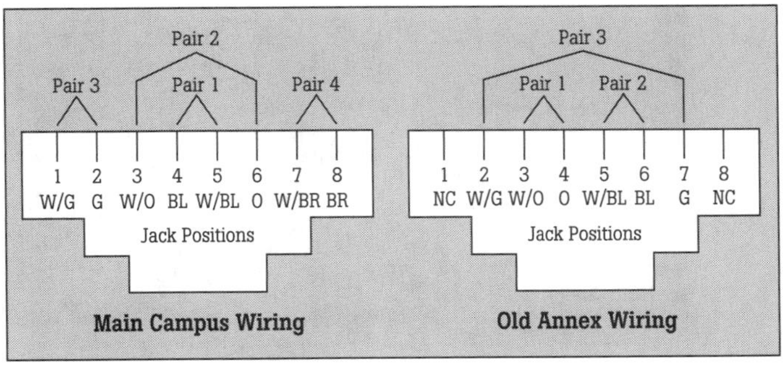

Figure 1-1. Wall jack labeling example.

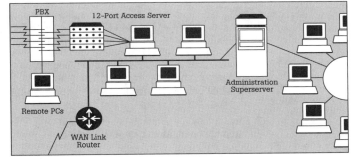

Figure 1-2. Example of pin-out documentation.

Station list

Like an insurance policy, a list of all stations on the network and the user associated with each station can be invaluable. By referencing such a station list, the network maintenance staff will be able to locate the source of problems indicated by errors much more quickly. And, for network administration purposes, this type of list will immediately highlight stations that have been moved without anyone notifying network management. As a less desirable but valid alternative, a nearly complete list of stations can be obtained by simply monitoring the network traffic for several hours and recording the source and destination MAC address listed in all traffic.

When compiling such a list, it's important to remember that the Ethernet protocol does not require a station to transmit, and the station can therefore join, monitor, and leave a segment without being detected by network monitoring tools. A physical inspection conducted at the time the list is compiled is recommended. If notes are made indicating which hub ports are inactive, future tests (such as the **NIC Test**) can be performed later when those ports become active.

Figure 1-3. Simple functional block diagram example.

For Token Ring networks, having the printed list appear in "ring order" will ensure much faster problem resolution because the list will allow the technician to quickly identify and bypass inactive stations by comparing the fault domain with the list.

Note: *Some monitoring tools do not abide by all of the Token Ring protocol rules, and will not identify themselves during the neighbor notification process. You will not know they are present and monitoring unless they transmit the required "trace tool present" frame.*

For Ethernet and Token Ring networks, the LANMeter test tool allows all of the station addresses detected over a measurement period to be added to the current station list in the instrument, or output as an ASCII list to a PC or printer. If a detected station has a symbolic name associated with its station address, the test results screen will automatically display the station by the symbolic name. This information can be used to assemble a complete list over time.

```
┌──────────────────────────────────────┐
│░░░░░░░░░░░░░░░░ Ring Stations ░░░░░░░░░│
│▶ Stations: 66  Average: 53  Maximum: 66  ◀░│
│  List: Complete      Time: Tue 14:33:32    │
│    1  400041413504 (AM)                    │
│    2  400041413301      LAKP3301           │
│    3  400041413112      LAKP3112           │
│    4 ! 400041413117     LAKP3117           │
│    5  0003e8a10090      ThisLANMeter        │
│    6  0000830b7079      Olicom0b7079        │
│    7  10005a43e5a9      IBM---43e5a9         │
│├────────────────────────────────────────┤│
│ NetMon: Running, SHIFT MORE = History     │
│┌────────┬────────┬────────┐              │
││Network │ Error  │ Ring   │              │
││Stats   │ Stats  │Stations│              │
│└────────┴────────┴────────┘              │
└──────────────────────────────────────┘
```

*Figure 1-4. Fluke LANMeter **Ring Stations** test results screen.*

 The LANMeter test tool provides a list of all active stations on a Token Ring segment. (See Figure 1–4.) The list is presented showing all active stations in physical ring order, beginning with the current active monitor. The test also keeps track of all stations that have performed the active monitor job since the test began.

Evaluate physical layer health

Results from tests at higher layers are meaningless if the network cabling or other physical layer equipment is faulty. This is a "micro" view of discrete parts of the network. A quick check of information available from the media access control (MAC layer) portion of the protocol stack can be very helpful for this purpose. Information available from the MAC layer is never seen by the average network user, but can be viewed by special software and/or monitoring tools.

Top error reporting stations

Every network will experience a certain number of errors. After one observes the behavior of a specific network for a period of time, the "normal" level of errors will become evident. Any sudden or intermittent rise in the number of errors should be viewed as a warning that a problem is developing on the network, and should be investigated. The second factor to consider is the ratio of error frames to normal data frames. If a particular station is identified as being involved in a disproportionate number of errors, then that station should be investigated for possible misconfiguration, malfunction or failure. One exception

to this would be if that station is generating a majority of the valid network traffic, and the ratio of errors to good traffic is similar to that of other stations. A third factor that should also be investigated is whether a specific station is associated with errors regularly. (See Appendix A for more information on Ethernet and Token Ring errors.)

Collisions

For Ethernet, the number of local and remote collisions (collisions occurring within the first 64 bytes of a frame) will depend on a relationship between the number of stations attempting to transmit at a given moment, the number of repeaters (including hubs) separating transmitting stations, and the size of the frames they are transmitting. Note that on an Ethernet segment, a reduced traffic level will conceal many problems that could be totally debilitating at higher traffic levels. Also note that certain types of problems may not be "visible" unless the measuring device is transmitting from the measurement point at the same time that monitoring is being performed.

Since some collisions are considered a normal part of Ethernet operation, a relative measure indicating what impact the collisions are having is more important than a simple collision count. Equally important is a measure of whether the energy measured on the cable is actually in the form of valid data frames, or if it is simply noise that is causing other stations to believe that valid frames are present when they are not. The term "ghost" will be used to describe this type of noise. Network bandwidth is reduced by an amount somewhat greater than the amount of ghosting that is present, because stations are required to wait a brief time after the cable becomes free (the interframe gap) before transmitting. Ghosts will not be observed as errors by NIC cards, because the signal appears to be a transmission from another station.

The **Collision Analysis** test relates bandwidth lost to collisions and ghosts to the amount of bandwidth in use. A direct correlation is therefore possible between consumption of available bandwidth and the amount of that consumed bandwidth that is lost to errors over the same time interval.

A normally operating Ethernet will lose less than 1% bandwidth to collisions (preferably less than 0.5%). The example network shown in Figure 1-5 is experiencing an average bandwidth loss of 7.76% (6.50 + 1.26), which is excessive. Unless there are a large number of stations frequently attempting to transmit at the same time, then the peak measurement of 64.2% collisions and current measurement of 23.5% suggest a probable cabling problem associated with one or two stations, or an Ethernet limit violation somewhere (such as too many repeaters).

Ghosting is never acceptable, and should always be viewed as a medium- to high-priority problem, depending on the quantity detected. In Figure 1-5, if any ghosting had been detected, it would indicate that an equivalent percentage of bandwidth was not available because the cable was already busy. The presence of ghosts causes stations to back-off the same way they would if another station were already transmitting. This type of error often indicates problems such as ground-loops, noise sources near the cable, or bad repeaters.

Ethernet errors

Errors other than collisions occurring within the first 64 bytes of a frame (such as Late Collisions, FCS errors, Jabber, Short Frames, etc.) should be considered an indicator that something is wrong, and should always be investigated. Unfortunately, despite the common bus structure of Ethernet, a simple check of the segment from a single connection point can be misleading. Certain types of physical layer problems that range from noise sources near a cable, to ground loops and cable installation errors, will exhibit different symptoms depending on where measurements are made in relation to the fault. If an error is detected, be sure to check the problem from several locations on the segment—otherwise you could waste time looking for the wrong problem.

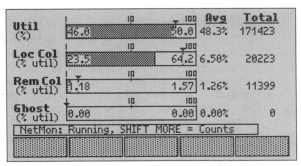

Figure 1-5. Fluke LANMeter **Collision Analysis** test results screen.

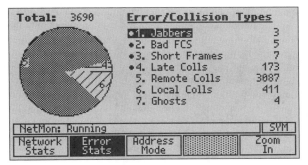

Figure 1-6. Fluke LANMeter **Error Stats** test results screen.

Use the **Error Stats** (Figure 1-6) test to discover the types of errors present on the segment and the rate that they are being reported, to gain an immediate feeling for how healthy the network is at that time. **Network Stats** and **Error Stats** automatically run concurrently so the network manager can switch between screen displays to determine which stations are involved in the errors detected, and relate those errors to the utilization at that moment. Optionally, the LANMeter test tool can be configured to simultaneously add traffic to the segment, including illegally long or short frames, at a specified number of frames-per-second. By stressing the network with extra traffic, problems that are hidden by automatic retransmissions and error recovery processes can be revealed.

Token Ring soft errors

For Token Ring, the number of "normal" soft errors depends on how often stations insert and deinsert. For example, a small number of errors such as Purge, Line and Burst Errors are expected when the network reconfigures because of station insertion and deinsertion. Congested Receiver errors are expected when a station is soft-booted, because the network adapter card is often still active on the ring, but the network drivers have not been reloaded.

In general, the presence of soft errors is not cause for immediate alarm. However, if the ring is stable (no insertions or deinsertions) then the presence of soft errors should be investigated to discover which stations are identified in the fault domain of those errors. A Token Ring network can operate at near 100% capacity without any errors (as long as no insertions or deinsertions occur) if the physical layer is well designed and carefully installed.

Use the **Error Stats** (Figure 1–7) test to discover the types of errors present on the ring and the rate that they are being reported, to gain an immediate feeling for how healthy the network is at that time. **Network Stats**, **Error Stats**, and **Ring Stations** are automatically run concurrently so the network manager can switch between screens to evaluate whether station insertions and deinsertions are responsible for the errors detected. If there is cause for concern, the network manager can display the reported errors by fault domain—reducing the scope of the problem to two stations and the cable path between them.

Optionally, the LANMeter test tool can be configured to simultaneously add traffic to the segment, at a specified number of frames-per-second and frame size.

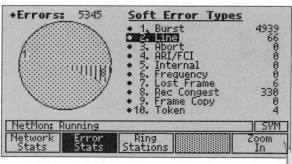

Figure 1-7.

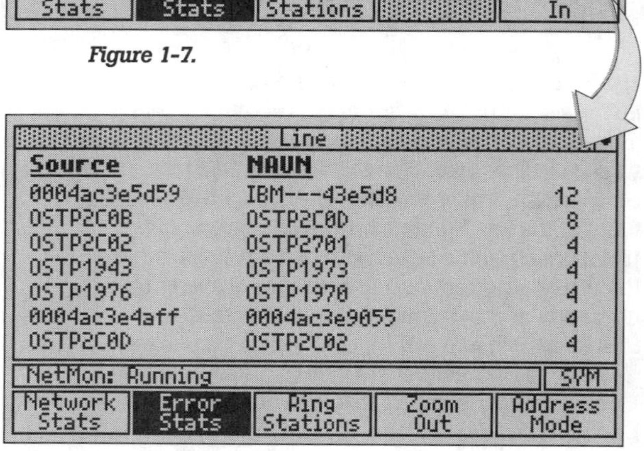

Figure 1-8.

Figure 1-7 and 1-8. Fluke LANMeter Token Ring **Error Stats** *test results screen (Figure 1-7) and "zoomed" line error results screen showing the fault domain for the greatest sources of line errors detected (Figure 1-8).*

Verify secondary ring path

If your network implements IBM Type 1 cables, it is very easy to determine whether or not the secondary ring path is operational.

Note: *This test should be performed during low network usage or non-critical times only.*

Simply insert the LANMeter test tool into the ring and monitor the **Network Stats** screen. While monitoring the network, remove the Ring-In (RI) or Ring-Out (RO) cable from one of the MAUs on the ring. If the ring does not begin sending beacon frames immediately and the number of active stations does not drop, then the secondary path is operational. If a beacon frame is detected, a pop-up window will be displayed, and the beacon LED on the front of the instrument will be illuminated. If you are already operating in the secondary ring path because of the way the ring was cabled or because of a pre-existing failure, then the number of stations shown on the **Network Stats** screen will drop within seven seconds after you disconnect the RI/RO cable. Try this test on a second RI/RO cable to ensure that the first cable was working properly too. If the secondary path test causes a ring failure, it is likely that one of the MAUs or RI/RO cables has failed.

If your network implements Type 3 cables, it is harder to test the secondary path. Type 3 cables use 8-pin modular (RJ-45) connectors, unlike Type 1 cables, which are made with self-shorting connectors. Also, if a failure occurs on a ring using Type 3 cables, it is likely that the ring will simply fail (beacon) and not switch to the secondary path.

To test the secondary path on a ring with Type 3 cables, build two RJ-45 connectors with the transmit and receive signal paths looped back into the same connector. Insert the tool into the ring and monitor the **Network Stats** screen. Then remove one RI/RO cable.

Note: *With some Type 3 MAUs the ring will enter a beaconing state while the RI/RO ports are disconnected. Do not be alarmed—as long as you are quick to replace the cable with the loopback connectors, the ring will recover from the beaconing state without a problem.*

Install the two loopback connectors where the cable had been. The beacon LED on the LANMeter test tool should stop reporting the presence of beacon frames immediately. If the ring resumes operation after the loopback connectors are installed *and* the number of active stations does not drop, then the secondary path is operational.

If you measure the token rotation time with the LANMeter test tool for either cable type, you will see an increase in the token rotation time while the ring is forced to use the secondary path—unless the ring is very small.

Phase jitter

Phase jitter is a symptom of problems with the synchronous data transfer technology implemented in Token Ring. Jitter refers to misalignment between the recovered clock and the incoming data stream. (See Figure 1-10.) Excessive jitter will cause improper sampling, which results in data errors and may be manifested as slow response time, dropped connections or inability to attach to a server. Stations may report an unusually high number of lost token, frame, and line soft errors.

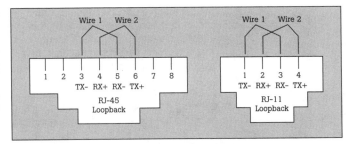

Figure 1-9. *Token Ring loopback connector pin-out for Type 3 cable systems.*

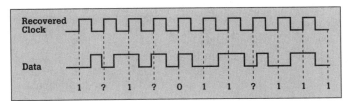

Figure 1-10. *Illustration of sampling misalignment due to signal jitter.*

The two types of phase jitter most frequently referenced are correlated and uncorrelated jitter. Correlated jitter is data-dependent (that is, the specific pattern of 1's and 0's causes the phase-locked loop (PLL) circuit to have trouble remaining synchronized), while uncorrelated jitter is the portion of the total jitter that is independent of the data pattern.

Because networks grow to include many different brands and design revisions of NIC cards, routers, and bridges, jitter problems tend to increase. Isolating the source is particularly difficult, both because there are few tools for measuring jitter and because the problem is very complicated. Often, the source of either jitter type can be isolated by monitoring the network for soft errors and then removing stations listed in the fault domain to see if the errors go away. For correlated jitter problems, transmitting a "worst-case" data pattern while monitoring for errors is usually necessary. To properly evaluate a *single* NIC card for either type of jitter requires a rack of lab-quality monitoring equipment, and is usually performed by networking equipment manufacturers only.

Never buy version 1.0 of any software. Wait for at least 1.1. Better yet, wait for 2.1.

A simple cumulative uncorrelated jitter measurement of an individual ring is made by the LANMeter test tool while transmitting frames of all 1's or all 0's. It displays an averaged cumulative jitter measurement, sampled late in the frame to allow the PLL circuit to stabilize. A low result indicates that there is relatively little cumulative jitter on the ring. And, a low result, along with no soft errors (while the topology is stable), generally indicates a solid network at the physical level.

There are some jitter removal techniques that will not affect this test. However, the presence of "jitter-busting" or other retiming circuits that reclock the data with their own crystal oscillator will distort the measured value. Media conversion (such as copper-to-fiber) will also retime the signal. Either case will cause the LANMeter test tool **Phase Jitter** test to be invalidated. However, the test results can still be used as an eliminating factor or an additional data point during troubleshooting.

To test for a correlated jitter problem, the LANMeter test tool offers several "worst-case" jitter patterns that may be sent with the traffic generator while simultaneously monitoring for soft errors. If an increase in soft errors can be related to when the traffic generator is running, then it is likely that the ring is susceptible to correlated jitter problems. Use the soft error fault domains to isolate the marginal NIC.

Healthcare tip:
If you don't have time to do it right the first time, when will you have time to do it later?

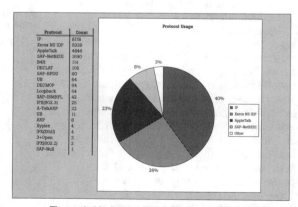

Figure 1-11. *Partial HealthScan results generated from LANMeter **Protocol Mix** test results.*

Evaluate data link layer health

After you have established confidence in the physical infrastructure, a more "macro" view of the network segment (taken as a whole) is appropriate.

Utilization

Utilization provides insight into the overall segment traffic and when usage peaks occur. Network utilization should not be confused with the utilization of any particular file server, though both numbers are good to know. In this case, utilization is a percentage of the total capacity, or bandwidth, of the network cable. There isn't really a "good" or "bad" amount of average utilization. You must first determine what is normal for your network, then decide if the network performance is acceptable at that level of utilization. However, sudden high utilization bursts can cause problems for Ethernet networks.

The LANMeter test tool provides a current, average and peak utilization measurement in the **Network Stats** screen, as well as an LED bar graph that constantly displays network utilization whenever the instrument is inserted into a segment, no matter what measurement is being made.

Traffic analysis

Traffic on a segment is categorized in several different ways. Traffic can be analyzed in terms of MAC layer versus higher-layer traffic. Ethernet MAC layer errors are detected, resolved and generally reported by each station to higher-layer protocols, while Token Ring MAC layer traffic is made up of media access management frames and error information describing problems within data frames and the physical layer. Higher-layer traffic is mostly actual data transfers.

Another way to categorize traffic is by protocol (IPX vs. SNA, for example). (See Figure 1-11.) Network operating systems, network management software, and protocol analyzers can provide some or all of this type of information, depending on their capabilities. Network operating systems usually offer statistics such as bytes sent and received by a particular server. In most cases, protocol analyzers will provide information about the distribution of different protocols within the total utilization. Network management software itself knows nothing about the network, but gathers information from custom hardware probes, other devices on the network (LAN or WAN), or both. The quantity and quality of information from network management software is limited only by the capabilities of the devices supplying information to it, and is usually easier to interpret than information from protocol analyzers.

Network support staff should have a general idea of how much traffic, which protocols, any "typical" types and amounts of errors, etc., are expected at different times of the day or week. This "normal" level of network activity is vital for providing a reference point against which any new measurements can be compared.

Each major network audit should monitor traffic patterns over several days to observe short-term, high-volume traffic periods that may occur first thing in the morning when all employees are getting started, or right after lunch. Because of software timers, scheduled late-night backups, and other regular maintenance activities, it is important to collect and analyze data for an entire week (24 hours per day, for seven consecutive days). This information also enables the network administrator to determine a down-time schedule for regular maintenance at times that will have the least impact. It also provides a baseline against which suspicious off-hour activity can be evaluated for security purposes.

The easiest format in which to present this information is in several graphs that represent the same time period, but in which different types of data are displayed on each graph. At a minimum, the graphs should include: network utilization, network errors, and protocols detected (shown by percentage of bandwidth used). With this information, various network management software programs can be configured for alarm levels. Support staff will quickly develop a feel for whether a spot check measurement is "normal" or not.

The LANMeter test tool can capture statistical data about utilization and errors for periods ranging from 24 minutes to five days. This data log file can be exported to a personal computer, and, with almost any spreadsheet program, the comma-separated variable (CSV) file can be used to produce graphs in a few minutes. The Fluke HealthScan application allows users to transfer and graph these CSV test results in Microsoft Excel with little more effort than three mouse clicks. (See Figure 1-12.)

Top senders/Top receivers

Network managers should know which specific stations are the greatest contributors to traffic on the network. This enables them to keep a close watch on the network resources that are relied upon most heavily, and identify the users who place the greatest demand on the network. This allows the network administrator to reconfigure network connections in order to isolate high-traffic users and resources onto sub-segments of the network, thus improving performance on the rest of the network. An example of this is where users of a Computer-Aided Design (CAD) program and the file server containing the application are connected to a local segment. Access to the rest of the network by the CAD users through a bridge or router would then prevent large local file transfers from affecting the performance of the rest of the network.

The network administrator also needs to know the number of frames and bytes transmitted on the segment to isolate applications that may be misconfigured. This information can indicate where to make changes to improve overall network performance and can identify individual stations where poor performance might be corrected by changing application or network driver

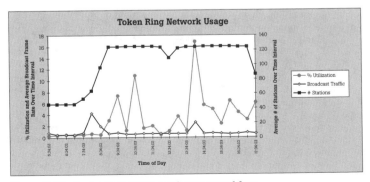

Figure 1-12. *Partial HealthScan results generated from LANMeter **Network Stats** test results.*

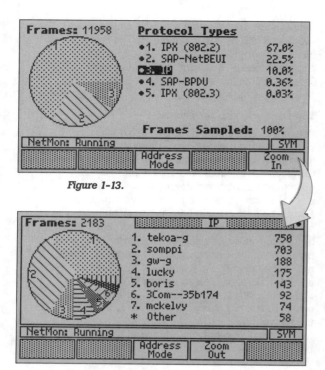

Figure 1-13.

Figure 1-14.

Figure 1-13 and 1-14. *Fluke LANMeter **Protocol Mix** test results screen (Figure 1-13) and "zoomed" detail screen on just the stations detected as sending TCP/IP traffic (Figure 1-14).*

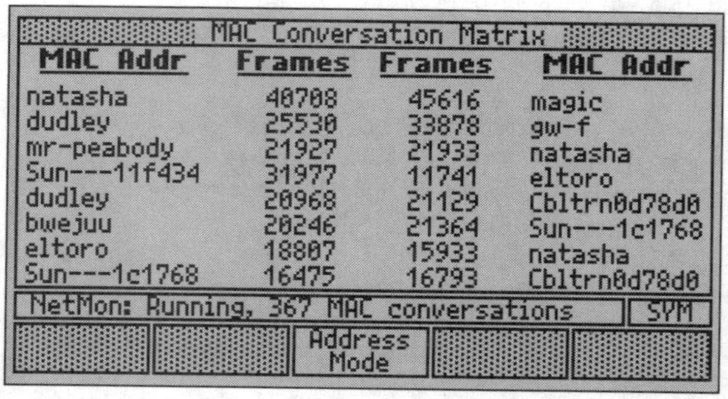

Figure 1-15. *Fluke LANMeter **MAC Matrix** test results screen.*

configurations. If maximum frame sizes on stations, bridges and routers do not match, then data may be lost. And, if they are set smaller than they could be, network throughput will be reduced.

The LANMeter test tool offers two ways to identify the heaviest users of network bandwidth. First, three tests run simultaneously and show a percentage-ranked list of top traffic source stations, top traffic destination stations, and top sources of broadcast traffic. The tool also has the ability to show a percentage-ranked list of top traffic source stations within each protocol detected. (See Figures 1-13 and 1-14.) Lists of stations from each of these screens can be output to a printer or PC, including percentage of traffic for each.

Top MAC pairs

A third and perhaps most useful way of monitoring MAC layer traffic is the ability to track the amount of traffic between any two stations. This will quickly identify the "power user," and significantly enhance the decision-making process for network improvements. When it is determined which users make the greatest demands on the network, and then identifying what applications they use, decisions about which segments or users should migrate to switch technology first, or which server should host a particular application are supported by observed demand. (See Figure 1-15.)

Slow response time

What can you do to determine the cause of slow response? The IEEE 802.2 Standard defines "XID Command PDU and Response PDU" frames (referred to here as a "ping"), for the logical link control (LLC) sublayer of the OSI data link layer. One simple test is to send this "ping" request to a network server or resource from the network connection that is experiencing difficulties. Besides ensuring that the connection is intact, a ping will report how long the addressed resource takes to reply. Nearly all Token Ring products respond to the special ping frame, while our experience indicates that Ethernet products usually don't respond to the ping frame—though the 802.2 response requirement applies to Ethernet as well (see 802.2 section 6.6). For both Token Ring and Ethernet networks, a protocol-specific

OSI network layer ping is almost always responded to. (See Network Layer response time testing later in this chapter.)

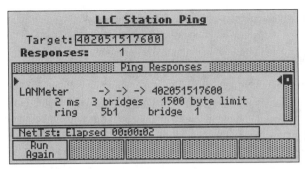

The response time is most adversely affected by the number of soft errors and utilization (of the local ring and any intermediate rings that the message must cross), the total number of intermediate hops that must be made, and how busy the destination station is. If the station being pinged is not on the local ring (when source routing is enabled), there will be delays caused by routing the message across additional rings to the destination resource and back. Each additional ring that the message crosses increments the number of "hops" by one. If the normal delay is known, later tests will aid the network maintenance staff in identifying where to look for the cause of "slow network" complaints by users.

Connectivity and response time can be checked with the LANMeter test tool using the **Station Ping** feature. (See Figure 1-16.) This command will solicit a response frame from any addressed station on the local ring, or on a remote ring of a source-routed network. To evaluate overall network performance and response times to critical network resources, try running this test during low and high network use times.

Token rotation time

Token rotation time, or the time required for the "token" to travel around the ring, can be affected by the total length of all cables, along with the number of active stations on the ring. Another influencing factor is the presence of fiber optic repeaters. Be alert for tests labeled "token rotation" that actually test token availability. Token availability is measurably influenced by the traffic load on the ring being tested, and is not suitable for the ARL calculations mentioned below.

The LANMeter test tool can measure average token rotation time, which should be no more than about 150 microseconds for good ring performance, though the standard permits a maximum of 2,000 microseconds. A description of how to calculate the Adjusted Ring Length (ARL) and Total Cable Length (TCL) based on the token rotation measurement is included in the Help text for the **Token Rotation** test.

Figure 1-16. Fluke LANMeter **Station Ping** test results screen.

Evaluate network layer health

Top senders/Top receivers

The need to know which specific stations are the greatest contributors of traffic at the network layer is very similar to that at the data link layer. The primary difference is that the stations so identified may be on the local segment, or on some distant segment—including places on the far side of a WAN connection. In these circumstances it becomes important to know which station is contributing traffic, and from where the traffic is coming.

The LANMeter test tool offers a set of two tests that run simultaneously, and shows a percentage-ranked list of top traffic source stations and top traffic destination stations within just the NetWare IPX, TCP/IP, VINES or NetBIOS traffic on the segment (depending on which protocol suite is used). For IPX, the display can be changed to show IPX stations by an associated symbolic name, IPX address (usually the same as the MAC address), or the IPX network number for that station. IP stations can be displayed by an associated symbolic name, or the "dotted-decimal" address. VINES stations are shown by the VINES IP address format, or by MAC address. The NetBIOS protocol is used by many network operating systems, such as Windows NT, Windows 95, Windows for Workgroups, IBM LAN Server, and OS/2. NetBIOS stations may be displayed by NetBIOS symbolic host name, by dotted-decimal IP address, or by MAC address, depending on

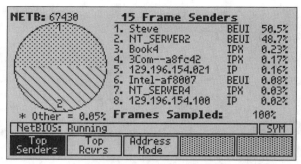

Figure 1-17. *Fluke LANMeter NetBIOS **Top Senders** test results screen.*

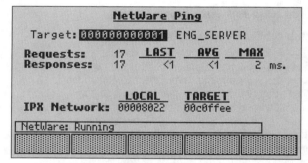

Figure 1-18. *Fluke LANMeter **NetWare Ping** test results screen.*

which network layer protocol is in use. (See Figure 1-17.) Lists of stations from these screens can be output to a printer or PC, including a count of frames transmitted by each station during the monitoring period.

Information from the **Protocol Mix** test can also be used similarly. (See Figure 1-12.) The Protocol Mix test can be "Zoomed" to show the top senders within virtually any protocol detected on the network segment, even new and potentially unknown or proprietary protocols. Protocol Mix is intended to give you as fine a resolution as possible on the protocol type. In descending order, it first attempts to show you the network operating system, then the protocol suite, and finally, the actual protocol code if nothing else is known. This is an extremely useful troubleshooting and management tool because it indicates what protocols are being used, and identifies the stations doing the most talking within each detected protocol.

Response time

It may be more important to test response time at the network layer than at the data link layer because network layer traffic is able to cross routers with ease, and cross WAN links and bridges transparently. As the path between stations becomes more complex, greater variations in the response time can be expected. Knowing the "normal" amount of time it takes to cross a specific path, or whether a specific path is still operational, is vital to network support staff. Without this information it is extremely difficult to locate the source of network slowdowns and failures.

Each network layer protocol will have some type of echo request and echo response frame available (also referred to as a "ping"). Two examples of using the ping function are provided, one for NetWare (Figure 1-18), and one for TCP/IP (Figure D-9).

For NetWare, the LANMeter test tool allows an IPX ping to be configured with the address, data link layer encapsulation (since NetWare permits multiple encapsulation types), and IPX network address. The default NetWare encapsulation changed between versions 3.11 and lower (802.3), and 3.12 and higher (802.2); trying different encapsulations can quickly reveal configuration problems. The test can also run in continuous mode, which will help isolate intermittent paths and interconnect devices by showing how often packets are dropped.

For TCP/IP, the LANMeter test tool allows an ICMP ping to be configured with the source and destination IP address, as well as the default router/gateway IP address. The test can also run in continuous mode, which will help isolate intermittent paths and interconnect devices by showing how often packets are dropped.

Depending on how a discovery packet is formed, it is possible to send a succession of frames out toward a specific destination. Each subsequent frame is permitted to get one hop closer to the destination station, and the response time for each frame is measured. By this means, often referred to as *traceroute* in TCP/IP, an exact listing of the routed path between two specific stations can be obtained. Failure of this process identifies the IP address of the router where the delivery of messages to the specified destination station fails. (See Figure 1-19.)

Routed traffic analysis

Unlike data link layer protocols (such as Ethernet), which only operate on a single segment at a time, network layer protocols include enough information in each frame to very clearly identify the logical source and destination network segment. In fact, the physical and data link layers are transparent to the network layer. The importance of this routing information relates to how efficiently data is moved between logical networks. The fewer routed connections a message must cross, the faster response time will be.

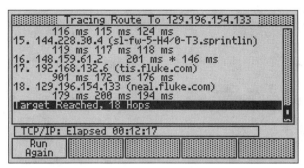

Figure 1-19. *Fluke LANMeter* **Trace Route** *test results screen.*

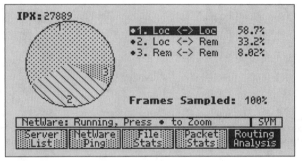

Figure 1-20. *Fluke LANMeter NetWare* **Routing Analysis** *test results screen.*

By examining routing information present in NetWare traffic, you can construct and display a view of how well load-balanced the NetWare traffic is on a given segment. The LANMeter test tool provides a list of the top senders within each of the three categories shown in Figure 1-20. Each entry in the "Zoomed" listing shows the source and destination address for a pair of stations, which may be displayed by symbolic name, IPX address, or IPX network number. When too much remote-to-remote traffic is present, providing a shorter alternate route will improve performance on the local segment by removing unnecessary traffic, as well as improving performance between the affected remote stations.

75% of a successful repair is "fixing" the user.

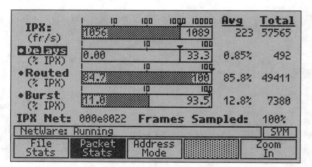

Figure 1-21. Fluke LANMeter **IP Matrix** test results screen.

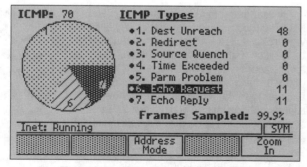

Figure 1-22. Fluke LANMeter NetWare **Packet Stats** test results screen.

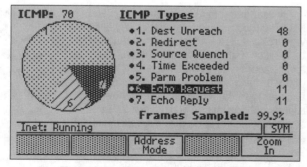

Figure 1-23. Fluke LANMeter TCP/IP **ICMP Monitor** test results screen.

TCP/IP address formatting offers its own method of determining whether or not an address is from another logical segment, and is thus passing through at least one routed connection. (See Figure 1-21.) By evaluating how much traffic is from the local subnet, and how much is from other subnets, it is relatively simple to determine whether moving one or more servers or users will improve performance. In many cases, it may be simpler or more practical to replicate a server or service on the local segment than to restructure connections. This is especially true if the high-use server or service is located across a WAN connection.

Network layer errors

Just as the network layer must provide *logical* station addressing services that duplicate the *physical* station addressing services provided by the data link layer, it must also provide for error handling and reporting. Each network layer protocol will issue, and respond to, a specific set of errors that control its operation. Many of these errors are related to proper delivery of messages between interconnected LANs and WANs—typically across routed connections, and to avoiding data loss because a receiving station is busy and unable to accept data at that moment. Two examples are shown below; for NetWare and for TCP/IP. (See Appendices D and E for more information on NetWare and TCP/IP errors.)

The LANMeter test tool has two tests for monitoring IPX error handling and frame delivery control traffic: **File Stats** and **Packet Stats**. Results from the two tests will help identify and isolate the sources of slow performance, and help quantify the general health of the Novell servers on your network. With these tests the tool monitors the IPX traffic for frame types that indicate an overloaded server, and for workstation traffic that indicates server loading. Monitored frame types include: burst mode traffic, delay frames, and routed traffic. (See Figure 1-22.)

The LANMeter test tool detects and displays ICMP error handling messages within the IP traffic. Results help to quickly identify and resolve problems related to misconfigured routers and hosts, and to identify congested devices. The IP address of the stations involved with each ICMP error is displayed by highlighting the desired category and "zooming." (See Figure 1-23.)

Chapter 2 — Solving Problems

Solving Problems

The basic troubleshooting sequence consists of five steps:

1. Collect all available information and analyze the symptoms of failure.
2. Localize the problem to within a single network segment, to a single complete functional unit or module, or to a single user.
3. Isolate the trouble to specific hardware or software within the unit, module, or user's network account.
4. Locate and correct the specific problem.
5. Verify that the problem has been resolved.

Theory and practical experience will determine which test to perform first. Consider experience with the same or similar equipment and related symptoms, as well as the probability of what is likely to fail or what suffers from repeated failures.

Never believe users...unless they confess. Verify everything yourself.

Can you eliminate several tests with a single test? A diagram of the parts of the network, as well as the signal flow paths between the various units, is enormously helpful in visualizing the problem and saving valuable time.

In general, it's best to subdivide or isolate a problem into a smaller functional section—removing the largest convenient section first (called the *divide-and-conquer* approach). Start at any convenient spot near the center point of the problem and divide the problem in half. Continue halving the problem until you've isolated it to the smallest possible section.

Don't assume that the user is providing complete and accurate information. It's best to verify it yourself, or have the user show you how the problem was discovered. In the confusion and stress that accompany a network failure, the little things are often overlooked.

Finally, if a component fails a second time, do not replace it until you have made absolutely certain that the source of the problem has been identified and corrected.

Troubleshooting Ethernet

When troubleshooting Ethernet, be careful to avoid spending time troubleshooting symptoms instead of the real problem. Many technicians have the tendency to assume that, because the theoretical model describes a specific error resulting from a specific problem, no other problem could cause that error. Marginal or failed equipment seldom obediently reads the appropriate standard. The technician then starts trying to solve the wrong problem.

Because of the common bus topology and potentially extended physical layout of Ethernet, a specific physical layer problem will often display different and conflicting symptoms, depending on where measurements are made, and depending on the conditions and location of the measurement.

Example 1

Two stations are located at opposite ends of an over-long thin coax segment (including repeaters). Assume that both stations begin transmitting at nearly the same instant and that collisions result. If measurements were made near the centerpoint between the stations, only normal local or remote collisions would be detected. But if measurements were made near the end of the cable, then late collisions would be detected.

Example 2

With 15 to 20 stations on several hundred feet of thin coax, a user rearranges his office, physically moving a station away from the BNC cable tap. To reconnect the station, a two-meter length of coax is attached from the station to the original BNC "tee" connector (the extra cable is called a "stub," see Figure 2-1).

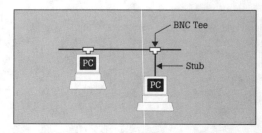

Figure 2-1. *Illegal coaxial cable system "stub" cable.*

Measurements taken on the cable when that station is not transmitting are likely to show no problems. But if the station is transmitting, the measurement is likely to show remote collisions or FCS errors. The theoretical model suggests that the measured signal in a collision fragment, where the voltage does not reach the collision detect threshold on coax, is indicative of a problem on the other side of a repeater. The technician is led to troubleshoot in the wrong area because the signal reflections generated by the stub are small enough that resulting problems appear to be from another segment.

Avoid misleading symptoms

If not identified, misleading symptoms can waste time and effort. To avoid them, take the following two steps whenever troubleshooting an Ethernet problem. First, make measurements from several locations along the segment. If the symptoms of the problem remain relatively constant regardless of where the measurement is made, then trouble-shoot according to what the detected problem suggests. If the symptoms are different at some or all of the locations along the segment where measurements are made, then direct your trouble-shooting toward a physical layer problem—no matter what the symptoms may suggest. Use the *divide-and-conquer* troubleshooting approach described in Appendix C. Look for bad cables, bad connections, failed or marginal hardware, noise sources, and ground loops. Check to see that station connections are properly fastened (BNC connectors rotated far enough to "latch," AUI slide latches are holding both connector posts firmly, etc.), that each individual piece of cable is of the correct characteristic impedance, that all cables are firmly crimped or clamped into the connectors, etc.

Second, to enhance the quality of measurements made, configure the measurement instrument to transmit a small amount of traffic from the measurement point while the measurement is being made. When using the LANMeter test tool to troubleshoot, the addition of 100 frames-per-second of 100-byte LLC frames to an unused MAC address is sufficient, and may be transmitted in the background while running **Network Stats, Error Stats** and **Collision Analysis**. Results obtained so far indicate that the quality of measurements made while traffic is being generated are enhanced by between 20% and 50% over a simple monitoring test. When traffic is added, many otherwise subtle and intermittent physical layer problems are revealed to the monitoring device. It is recommended that a low level of traffic be sent at all times when monitoring, even if network problems are not suspected.

Problem:
Cannot access server or service

The following procedures assume that this server or service has been operating properly prior to this problem, and you have already:

- Cold-booted the PC in question (a warm-boot does *not* reset all adapter cards).

- Verified that the PC does not have any hardware failures.

- Verified that all required network cables are present and properly connected.

- Verified that all required network adapter software driver files were loaded and that no errors were reported when they loaded.

- Verified that nothing has been changed on the PC, server or service recently that may have caused this problem, such as reconfiguring or adding software or hardware.

Determine whether the problem is isolated to this station (**local** problem) or if it affects many stations (**LAN** or **WAN** problem). Do this by attempting to log into the server or service from 1) other stations (and other user accounts) on the same segment or hub, and 2) from stations attached to other hubs or segments if the failure is present on additional stations attached to this hub or segment.

Is it a local problem?

Before troubleshooting the hardware, verify that other users are unable to log in from this station—thereby eliminating the possibility of problems with the user's account. Typically, problems limited to a single station are caused by a bad cable servicing the problem station, a bad NIC, bad software drivers, or improper configuration of the station.

Run the **Expert-T** test to determine whether the station is successfully accessing the network. In addition to voltage levels, the presence and polarity of link pulses, and which protocols are in use on the network and by the station being tested, the test will report any detected cable problems. During the protocol test, if IP or IPX traffic is detected the test will attempt multiple pings to ensure repeatable connectivity within those protocols. If the test fails a hub port, try another port.

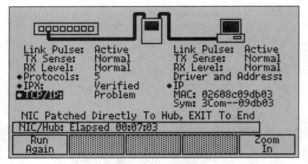

*Figure 2-2. Fluke LANMeter Ethernet **Expert-T** test results screen.*

If the Expert-T test passes both the network and the station, the problem is often related to the user's account. Try one of the ping tests described below in the WAN problem section; also try connecting somewhere else on the segment and pinging back to this station. If the ping fails in either direction, begin troubleshooting the software configuration there.

Is it a LAN problem?

Typically, if there is a physical problem on coax, the result is a catastrophic failure of the segment. This should be easily and quickly located, and the problem corrected using the *divide-and-conquer* troubleshooting approach. Intermittent problems, however, are more difficult to isolate.

First, check for connectivity. In most cases, the fastest method is to examine the status of LEDs found on most hubs, concentrators, transceivers, and recently even NIC cards. Be sure to check for link active indication on 10BASE-T hubs. The voltage levels and polarity of the link pulse can be verified for both the NIC and the Hub with the

Expert-T test. Next, check to ensure that all AUI cables are firmly seated, with the slide latch holding both posts properly. Many problems can be corrected by simply reseating cables that have become partially disconnected. As you perform your physical inspection, look for damaged cables, improper cable types (i.e., RG-62 or RG-59 cable on an Ethernet segment), and poorly crimped 8-pin modular plugs (RJ-45) and BNC connectors. If you can use a moderate amount of tension to pull the connector from the cable, then the cable should be reterminated—this is a particularly common problem on coax cables with BNC connectors. Suspect cables can be tested with the **Cable Scan** test, or a cable tester.

Run the **Network Stats** test to determine whether the network physical layer is currently experiencing high network utilization, excessive collisions, or unusual error conditions.

If the network utilization is not consistently high (above 60%), and the number of collisions is "normal," then you may have software configuration problems with the server or service.

If average collision counts seem excessive (over 5%), run the **Collision Analysis** test for more information. If the bandwidth lost to collisions averages greater than 0.5% (or you are seeing very high collision bursts), further testing is warranted. If possible, try to isolate the problem domain by breaking the segment into smaller pieces and using the LANMeter test tool to look for symptoms.

To track down collisions, it is necessary to have traffic on the network. Use the background traffic generator to add a small amount of traffic (100 frames-per-second, 100-byte frames) and observe the results with **Network Stats**. Some media-related problems are traffic-level dependent. Try varying the traffic level by using the cursor keys from the **Traffic Gen** screen and at the same time watching the ERROR and COLLISION LEDs. Be careful when doing this because you can easily saturate the network. Solving collision-related problems can be very tricky because the measurements are largely dependent upon the observation point. Results may vary between two observation points separated by only a few feet on the same cable. Make tests from multiple locations and watch for changes in the nature of the problem.

If collisions get worse in direct proportion to the level of traffic, if the amount of collisions approaches 100%, or if there is no good traffic at all, the cable system may have failed. For UTP, disconnect the cable from the hub and try a **Cable Scan** test. For coax try a DC continuity test. You should see about 25Ω if both terminators are present, or 50Ω if you are testing from an end. You could also go to one end of the coax, attach the LANMeter test tool in place of the terminator, and run the **Cable Scan** test (this test can be performed on a live coax segment if the *BNC termination* configuration is set to *on*).

If errors are present, run the **Error Stats** test and "Zoom" on problem categories to learn the MAC address of problem stations. Test these problem stations with the **Expert-T** test to isolate the specific failure. Try replacing the software driver files with fresh copies from the source diskettes or by downloading the latest drivers from the manufacturer's BBS or Web site, making certain to completely reconfigure them since the configuration may be the problem. Try replacing the suspect NIC.

If utilization is high (averages over 40%, or sustained peaks that are over 60%) then the segment may be saturated. Consider installing a switch, bridge or router to reduce the amount of traffic on the segment or to break the segment into smaller sections.

Is it a WAN problem?

If there are no significant errors detected by monitoring the physical layer, then attempt a continuous network layer ping (IP, IPX, NetBIOS, etc.) to the server or service that is not responding. Marginal or failed bridges and routers, and corrupted, incomplete, or bad bridge or router configurations are quickly located this way.

Run the **Server List** or **Novell Ping** test (if using Novell) to verify that the desired server or service can be reached from the current network connection point. If the server responds, restart the server from a cold-boot and watch to ensure that all required software driver files load without error. The LANMeter test tool will help identify configuration problems related to encapsulation. Novell versions 3.11 and below default to 802.3 encapsulation, while versions 3.12 and higher default to 802.2 encapsulation.

Also try running the Novell Ping test configured for *continuous*. Then ensure that the number of requests is equal to the number of responses. Discrepancies may indicate a marginal NIC or hub port, and that frames are being dropped. Marginal or failed switches, bridges and routers are quickly located this way.

Run the **File Stats** or **Packet Stats** test (if using Novell) and check for Delays coming from the desired server (highlight the *Delays* field and press the "Zoom" key). If these are present they indicate that the server is unable to keep up with the load, and some requests are being ignored.

Run the **ICMP Ping** test (if using TCP/IP) to verify that the desired host can be reached from the current network connection point. It is important to run this test at least twice, as some network devices improperly fail to reply to the *first* ping request. Verify that the default gateway address is configured correctly if the desired host is not on the local segment.

Also, try running the ICMP Ping test configured for *continuous*. Be sure to verify that the number of requests is equal to the number of responses. Discrepancies may indicate a marginal NIC or hub port, and that frames are being dropped. Marginal or failed bridges and routers are quickly located this way.

If repeaters are present on the local segment, if repeaters are connected to hubs, or if hubs are cascaded, check to see that *signal_quality_error* (SQE, sometimes known as "heartbeat") is set properly. SQE should never be enabled between repeater devices—including hubs. A repeater will misinterpret an SQE signal coming from another device, and improperly generate a collision jam signal. The worst-case symptom of this problem is a reported collision rate of exactly 50%. Usually, there is other traffic present and the percentage is reduced (diluted by the other good traffic). These events are not really collisions though, and the network will operate without apparent problem other than some slowness at high utilization levels.

Problem:
Connections that drop

The following procedures assume that this connection has been operating properly prior to this problem, and you have already:

- Cold-booted the PC in question (a warm-boot does not reset all network adapters).

- Verified that the PC does not have any hardware failures.

- Verified that all required network cables are present and properly connected, and fastened firmly.

- Verified that all required network adapter software driver files were loaded, and that no errors were reported when they loaded.

- Verified that nothing has been changed recently on the PC, server or service, or the problem station that may have caused this problem, such as reconfiguring or adding new software or hardware.

- Eliminated potential PC memory allocation problems on the station by loading only the minimum software required to operate a test application across the network. Be sure to unload "TSR" type programs.

Determine if the problem is isolated to this station (local problem), multiple stations on this segment (**LAN** problem), or if it affects stations connecting to servers or services across a router or WAN connection (**WAN** problem) by asking other users in the area if they have had similar problems.

The reason for dropped connections is a logical or physical connectivity loss. This will be manifested by difficulties getting through a switch, bridge, router or WAN connection, or by cable-related problems. Upper-layer protocols like NetWare implement "watchdog" timers that will disconnect a station's logical connection if the timer expires without having heard from that station recently. Thus, if packets are being dropped across a switch, bridge, router or WAN connection, it is possible to lose your connection to the server or service while still operating perfectly on the local segment. Also, if there are particularly bad problems on the local segment, it can cause problems that affect users in other parts of the WAN.

Is it a local problem?

Typically, lost connections on a local segment are related to high error levels, or a bad cable. At times of very high collision or error rates, some interconnect devices (repeaters, switches, bridges, and routers) may shut a port down briefly, then re-open it. This can result in dropped sessions. If the errors and collisions are not excessive, then it's not likely to be a media-related problem unless they can be correlated to when the problem station transmits.

Run the **Network Stats** test and check for high network utilization or abnormally high collisions. Run the test again with a moderate amount of background traffic enabled (100 frames per second, 100-byte frames is enough). If you notice the collision counts or errors increase at the same time that the tool transmits, then you should run **Cable Scan**.

If errors are present, run the **Error Stats** test and "zoom" on the error to learn the MAC address of the problem station(s), then use the **Expert-T** test to isolate the specific problem, or **Cable Scan** to check the cabling. Try replacing the suspect NIC if the problem is intermittent, since these problems may not show themselves when the test is run.

If the number of collisions is high (over 5%), then use the **Collision Analysis** test to determine how much bandwidth is actually being lost to collisions. Add the total average bandwidth that is being lost to local and remote collisions to see if the average is greater than 0.5%. Also check to see if collisions are "bursty," where a noticeable increase in collisions does not follow a similar increase in traffic. That is, if there is a large change in the number of collisions without a corresponding increase in the traffic level, then you have a serious problem in the physical layer somewhere—usually related to when one specific station transmits. Excessive collisions are most often caused by a problem with the physical media, such as missing or incorrect terminators, impedance discontinuities (bad connectors, cable "stubs," crushed cables, etc.), and marginal or failed network interface cards. There should be no ghosts at all. If there are any ghosts, use the *divide-and-conquer* method of troubleshooting described in Appendix C to isolate the source *before* troubleshooting other symptoms.

Run the **Expert-T** test to determine whether the station is successfully accessing the network. In addition to voltage levels, the presence and polarity of link pulses, and which protocols are in use on the network, and by the station being tested, the LANMeter test tool will report any detected cable problems. During the protocol test, if IP or IPX traffic is detected the tool will attempt multiple pings to ensure repeatable connectivity within those protocols. If the tool fails the hub port, try another port. (See Figure 2-2.)

Corrupted NIC card drivers and software, and interrupt conflicts within the station may cause the station to ignore or fail to respond to the watchdog timer pings. Use a continuous **NetWare Ping** or **ICMP Ping** to isolate whether the problem is occurring at the station (local), or the server or service (LAN or WAN). Reinstall and configure new driver files from source diskettes, or obtain a more recent version from the manufacturer of that NIC.

If repeaters are present on the local segment, if repeaters are connected to hubs, or if hubs are cascaded, check to see that SQE (sometimes known as "heartbeat") is set properly. SQE should never be enabled between repeater devices—including hubs. A repeater will misinterpret an SQE signal, and improperly generate a collision jam signal.

Is it a LAN problem?

Run the **Network Stats** test and check for high network utilization and abnormally high network errors.

If the network utilization is not consistently high (average above 40% or sustained peaks above 60%), and the number of errors is very small, then you may have software configuration problems with the server or service.

If the number of errors is high, use the **Error Stats** test to isolate the source of the fault. Use the **Expert-T** test to verify the station(s) reported by Error Stats. (Follow instructions for **local** and **LAN** problems starting on page 2-3.)

Run the **File Stats** or **Packet Stats** test (if using Novell) and check for Delays coming from the desired server (highlight the *Delays* field and press the "zoom" softkey). If these are present it indicates that the server is unable to keep up with the load, and a request was ignored for each Delay issued.

Is it a WAN problem?

Run the **Novell Ping** test (if using Novell) configured for *continuous*. Then ensure that the number of requests is equal to the number of responses. Discrepancies may indicate a marginal NIC or MAU port, switch, bridge or router, and frames are being dropped.

Run the **ICMP Ping** test (if using TCP/IP) configured for *continuous*. Ensure that the number of requests is equal to the number of responses. Discrepancies may indicate a marginal NIC or MAU port, switch, bridge or router, and frames are being dropped.

If the connection is made through a switch, bridge, router or WAN link, monitor response times while sending a continuous ping across the WAN connection, using **NetWare Ping** or **ICMP Ping** as appropriate. If a slowdown in response time is noted, check what else is happening with that WAN connection during the slowdown. Verify the configurations for time-out values and check the utilization of the intervening medium. Ensure that the number of requests is equal to the number of responses. Discrepancies indicate that frames are being dropped.

If TCP/IP frames are being dropped, try running **Trace Route** or **Path Discovery** several times to learn where along the path the problem is occurring. Use the SNMP **Toolkit** tests to check the problem router's interface for detected errors. Watch also for changes in the path that indicate intermittent WAN links that the routing protocols are trying to compensate for.

Use the LANMeter **Traffic Generator** to send IP or IPX traffic across the router or WAN connection and then monitor the distant LAN segment with another tool to ensure that the traffic is arriving at all, and that the expected amount of traffic is arriving. Also vary the frame size to ensure that there is no size-related problem.

Problem:
Slow or poor performance

When the network shows signs of slow or poor performance, first determine whether the problem is related to the network media, or if it's related to a particular station, server or service. Next, try accessing the same server or service from other nearby stations, and asking users on the same and other network segments to do likewise. If the problem is not **media**-related, determine if the problem is related to the **hardware** or **software**. Check the network utilization, bandwidth lost to collisions, and errors *while the network is performing poorly*.

Is it a media problem?

Run the **Network Stats** test and check for high network utilization and abnormally high collisions. Run the test again with a slight amount of background traffic enabled (100 LLC frames per second, 100-byte frames is sufficient). If you notice the collision counts or FCS errors increase at the same time that you transmit, then run **Cable Scan**.

If the average number of collisions is high (over 5%), then use the **Collision Analysis** test to determine how much bandwidth is actually being lost to collisions. Add the total average bandwidth that is being lost to local and remote collisions, and troubleshoot if the average is greater than 0.5%. Also check to see if collisions are "bursty," where a noticeable increase in collisions does not follow a similar increase in traffic. That is, if there is a large change in the number of collisions without a corresponding change in the overall traffic level, then you may have a serious problem in the physical layer somewhere. There should be a relationship between the traffic level and the collisions. If the collision count remains too large for acceptable network performance all the time, there may be too many stations transmitting within this collision domain, or the network architecture may need optimizing for shorter distances between distant stations. Excessive collisions are most often caused by a problem with the physical media, such as missing or incorrect terminators, impedance discontinuities (bad connectors, cable "stubs," crushed cables, etc.), and bad network interface cards.

If the utilization is high (sustained peaks in excess of 60%) and collision counts are acceptable (average is below 5%), then the network may be saturated. This is somewhat unlikely as an Ethernet segment will normally experience very high collision rates if there is too much utilization. As utilization approaches 100%, the number of collisions can grow exponentially until they far exceed the number of good frames. It may be necessary to install a switch, bridge or router to divide the segment into small enough groups to support the traffic load.

Is it a hardware problem?

Run the **Network Stats** test and check for errors (other than collisions). If errors are present, run the **Error Stats** test and "zoom" on the error to learn the MAC address of the problem station(s), then use the **Expert-T** test to isolate the specific problem, or **Cable Scan** to check the cabling. If the problem is intermittent, try replacing the suspect NIC, since these problems may not show themselves when the test is run.

Check to see if the server or service that the user(s) are connecting to is on the far side of a WAN or routed connection. If so, then check response times through those segments by using a ping test (**NetWare Ping**, **ICMP Ping**, etc.), and comparing the results with your baseline or audit results. To ensure that frames are not being dropped, try using the ping test set to continuous, and verify that the number of requests matches the number of responses (IP hosts often fail to respond to the first ping, so try at least several). If the numbers do not match, the remote media or interconnect devices (bridges, routers, etc.) may be at capacity or may have problems. Dropped frames are also a symptom of a cable fault, such as a split pair on UTP or a ground loop on coax. If dropped frames are suspected, run **Cable Scan** to test the cable attaching the slow stations (also the file server they are communicating with) to the network, or the cables connecting any bridges or routers in the path between them.

Is it a software problem?

Run the **Network Stats** test. If there is high network utilization, low collisions, and few if any errors, run the **Top Senders** test to learn which station(s) are contributing the most traffic. Go to the station(s) identified and discover what the user is doing on the network. It may be necessary to ask that the action be performed during off-peak times, or it may be necessary to move user(s) to another segment in order to improve network service for remaining users.

If utilization, collisions, and errors are low, ask the user(s) complaining about performance which server(s) or application(s) they are using. Check the server(s) identified to see if they are experiencing high utilization (which will be different than the network utilization). Configure the Network Monitor, **Top Senders** test filter for the address of the server or service and check to see which stations are making the most requests of that device. The **Top Senders** test could also be configured to filter on the address of users suffering poor performance to learn which server(s) they are connected to. Check with the user to determine the requirements being made of the server or service.

Run **Protocol Mix** to learn which protocols are consuming the most bandwidth. Configure the upper-layer **Top Senders** test filter (such as NetWare, TCP/IP, NetBIOS, Banyan, etc.) the same way as the Network Monitor, **Top Senders** test above to establish which stations are making the greatest demand on a particular network resource. Then check to see if the job can be moved to a less-used server or shared between several servers.

Problems relating to high or low network utilization—but low collision rates and no errors—tend to be related to the application software or file server. The server could have too small of a setting for the cache, insufficient buffers reserved, insufficient RAM in the server, limited free space on the server hard disk, an 8-bit NIC card, etc. Also, a software program may be running that makes an abnormal number of "network disk requests." It may be necessary to move an application to another server, upgrade the existing server, or add a new server.

If the server is running NetWare or TCP/IP, run **File Stats** and look for *delays*, or run **ICMP Errors** and look for *source quench* errors. If either of these errors is coming from the slow server, it may be overloaded. If source quench errors are coming from a router located between the problem station and the desired server or service, it may be overloaded, unable to handle the load, or an intermediate hop may be overloaded or experiencing errors.

Run the **Top Broadcasters** test and check for unusually high broadcasts (other than the "Non-Broadcast" category). If there are a significant number of broadcasts present, check the source of the broadcasts to see if the slow station or the server or service appears in the list. If so, check the configuration of the station and server or service.

If the server or service in use is separated from the user connection by a bridge, router or WAN connection, then check the frame size in use locally and the maximum transmission unit (MTU) through the WAN connections. The speed of such interconnections is determined more by the number of frames than by the size of the frame. If a station is sending many small frames, it will cause the interconnection device or path to clog up. Reconfigure the application to utilize the optimum frame size for the path between the source and the server or service to improve the response time.

Troubleshooting Token Ring

It won't install because the instructions are wrong. When phoning for help, ask for the software patch too.

The key to troubleshooting Token Ring is in understanding the importance of soft errors. If a station joins or leaves a ring, there will be some number of "normal" soft errors generated (most frequently Burst and Token errors). The ring will quickly stabilize after this topology change, and there should be no further soft errors.

If there are no soft errors present, then in almost all cases the ring is operating satisfactorily and whatever problem is being reported by users is the result of some upper-layer software problem.

This situation is especially true with "jitter" problems. If there are no errors reported, then there is very little likelihood that a jitter problem is manifesting itself at that time. The easiest way to locate a jitter-related problem is to monitor the soft-error fault domains while subjecting the problem ring to troubleshooting efforts (such as contributing traffic that has jitter-inducing data patterns).

The fault domain information found in all error frames will quickly help to isolate the source of most problems. To take advantage of this information, you need to have good network documentation available. (See Chapter 1.)

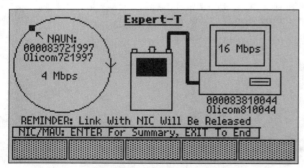

Figure 2-3. *Fluke LANMeter Token Ring Expert-T test results screen.*

Avoid misleading symptoms

Some number of soft errors are to be expected. They are "normal" only when stations join or leave a ring, so be sure to monitor the number of stations currently on the ring. Unless the station count is changing in an abnormal pattern, such as when an intermittent connection is present, then you may safely disregard soft errors associated with changes in station counts. All other soft errors should be investigated.

If soft errors appear to be coming from all over the ring, they are probably the result of an environmental problem such as bad ac power to the wiring closet, or a strong electrical noise source near a major cable run. Do not troubleshoot the individual stations when the fault domain appears to encompass the whole ring—troubleshoot the office or building. Try to determine whether the fault domains include just one section of the ring or the whole ring. By doing so, you may be able to eliminate parts of the ring as suspect. Also, be sure to consider the possibility of a bad MAU, of bad RI/RO cables, and of bad ports on MAUs that join other floors or buildings. They are frequently the source of problems.

Problem:
Cannot access server or service

The following procedures assume that this server or service has been operating properly prior to this problem, and you have already:

- Cold-booted the PC in question (a warm-boot does *not* reset all adapter cards).

- Verified that the PC does not have any hardware failures.

- Verified that all required network cables are present and properly connected.

- Verified that all required network adapter software driver files were loaded, and that no errors were reported when they loaded.

- Verified that nothing has been changed on the problem PC, server or service recently that may have caused this problem, such as reconfiguring or adding software or hardware.

Determine whether the problem is isolated to a specific station (**local** problem), or if it affects many stations (**global** problem). Do this by attempting to log into the server or service from other stations (and other user accounts) that are attached to the same MAU. If the failure is present on additional stations attached to this MAU, log into the server or service from other stations attached to other MAUs (or other rings).

Is it a local problem?

Run the **Expert-T** test to determine whether the station is correctly and successfully inserting into the ring. In addition to insertion speed, phantom voltage and station address problems, any detected cable problems will be reported. (See Figure 2-3.) If **Expert-T** is unable to insert into the ring, run the **Network Stats** test as described below.

If the lobe test portion of the LANMeter test tool insertion process or the station insertion process fails, use the **Cable Scan** test to verify the lobe cable for the problem station.

If the station lobe cable includes mixed cable types, then additional testing may be necessary because cable tests cannot be made on a cable that includes a media filter. All junction points between the 8-pin modular (RJ-45) and Type 1 cable systems require impedance matching circuitry, or the resulting cable faults will cause intermittent or hard failures of the attached ring.

Many people do not understand the purpose of media filters. As a result, they are often looked upon as simply a mechanical adapter to allow 100Ω 8-pin modular (RJ-45) style NIC cards to connect to legacy 150Ω Type 1 (IBM's large hermaphroditic connector) style MAUs. There are several different types of adapters that permit modular cables to be connected to Type 1 cable systems. Some are simply a mechanical adapter with no other circuitry or wiring. Others have all of the impedance-matching circuitry to properly join 100Ω and 150Ω cable systems.

It is not possible to perform cable testing through a media filter, because of the impedance-matching circuitry. However, by using the LANMeter test tool **Lobe Test**, you can make a simple performance check of the lobe and get a fair indication of whether the media filter is performing satisfactorily. Connect the tool to the cable in place of the problem station, with the far end of the cable still attached to the MAU. Run the **Lobe Test**, configured for testing both 4 and 16 Mbps operation—even if you are running the ring at only 4 Mbps! (The test does not actually cause the connection to join the ring, and thus will not disrupt normal ring operation.) If the test fails then either the cable, the media filter, or both should be replaced.

Run the **Network Stats** test. If the LANMeter test tool is unable to insert into the ring it is likely due to one of three causes: one of the NICs is failing to participate properly in the neighbor notification process, a station is attempting to perform the Ring Parameter Server job but is not performing the job correctly (see Appendix B on Token Ring operation), or there is a problem on the local lobe. Due to the nature of this problem it may be necessary to use the *divide-and-conquer* approach to troubleshooting described in Appendix C.

If the LANMeter test tool timed-out during the insertion process, use a spare empty MAU and insert locally, or insert into a Type 1 cable that is not attached to a MAU (the unattached square IBM connector acts like an empty ring for one station). Once the tool is inserted locally, *quickly* attach the tool to the problem MAU connection. By doing this the tool will skip past insertion-related MAC layer problems, and it will permit you to troubleshoot. Observe the Ring Error LED, verifying that when it flashes there is a corresponding increase in the soft error counts. If the soft error counts do not increase, or if you cannot tell if the increase corresponds to the flashing LED, run the **Ring Stations** test and watch for the station count to change radically or for "bracketing" to appear on the far left of the stations in the list. (See Figure 2-4.) Bracketing indicates an incomplete list. Use the cursor down key to pause screen updates of the station list, and continue down through the list to learn which is the last station to participate correctly (the last station within the first major bracket—in Figure 2-4 the last "good" station is the fifth one shown). Then be sure to resume screen updates by pressing the Enter key. Repeat this process several times to see if the same stations are identified. If so, the active station located downstream (to the right when looking at your MAU) of the last station within the first major bracket is probably the marginal or

Figure 2-4. *Fluke LANMeter* **Ring Stations** *test results screen showing "bracketing."*

failed NIC. Either disconnect it from the MAU or turn it off, then check for continued bracketing of the Ring Stations list or attempt to insert into the ring normally. If you can again insert normally and bracketing of the station list stops, replace the marginal NIC.

If the Ring Stations list is normal (and showing the expected number of stations), try sending an **Adapter Stats** request to each station on the ring. Look for a station that is performing the additional job of Ring Parameter Server. If you find such a station, either disconnect it from the MAU or turn the station off, then attempt to insert into the ring normally. Many bridges (but sometimes switches, routers, and network management stations too) have default configurations that cause them to assume the job of Ring Parameter Server unless explicitly enabled or disabled. Sometimes this problem occurs after upgrading the software in one of these devices. Another symptom of this problem is when a station is able to insert into the ring *only* through LANMeter test tool Expert-T mode, and not directly into the ring on its own. (The LANMeter test tool itself may not be able to insert normally into the ring when this problem

is present. If this is true, use an empty MAU or a Type 1 lobe cable that is not attached to a MAU to allow the tool to get past the insertion problem, then quickly move the tool's connection into the problem MAU—then start searching for the station performing the Ring Parameter server job.) If you can again insert into the ring normally after removing or disabling the station performing the Ring Parameter Server function, replace the failed NIC or reconfigure the device.

If you are attaching to an intelligent MAU or concentrator, and the LANMeter test tool inserts into a ring containing only itself, then verify the speed of your ring and the tool's setting for ring speed. The LANMeter test tool will perform the lobe test at 16 Mbps when set to either 16 Mbps or Auto Speed Detect, and will perform the lobe test at only 4 Mbps if it is configured for 4 Mbps operation only. An intelligent MAU or concentrator will see the lobe test being performed at the wrong speed for the ring, and will lock-out the port before the LANMeter test tool is able to autosense the ring speed.

Is it a LAN problem?

Run the **Network Stats** test and check for high network utilization and abnormally high network errors.

If the network utilization is not consistently high (above 75%), and the number of network errors is "normal" then you may have software configuration problems with the server or service.

If the number of errors is high, use the **Error Stats** test to isolate the fault domain.

If the fault domain is relatively stable, use the **Expert-T** test to verify the station(s) reported in the fault domain. Also, use the **Cable Scan** test to verify each cable identified in the fault domain. Try replacing the suspect NIC.

If the fault domain shows numerous stations, or it jumps around a lot, then run the **Phase Jitter** test. A side effect of this test is to cause the Active Monitor to change, which may temporarily solve the problem. If the Phase Jitter test result is higher than "normal" (and there are no retiming devices on the ring), turn off each station on the local ring one at a time until the measurement returns to "normal," then replace the NIC card or software drivers in the suspect station.

If the fault domain shows numerous stations, or it jumps around a lot, it may be an environmental problem, such as a noise source near a cable bundle or bad ac power being supplied to a wiring closet, electrical circuit, or building. Refer to your network documentation and see if the fault domains are limited to a single wiring closet or MAU. If a single MAU is indicated, try swapping the MAU to determine if it has become marginal or failed.

As a special case try using the LANMeter test tool **Phase Jitter** test from different locations on the ring to isolate a position dependent problem. If the problem clears up when the tool is in a particular area, then it's most likely an uncorrelated jitter problem. For a short-term solution, install a device that provides signal retiming in this location.

Also try using the LANMeter **Traffic Generator** to send LLC traffic configured for each of the three available jitter data patterns. Once configured, enable the *Run In Background* feature and then start the **Network Stats** test with and without traffic. Watch for increases in the number of soft errors that can be directly associated with the presence of one of the three jitter patterns. Use the soft error fault domain to locate the station that is sensitive to correlated jitter. Verify by turning the suspect station off and repeating the test. The errors should not resume. Replace the suspect NIC.

If the network utilization and number of network errors are not high, run the **Station Ping** test (source routing must be enabled, and even then some devices have not fully implemented the 802.2 requirements and will not respond) to ensure that the server can be reached. If source routing is not enabled, use the **Adapter Stats** test from the ring to which the server is attached. If the server responds, restart the server from a cold-boot and watch to ensure that all required software driver files load without error.

Run the **Station Ping** test (source routing must be enabled for this test, and even then some devices have not fully implemented the 802.2 requirements and will not respond) to verify that the desired server or service can be reached from the current network connection point. If source routing is not enabled, use the **Adapter Stats** test to reach stations on the local ring only.

Is it a WAN problem?

Run the **Server List** or **Novell Ping** test (if using Novell) to verify that the desired server or service can be reached from the current network connection point. Also try running the Novell Ping test configured for *continuous*. Then ensure that the number of requests is equal to the number of responses. Discrepancies may indicate a marginal NIC or MAU port, and that frames are being dropped.

Run the **File Stats** or **Packet Stats** test (if using Novell) and check for Delays coming from the desired server (highlight the *Delays* field and press the "zoom" softkey). If these are present it indicates that the server is unable to keep up with the load, and that for each Delay issued a request was ignored.

Run the **ICMP Ping** test (if using TCP/IP) to verify that the desired host can be reached from the current network connection point. Be sure to run this test at least twice, as some network devices fail to reply to the *first* ping request. Verify that the default gateway address is configured correctly if the desired host is not on the local ring.

Also try running the ICMP Ping test configured for *continuous*. Then ensure that the number of requests is equal to the number of responses. Discrepancies may indicate a marginal NIC or MAU port, and that frames are being dropped.

Problem:
Network is beaconing

Determine whether the problem is a persistent **hard failure**, or an **intermittent** network interruption. If the ring is totally inoperable, and doesn't recover itself even briefly after 30 seconds, then it is likely that a cable or hardware component has spontaneously failed or has been damaged in some way. If the problem appears and disappears intermittently, it's the sign of a bad or marginal connection, NIC, or improperly configured station. In most cases, once beaconing has started the fault domain remains stable for some period of time, and troubleshooting is relatively simple. There are conditions though that will cause an **unstable fault domain**, usually because of external interference or other environmental problems in the building.

When learning new networking skills always study the standards before resorting to the popular press. They may be hard to understand— but they have the advantage of being accurate.

Is it a hard failure?

Run the **Network Stats** test to identify the domain of the failure. If the fault domain is stable, use **Expert-T** to isolate the failure. Refer to your network documentation to identify the location of the devices listed in the fault domain, or use the **Ring Stations** test to help locate them.

Is it an intermittent failure?

Run the **Network Stats** test continuously until the intermittent failure occurs. If the fault domain for the intermittent failure is stable, run the **Expert-T** test on the two stations identified in the fault domain to isolate the problem.

Is the fault domain unstable?

Run the **Network Stats** test continuously. Even in situations where the beacon fault domain is "walking" around the ring, the LANMeter will properly identify the original failure point as long as one of the Network Monitor tests was running prior to, or close to, the onset of beaconing. ("Walking" usually will not occur until beaconing has been present long enough for application software on workstations to fail due to loss of network connectivity. At that time the station will deinsert, causing the beacon fault domain to shift to the next still-active device.

In this manner, the beacon fault domain will "walk" around the ring at the rate that stations deinsert, are rebooted, or are turned off.)

If the fault domain is not stable due to "walking," then segment the ring while continuing to monitor **Network Stats**. Do this by recabling to bypass one MAU (or a group of MAUs) at a time until the MAU containing the failure has been isolated. Then, while running **Network Stats** on the bad part of the ring, disconnect stations one by one to find the problem connection. Use **Expert-T** to isolate the specific failure. Verify all ring cabling and connectors.

If the failure has been present for an extended period of time, all stations on the network except for bridges, routers, servers, etc., may have deinserted. If so, run the **Network Stats** test continuously while you restart the ring. It may be necessary to isolate individual or groups of MAUs in order to get a part of the ring started, before you add additional MAUs. During the startup process you should discover the source of the failure by monitoring the fault domain of any resulting beacons. Then use **Expert-T** to isolate the specific failure.

Problem:
Connections that drop

The following procedures assume that this connection has been operating properly prior to this problem, and you have already:

- Cold-booted the PC in question (a warm-boot does not reset all network adapters).

- Verified that the PC does not have any hardware failures.

- Verified that all required network cables are present and properly connected, and fastened firmly.

- Verified that nothing has been changed on the problem PC, server or service recently that may have caused this problem, such as reconfiguring or adding new software or hardware.

- Eliminated potential PC memory allocation problems on the station by loading only the minimum required to operate a test application across the network. Be sure to unload "TSR" type programs.

- Verified that all required network adapter software driver files were loaded, and that no errors were reported when they loaded.

Determine if the problem is isolated to this station (**local** problem), or if it affects many stations (**LAN** or **WAN** problem) by asking other users in the area if they have had similar problems.

Is it a local problem?

Run the **Expert-T** test to determine whether the station is correctly and successfully inserting into the ring. In addition to insertion speed, phantom voltage and station address problems, any detected cable problems will be reported.

If the problem is isolated to a single station, try replacing the software drivers and NIC card.

Is it a LAN problem?

Run the **Network Stats** test and check for high network utilization and abnormally high network errors.

If the network utilization is not consistently high (above 75%), and the number of network errors is "normal" then you may have software configuration problems with the server or service.

If the number of network errors is high then use the **Error Stats** test to isolate the fault domain. (Follow instructions for **LAN** problems. See page 2-12.)

Observe the Ring Error LED, and verify that the error counts correspond closely to the flashing of the LED. If the LED flashes, and there is no corresponding increase in soft errors then check the Ring Stations test for bracketing on the left side of the display. If the Ring Error LED is flashing without incrementing the soft error counts, or bracketing is present in the Ring Stations list, then follow the instructions for a **local** problem. (See page 2-11.)

If the number of network errors is high then run the **Phase Jitter** test. If the Phase Jitter test result is higher than "normal," segment the ring while continuing to monitor the Phase Jitter test. Do this by recabling to bypass one MAU (or a group of MAUs) at a time until the MAU containing the failure has been isolated. Then connect one station at a time until the jitter measurement jumps to isolate the specific station failing. Replace the NIC or interconnect device.

Is it a WAN problem?

If the connection is made through a bridge, router or WAN link, monitor response times while sending a continuous ping across the WAN connection using **Station Ping**, **NetWare Ping**, or **ICMP Ping** as appropriate. If a slowdown in response time is noted, check what else is happening with that WAN connection during the slowdown. Verify the configurations for time-out values and check the utilization of the intervening medium. Ensure that the number of requests is equal to the number of responses. Discrepancies indicate that frames are being dropped.

Problem: Slow or poor network performance

Determine whether the problem is related to the network **media**, or if it's related to a particular station, server or service. Try accessing the same server or service from other nearby stations, and asking users on the same and other network segments to do the same. If the problem is not media-related, determine if the problem is **software** or **hardware**-related. Check the network utilization and soft error counts while the network is performing poorly.

Is it a media problem?

Local media (where you are now).

Run the **Network Stats** test and check for high network utilization and abnormally high network errors.

If the number of network errors is high then use the **Error Stats** test to isolate the fault domain. If the fault domain is relatively stable, use the **Expert-T** test to verify the stations reported in the fault domain, use **Cable Scan** to check the cabling, verify that the software drivers load properly, or try replacing the suspect NIC. Also try the jitter tests described under **LAN** problems on page 2-13.

If the number of network errors is low, but network utilization is consistently high (above 90%), then the network may be saturated. Resolve this by splitting large rings into smaller rings, changing the network speed from 4 Mbps to 16 Mbps, installing a switch, etc.

Run the **Token Rotation** test, then make the adjusted ring length calculation described in the Help text for this test. For good performance, we have found that token rotation should be below 150 microseconds, though the Standard permits much longer times.

Remote Media (slow station is on the far side of a spanning device like a switch, bridge or router).

Run the **Error Stats** test and check for high network utilization and abnormally high network errors. If there is a high number of Congested Receiver errors use the "zoom" softkey to check whether the source address in the fault domain is the address of a bridge, router, etc., between the slow station and the server or service. If so the problem could be that the bridge, router, or other device has reached its capacity or the capacity of the remote medium. The spanning device could also be misconfigured.

Run the **Top Senders** test, configured to filter on the address of the server or service, or first router leading to that server or service.

If a disproportionate amount of traffic is addressed to that server or service, it may be overloaded, or the remote media may be at capacity.

Is it a software problem?

Run the **Network Stats** test and check for high network utilization and abnormally high network errors.

If the network utilization is not consistently high (above 75%), and the number of network errors is "normal," you may have software configuration problems with the server or service. Check the server for utilization (which will be different than the network utilization). The server could have too small of a setting for the cache, insufficient buffers reserved, insufficient RAM in the server, limited free space on the server hard disk, an 8-bit NIC card, etc. Also, many programs are not "network savvy," and may be making an abnormally high number of network requests. Check top frame and top byte senders. If one station is very high on the "frame" list, but very low on the "byte" list, it may be running such a program.

If the server is running NetWare or TCP/IP, run **File Stats** and look for *delays,* or run **ICMP Errors** and look for *source quench* errors. If either of these errors is coming from the server, it may be overloaded. If source quench errors are coming from a router between the problem station and the desired server or service, it may be overloaded.

If the number of network errors is low, but the network utilization is high (above 90%), then the network may be saturated. Determine if the slow-down is application-specific.

Run the **Top Broadcasters** test and check for unusually high broadcasts (other than the "Non-Broadcast" category).

If there are a significant number of broadcasts present, check the source addresses for the broadcasts to see if the slow station or the server or service appears in the list. If so, check the configuration of the station and server or service. Also check to see if the server or service is operating at full capacity.

Is it a hardware problem?

Run the **Network Stats** test and check for high network utilization and low network errors.

If the number of network errors is low (other than congested receiver errors), but the network utilization is high (above 90%) then the network may be saturated. Resolve saturation by splitting the network into smaller rings, increasing the network speed from 4 Mbps to 16 Mbps, etc.

If the number of network errors is high then use the Error Stats test to isolate the fault domain. (Follow instructions for LAN problems beginning on page 2-12.)

Chapter 3 — Forming a Strategy

A Strategy for Network Maintenance

There was a time when a certain type of computer network was defined as "mission-critical." This term usually referred to a system whose failure would be considered catastrophic to the organization relying on its application. Air traffic control networks, money transfer exchanges and hospital local- and wide-area networks (LANs and WANs) are examples of what were commonly referred to as mission-critical networks.

Today, however, companies and organizations worldwide are discovering that nearly every computer network that links people and information is critical to the overall success of the business or institution. A survey conducted by Infonetics Research, Inc., found that 83% of network managers had applications running on their networks that were deemed critical to their business.

But while networks become integral to businesses, complications continue to arise. Technology and application advancements must be continually implemented; networks are becoming distributed, with more and more remote sites and users; components from multiple vendors must be made interoperable; and end users untrained in networking have increasing access to the network, thereby adding more variables. These issues, combined with the on-going growth of the network, place a tremendous burden on network support staff, from the Help Desk operator to the network engineer. The 1993 Infonetics study found that network size and complexity is growing at almost twice the rate of network support staff. (See Figure 3-1.)

Network downtime and poor performance is costly to business. Productivity losses due to network downtime and poor performance are calculated to be as high as $3.3 million per year for some companies.

One way to handle the burden of increasing network complexity, along with the high cost of network downtime and poor performance, is to implement a Network Maintenance Strategy—an integrated, holistic approach to maintaining the network to increase reliability, facilitate implementation of technology advancements, and ease the burden of network support.

Perhaps the best way to understand what Network Maintenance Strategy is would be to use an analogy: Just as the local fire department spends 95% of its time preventing fires (by inspecting potentially dangerous areas, preparing plans of buildings, checking equipment), and only 5% of its time actually fighting a fire, so should a network staff plan and prepare to minimize the frequency and effects of emergencies.

To arrive at such a strategy, Fluke Corporation, a company that for nearly 50 years has been recognized as a world leader in understanding and recommending maintenance processes for electrical, HVAC, and dc calibration systems, commissioned research to arrive at such a plan for today's networks.

The research studies

The strategy outlined in this chapter is based on data from a number of sources. Fluke Corporation commissioned several studies over the past year, including one in conjunction with Infonetics Research, Inc. In all, this research has drawn from the experience of over 200 network engineers and Information Systems (IS) managers from organizations large and small. The primary sources of data include:

- *Battling Downtime: Network Management Tools and Practices,* Infonetics Research, Inc., 1996

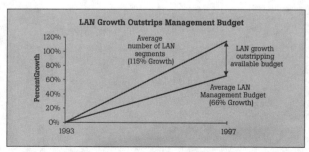

Figure 3-1. *LAN growth rate compared to the budget allocated to support the LAN. (Data from The Real Cost of Network and Systems Management, 1993. Chart © 1996 Infonetics Research, Inc.)*

- Fluke Corporation analysis of Infonetics Research, Inc. data from *Battling Downtime,* 1996

- Martin Research, *Network Maintenance Strategies and Practices,* 1996

Based on this research, Fluke has identified seven "best practices" that any network from 100 nodes up can implement to increase uptime and save network support costs. We call it a Network Maintenance Strategy.

Network maintenance strategy

The seven practices Fluke identified as constituting a successful Network Maintenance Strategy are:

Practice 1. Management involvement in network decision making
Practice 2. Preparation and planning
Practice 3. Problem prevention
Practice 4. Early problem detection
Practice 5. Quick problem isolation and resolution
Practice 6. Investing in tools and training rather than additional staff to accommodate growth
Practice 7. Quality improvement approach to network management and maintenance

And what exactly is gained by implementing these practices? Fluke research has found that companies that employ these "best practices" accrue the following benefits:

- A 35:1 difference in total downtime for the high-downtime group compared to the best-practice group. (See Figure 3-2.)

- More than 10% fewer support staff per node than average.

- Over $227, 000 support cost savings per year.

- Higher morale and less turnover of network support staff.

- Perhaps the most surprising finding of the Fluke-sponsored research is that those managers most satisfied with the operation of their network actually have less staff to maintain the network than those who are dissatisfied with their network. (See Figure 3-3.)

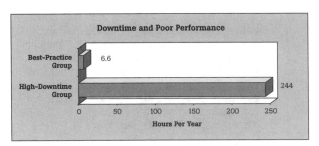

Figure 3-2. Comparison of total network downtime between the "Best-Practice" group and the "High-Downtime" group. (Chart © 1996 Infonetics Research, Inc.)

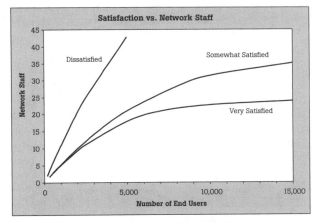

Figure 3-3. Network operation satisfaction level based on staffing level presently maintaining the network. (Martin Research)

Now let's look at the practices a little more in depth.

1. Management involvement

Upper management must demonstrate that they care about the network performance by creating a framework that facilitates problem prevention and resolution. They must also be part of a regular review process to ensure that the network is fulfilling its promise to the organization. Research indicates that network managers in the best networks report to management nearly 10% more often than average.

Additionally, management must collaborate with technical managers to ensure that network objectives match business objectives. Together, they should arrive at reasonable guidelines for establishing which portions of the network are high-priority operations. For example, in a major manufacturing company, it is clear that the network associated with the manufacturing line has higher priority than the president's PC.

2. Preparation and planning

Having a documented plan as to who is responsible for each area of the network, criteria for preventative maintenance and types of performance metrics that are monitored, how problems are escalated, and what tools are used to troubleshoot the network, is essential.

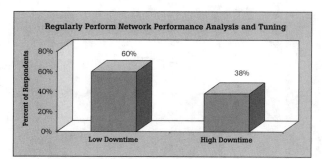

Figure 3-4. *Regular performance tuning is an important step in maintaining low downtime. (Chart © 1996 Infonetics Research, Inc.)*

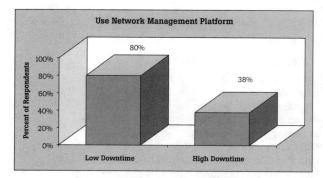

Figure 3-5. *On-going performance monitoring is an important step in avoiding downtime and for providing rapid problem detection. (Chart © 1996 Infonetics Research, Inc.)*

The "best practices" companies have agreed upon guidelines for problem detection, isolation and resolution, as well as day-to-day operations like moves, adds and changes.

3. Problem prevention

Companies that have a Network Maintenance Strategy realize that the earlier a problem is identified and fixed, the less expensive it is.

Educating end users on do's and don'ts qualifies as an important element of problem prevention. Examples include telling users to contact the Help Desk to move their computer or asking end users to be careful about running over cables with equipment or furniture. In the same vein, network devices such as routers, hubs and switches should not be accessible to end users.

Another aspect of problem prevention is the testing and certifying of network cable during installation and after moves, adds and changes.

Finally, the network should be documented and regularly monitored for performance. Sixty percent of the low-downtime respondents regularly do performance analysis and tuning, as opposed to only 38% of the high-downtime respondents. (See Figure 3-4.)

4. Early problem detection

Even with the best problem prevention plan, some problems will inevitably occur. To reduce the impact of the problems, the network should be monitored so that performance deviations can be identified immediately.

This means using network management systems such as HP's *OpenView*, Sun's *SunNet Manager*, and Cabletron's *SPECTRUM* to monitor routers and switch performance, and RMON probes to monitor remote segment performance. Eighty percent of the low-downtime group have network management platforms; whereas only 38% of the high-downtime respondents do. (See Figure 3-5.)

It is essential to have a single, centralized Help Desk to quickly receive and respond to problems reported by individual users. Trouble-ticketing applications are used by Help Desks to log and track network problems. Forty percent of the low-downtime respondents use a trouble-ticketing application while only 25% of the high-downtime respondents use a trouble-ticketing application. (See Figure 3-6.)

5. Quick problem isolation and resolution

The previously mentioned centralized Help Desk will discuss the problem with the caller and, if needed, dispatch a front-line troubleshooter, who, armed with the right tools, should be able to quickly diagnose and fix all single-user problems.

When the front-line staff cannot solve the problem, he or she should escalate the problem to a more experienced staff member.

For quick problem isolation and resolution, it is important that the support staff be armed with the appropriate tools. Protocol analyzers, handheld network testers, and cable testers are used by the different levels of network staff to troubleshoot network problems. Seventy-three percent of the low-downtime group use these tools while only 58% of the high-downtime group use these tools. (See Figure 3-7.)

6. Invest in tools and training rather than staff to accommodate network growth

The old saying, "Sometimes you have to spend a little money to save a lot of money," is also true for successful network maintenance. From Figure 3-3, Fluke's research shows that the best run networks are maintained with less staff. However, those companies employing "best practices" invest in training and tools for their staffs. In fact, putting the right tool to fit the function and experience level of the staff member empowers him or her to maximize his or her efficiency. Seventy percent of the low-downtime group purchase labor-saving tools rather than adding staff, while only 54% of the high-downtime group use this strategy to accommodate network growth. (See Figure 3-8.)

The result is that the best run networks achieve better results with less staff per node!

7. Quality improvement approach to network management

A quality improvement approach means taking metrics such as the number and nature of network failures and problems. Network performance is measured and compared against goals (which were set in conjunction with upper-level management). Reports are regularly provided to management.

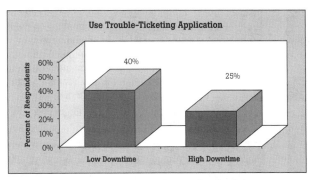

Figure 3-6. Use of a trouble-ticketing application helps ensure problems are resolved, and can provide statistics that highlight problem areas. (Chart © 1996 Infonetics Research, Inc.)

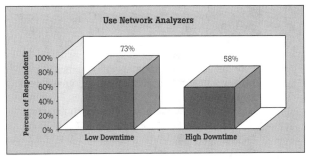

Figure 3-7. Providing sufficient and appropriate diagnostic tools allows network support staff to locate problems faster, and thus maintain lower downtime. (Chart © 1996 Infonetics Research, Inc.)

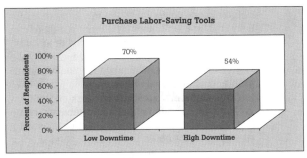

Figure 3-8. On-going training programs and appropriate tools allow support staff in the "best-practices" group to perform better than staff from companies that experience high downtime. (Chart © 1996 Infonetics Research, Inc.)

Conclusion: As networks begin to play a critical role in all enterprises, it is important to move from a reactive model of network fire-fighting to a proactive model of network management and maintenance. Fluke has identified some "best practices" that, when implemented correctly, can not only improve network efficiency and productivity, but also have a positive, real impact on a company's bottom line.

Tools: A key element of the Network Maintenance Strategy

Practice 6 of the Network Maintenance Strategy is investing in tools and training rather than in additional staff to accommodate growth. Buying labor-saving tools is not only less expensive than adding staff; it makes existing staff more efficient. By using these tools, the network management staff is able to spend more time managing proactively, thus supporting practices 2, 3 and 7 of the strategy—preparation and planning, problem prevention, and quality improvement, respectively.

Seventy percent of the low-downtime respondents purchase labor-saving tools rather than adding additional staff, whereas 54% of the high-downtime group follow this practice.

Examples of labor-saving tools include:

Network management systems

A network management system uses intelligent managed devices and software to collect critical network parameters and then report them back to a central location where a network manager can view what's happening on the network in real-time. Network management systems also include alarms to indicate the occurrence of performance problems on the network.

These systems provide a network engineer with a good overall picture of the network's performance. Consequently, they are an important strategic tool for network monitoring and planning. However, purchasing one is only a first step. These tools typically require on-going maintenance in order to be effective. One unconfirmed estimate is that only 10% of all Network Management Systems are fully configured and maintained, and therefore providing their optimum usefulness, one year after purchase.

Protocol analyzers

Protocol analyzers are also an important part of a large network's maintenance "tool box." With their capability to capture and decode data packets, they are necessary for troubleshooting a class of very complex (but rarely occurring) problems, such as software application debugging. Complex and powerful, protocol analyzers require trained experts to run and, in the interest of a more rapid return to service, are probably better used when other faster tools fail to identify the problem.

Handheld network analyzers

Fluke pioneered a new category of handheld network analyzer with the introduction of the LANMeter series test tool, receiving its first industry award in January, 1993, and has expanded both the category and the available feature set regularly since that time. From a very basic pair tester to a portable network management system, each product is designed for a specific role in the Network Maintenance Strategy.

The 680 Enterprise LANMeter series of portable network management tools are designed to complement network management systems. They are used by network professionals to diagnose and troubleshoot enterprise elements of the network including routers, switches, and hubs. The network health monitoring capability of the tool aids in problem prevention (practice 3), while its fast diagnosis of network failures supports the quick problem isolation and resolution aspect of the strategy (practice 5). It also has SNMP capability to query management information bases (MIBs) including remote monitoring agents (RMON) to gather vital information from remote sites, even on the other side of routers and switches.

The OneTouch Network Assistant series offers portable diagnostics for installing and troubleshooting 10 and 100 Mbps Ethernet network connections. For use by front-line support staff, the tool supports the quick problem isolation and resolution (practice 5) by empowering network support staff to resolve most problems on the first visit. In addition to being a first response troubleshooting tool, the tool is also used to help prevent network connection problems (practice 3) during moves, adds and changes.

Cable testers

With fast network technologies (Fast Ethernet and ATM, for example) it is critical that the network media be the highest grade components, such as Category 5 UTP and connectors, supporting practice 2, preparation and planning, of the Network Maintenance Strategy. In addition, the installation of these components should be certified to the appropriate industry standards to ensure that unexpected problems are not experienced later, thus supporting practice 3, problem prevention, of the strategy.

The DSP-100 is the first digital network media tester. The fact that it's digital gives it significant advantages over older analog testers, including test speed and its Time Domain Crosstalk (TDX) feature which locates near-end crosstalk (NEXT) faults. The DSP-100 is the first field tester to receive Underwriters Laboratories' UL Listing and Classification label. The classification states that the DSP-100 fully complies with all requirements set forth in TIA/EIA-568-A, TSB67 for accuracy Level II (the highest) for both the basic link and the channel configurations—the only tester that can make that claim.

Conclusion: While tools are specifically mentioned in only one of the "best practices," it can be seen that their use positively contributes to many of the practices in the Network Maintenance Strategy. While improving network quality, the use of labor-saving tools can save hundreds of thousands of dollars. There is a quick payback on an investment in tools, and the training required to make them useful.

Self-Assessment Questionnaire

This self-assessment questionnaire is designed to provide you with a simple means of assessing your organization's progress in adopting the seven best practices of a successful Network Maintenance Strategy. It allows you to compare

your network management and maintenance practices with those of your peers. In addition, it provides you with feedback that will help you focus on those areas that are likely to help you improve your maintenance practices and reduce network downtime.

Scoring

Table 3-1 shows the points to be applied to each of the statements checked on page 3-8. These points were statistically derived by correlating the downtimes of various organizations and the network management and maintenance practices used at those organizations. Your total score is the sum of all the points for each statement.

1. 4 points		4. 4 points	12. 3 points
2. a. Daily .... 4 points		5. 2 points	13. 4 points
b. Weekly .... 3 points		6. 4 points	14. 4 points
c. Monthly .... 2 points		7. 3 points	15. 4 points
d. Quarterly .... 1 point		8. 3 points	16. 5 points
e. Less than quarterly ...... 0 points		9. 5 points	17. 2 points
3. a. Very supportive ...... 6 points		10. 5 points	18. 3 points
b. Moderately supportive ...... 3 points		11. 5 points	19. 3 points
c. Not supportive ...... 0 points			

Table 3-1. How to score your results.

Comparison with other organizations

Now that you've checked the statements that apply, and scored the questionnaire, you can compare your network management and maintenance practices score with the those of other organizations.

Table 3-2 below summarizes the scores of other organizations. Ten percent of previous respondents scored 60 or above. Twenty percent scored 50 or above. Seventy-five percent scored 35 or above, and 25% scored less than 35.

Score	Percentile
60 or more	90th percentile
50 to 59	80th percentile
35 to 49	25th percentile
less than 35	bottom 25%

Table 3-2. Scoring comparison.

Questions

To use the questionnaire, first check those statements below that describe the network management and maintenance practices that currently apply to your organization.

Practice 1: Management involvement in network decision making

☐ 1. We know what our organization's business objectives are, and our network objectives match our organization's objectives. When responding to network problems, we know which portions of the network have highest priority.

2. Our department provides network status reports to upper management:
   ☐ a. Daily
   ☐ b. Weekly
   ☐ c. Monthly
   ☐ d. Quarterly
   ☐ e. Less than quarterly or not at all

3. Upper management is:
   ☐ a. Very supportive
   ☐ b. Moderately supportive
   ☐ c. Not supportive of the network management department's budget, allowing the network to contribute toward achieving corporate business goals.

Practice 2: Preparation and planning

☐ 4. We plan for future growth and changes, and buy network equipment that is upgradable and/or expandable.

☐ 5. We have a documented plan that spells out who is responsible for handling specific network problems that may occur.

☐ 6. We have a documented plan for preventive network maintenance.

Practice 3: Problem prevention

☐ 7. We educate end-users regarding the do's and don'ts of networks.
   (E.g., don't connect yourself to the network.)

☐ 8. We test and certify network cable during installation and after moves, adds and changes.

☐ 9. We locate network devices (routers, hubs, switches, etc.) in areas not accessible to end-users.

☐ 10. We do regular network performance analysis and tuning.

Practice 4: Early problem detection

☐ 11. We have a single centralized help desk, staffed with knowledgeable personnel, to encourage end-users to immediately report network problems.

☐ 12. We use a network management system to continuously monitor the status of critical network components.

Practice 5: Quick problem isolation and resolution

☐ 13. We use a Trouble Ticketing Application to log and track network problems.

☐ 14. Our front-line troubleshooting staff is able to quickly diagnose and repair most single user-problems, on the first trip to the end-user.

☐ 15. Our network support staff is armed with appropriate tools. Network analyzers, including both handheld network testers and protocol analyzers, are used by different levels of staff to troubleshoot network problems.

Practice 6: Invest in tools and training rather than additional staff to accommodate growth

☐ 16. We purchase labor-saving tools and provide training for existing network staff rather than adding additional staff to accommodate growth.

Practice 7: Quality improvement approach to network management and maintenance

☐ 17. We track the number and nature of network failures and problems.

☐ 18. We track time-to-repair network problems.

☐ 19. We periodically review and modify our network maintenance practices to prevent future network failures and to reduce the time to repair those failures.

Appendix A — Errors

Ethernet Errors

A certain number of "normal" errors can be expected on Ethernet under standard operating conditions. The most common error experienced on an Ethernet segment is a collision. Collisions are so common that the rules of Ethernet operation not only define collisions as being normal, but provide an explanation of how the segment should operate in the presence of a variable amount of collisions. The rules further explain that performance should not be adversely affected unless relatively heavy loads are experienced. The MAC layer of the NIC card is not expected to report collisions to the next higher layer.

Diagnosing Ethernet problems

Troubleshooting errors on Ethernet presents special problems, almost all of which are related directly to the "bus" structure of Ethernet. For messages to get from one station to another quickly, the bus structure delivers all messages nearly simultaneously to all stations within a collision domain (up to 1024 stations within approximately 2500 meters of each other). This also results in problems anywhere within the system appearing at all other parts of the system nearly simultaneously. Making the distinction between errors that are nearby and more distant errors requires a degree of skill, and often requires the *divide-and-conquer* approach to troubleshooting. To aid this process, it is important to understand the often minor differences between errors.

Table A-1 gives a summary of common errors and many of their most likely causes. The sections following the table describe the errors in detail and their causes and cures.

Causes	Error Type						
	Local Collision	Remote Collision	Late Collision	Short Frame	Jabber	FCS	Ghost
Normal CSMA/CD	•	•					
Overloaded Segment	•	•					
Bad SW Drivers				•	•	•	•
Faulty/Marginal NIC	•	•	•	•	•	•	•
Transceiver Fault	•	•	•		•	•	•
Repeater Fault	•	•	•	•	•	•	•
Too Many Repeaters			•				
Taps Too Close						•	•
Illegal HW Configuration	•	•	•		•		•
Cable Too Long			•			•	
Cable Fault	•	•	•		•	•	•
Termination	•	•	•		•	•	•
Bad Grounding	•	•	•		•	•	•
Induced Noise	•	•	•		•	•	•

Table A-1. Ethernet errors chart.

Description of error types

Collision

Collisions occur when two nodes transmit at the same time, because of different cable types, and because interim devices between source and destination stations delay the signal. And, since not all equipment operates properly forever, and not all networks are constructed exactly according to the specifications, there are predictably some minor variations between one collision and another. These differences allow the distinctions listed below to be made.

If the collision is detected by the transmitting station(s) early enough, there may not be even a start frame delimiter (SFD) in the aborted message. Many network monitoring tools are unable to "see" collisions that occur in the preamble (before the SFD is transmitted) because they rely on the Ethernet chipset to pass information up the protocol stack. In normal Ethernet operation, the physical layer in the network interface card (NIC) does not forward any data to the data link layer until after the SFD has been seen. Special hardware is required to observe signals prior to the SFD.

When a collision is detected by a station that is transmitting, it will send a "jam" signal that is at least 32 bits long. The standard does not specify what the jam signal should look like (except it should not form a proper frame check sequence (FCS) for what *was* sent), so most NIC cards simply use a 10 MHz clock signal. If this clock signal is sent early in the message and replaces just the right part of the header, the destination or source address may translate to all A's, or all 5's. Repeaters detecting a collision on one port will send a jam signal on all other ports to ensure that all stations detect the collision.

The portion of a message that is left over after a collision is sometimes known as a **collision fragment**, because the original message has been damaged and is no longer complete.

Local collision

On coax cable (10BASE2 and 10BASE5) the signal travels down the cable until it encounters the signal from the other node. The waveforms then overlap, canceling some parts of the signal out, and reinforcing (doubling) other parts. The "doubling" of the signal pushes the voltage level of the signal beyond the maximum-allowed transmit level. This over-voltage condition is then sensed by all of the nodes on the cable segment as a local collision. On UTP cable (10BASE-T) a local collision is detected only when a node detects a signal on the RX (receive) pair at the same time it is transmitting on the TX (transmit) pair.

Remote collision

If a collision occurs on the far side of a repeater, the over-voltage state will not be observed on the near side of the repeater. What will be seen on this side of the repeater is the beginning of an incomplete message. Note that this shortened message will not have a proper FCS checksum, and will not be long enough to meet the 64-byte (after the preamble) minimum requirement. It will likely be so short that the entire header block (with source and destination address) cannot be seen. There will also be the characteristic "jam" signal occupying the last four octets of the shortened message (an octet is a grouping of 8 binary bits, and is sometimes imprecisely known as a byte).

This type of foreshortened frame is referred to as a remote collision. The key features are that the over-voltage state is not present, the frame is shorter than 64 bytes (after the preamble), and it does not have a valid FCS.

Since a 10BASE-T hub is essentially a multi-port repeater with a "segment" dedicated to each station, collisions on 10BASE-T are nearly always detected as remote collisions (a station would have to be transmitting to sense a "local" collision).

Late collision

A late collision is one that occurs after the first 64 bytes in a frame, but only when the other symptoms of a "local" collision are present at the same time (over-voltage or simultaneous transmit and receive). That is, it is detected exactly the same as a local collision; it just happens too far into the frame. Generally, late collisions are seen only on a coaxial segment (in 10BASE-T networks, the monitoring station must be transmitting simultaneously in order to see a late collision). Late collisions are usually caused by a faulty NIC or network that is too long. A network that is too long is one in which the end-to-end signal propagation time is greater than the minimum legal-sized frame, which is unlikely. The usual cause of late collisions is marginal or failed hardware. In 10BASE-T networks late collisions are often detected simply as FCS errors.

The problem with late collisions is that they do not cause the NIC card to automatically attempt to retransmit the collided frame. As far as the NIC is concerned, everything went out fine, and the upper layers of the protocol stack must deduce that the frame was lost.

Late remote collision

A late remote collision is one that takes place after the first 64 bytes in a frame, and on the far side of a repeater. However, since the repeater would prevent observation of the over-voltage state, monitoring hardware would have to be present on the distant segment in order to detect a late collision and report that information back to your monitoring station. It is also possible to infer that a late remote collision took place somewhere on the other side of a repeater by analyzing the last few octets of a bad frame for the presence of a jam signal. Typically, this type of collision would be detected on the local segment simply as an FCS error.

Short frame

A short frame is a frame smaller than the minimum legal size (less than 64 bytes after the preamble) with a good frame check sequence. Some protocol analyzers and network monitors call these frames "runts," but the term is imprecise. In general you should not see short frames, though their presence is not a guarantee that the network is failing. The most likely cause of a short frame is a faulty card, or an improperly configured or corrupt NIC driver file.

Runts

Many protocol analyzers and network monitors count runts. Unfortunately, the term *runt* is not standardized, and its definition carries different meanings in different products. A runt could be any type of frame that is shorter than the legal minimum, including: local, remote or preamble collisions, and short frames with a good or bad FCS.

Jabber

Jabber is defined in the 802.3 standard as a frame longer than the maximum legal size (greater than 1518 bytes). However, there is no indication as to whether the frame has a good or bad FCS. In general, you should not see jabbers. The most likely causes of jabber are a faulty NIC card and/or faulty or corrupt NIC driver files, bad cabling, or grounding problems. See also Long Frame and Frame Check Sequence.

Long frame

A long frame is one that is longer than the maximum legal size (greater than 1518 bytes), and has a valid frame check sequence. This is normally the result of improperly configured software or NIC driver files.

Frame Check Sequence (FCS)

A frame having a bad frame check sequence (also referred to as a **CRC error**) is known as a Frame Check Sequence (FCS) error. In an FCS error, the header information is *probably* correct (the addressing and such), but the checksum calculated by the receiving station does not match the checksum appended to the end of the frame. A high number of FCS errors from a single station usually indicates a faulty NIC card and/or faulty or corrupted software drivers, or a bad cable connecting that station to the network. If FCS errors are associated with many stations, it generally is traceable to bad cabling, a faulty version of NIC driver, a faulty hub port, or induced noise in the cable system.

Alignment error

A message that does not end on an octet boundary is known as an alignment error. That is, instead of the correct number of binary bits forming complete octet groupings, there are some additional bits left over (less than 8). This is often caused by bad software drivers, or a collision, and is frequently accompanied by a failure of the FCS checksum. See also Framing errors.

Framing errors

Framing errors can be one of two types, both of which indicate improperly assembled messages.

1. Maximum Frame Size—the received frame had more than the maximum legal number of octets. When this happens, the NIC is allowed to truncate the message and report an error. See also Jabber and Long Frame.

2. Integer Number of Octets in Frame—the frame format requires completely formed octets, and any frame that contains extra or missing bits constitutes an error. Such a frame is truncated to the nearest octet boundary, and if the FCS checksum fails, then an alignment error is reported. See also Alignment Error.

Ghosts

Fluke has coined this new term to mean energy (noise) detected on the cable that appears to be a frame, but without a valid SFD. To qualify as a ghost, this "frame" must be at least 72 bytes long (including preamble), otherwise it is classified as a remote collision. Because of the peculiar nature of ghosts, it is important to note that test results are largely dependent upon where on the segment the measurement is made.

Some types of noise will fool nodes on a network segment into thinking they are receiving a frame. However, the sensed frame never comes, so no data is passed up into the NIC to be processed. After awhile the sensed transmission ceases, and the NIC is able to resume sending its own messages. Different network interfaces will react differently, and there are no standards defining how or when an NIC should react to a noisy segment. Repeaters will sometimes propagate these signals into other segments of the network.

The visible symptom of ghosting is a network that is slow for no apparent reason. The file servers are nearly idle, and network monitoring equipment shows very low network utilization, yet users are complaining that the network is excessively slow or completely down. The symptom may be geographically limited, where one end of a large/long segment seems to operate, and the other is slow or completely down.

Ground loops and other wiring problems are usually the cause of ghosting. Ghosts cause some repeaters to respond as though a frame is being received. Since the repeater is only reacting to an ac voltage riding on the cable, there will not be a valid frame to pass on to the other ports. The repeater, however will transmit this energy on to its other port(s). The retransmitted ghost may appear as a jam pattern or a very long preamble.

Most network monitoring tools do not recognize the existence of ghosts, for the same reason that they do not recognize preamble collisions—they rely entirely on what the chipset tells them. Depending on the duration of the event, the LANMeter test tool will interpret the noise either as a ghost or a collision.

Range

A frame that had a legal-sized value in the Length field that did not match the actual number of octets counted in the data field of the received frame is known as a range error. This error also appears when the length field value is less than the minimum legal unpadded size of the data field (normally this would be a minimum value of 46).

Description of causes and cures

There are two factors to remember whenever trying to isolate Ethernet problems. First, test results are often influenced by where on the segment the measurement is made and are substantially enhanced if the test device is generating traffic while it is monitoring. Second, because an Ethernet collision domain can be described as a *distributed single point of failure*, you must always remember that a problem detected in one area could be coming from a failure that is hundreds, or even thousands, of feet away physically.

Knowing which specific errors are present will help you determine the causes of Ethernet network problems. However, because of the nature of a bus topology, your best approach in troubleshooting Ethernet is still the *divide-and-conquer* method of isolating problems. Keep dividing the segment until the smallest common denominator can be removed or replaced. As long as you can detect an error you have a good chance of isolating it. Refer to Appendix C for general troubleshooting guidelines.

Use Table A-1 to determine the most likely causes, then refer to the descriptions below to solve them.

Cabling

The majority of LAN problems are cable-related (see Appendix F). Cable problems can appear in many forms. If an FCS error is associated with many stations, it generally is traceable to bad cabling, a faulty hub port, or induced noise.

Noise source

Common sources of induced noise include fans, heaters, photocopiers, fluorescent lights, elevators, any type of electric motor, etc. These sources create short, powerful bursts or spikes of noise called *impulse noise*, which is what usually corrupts data.

The fastest way to isolate either cabling or noise problems is to test suspect cables with a cable tester. If the problem is intermittent, some cable testers can be used to run a long-term (i.e., 24 hours) test. Any noise "spikes" that occur during that period will be identified, helping to determine the cause of the noise by correlating the time of the event with what was occurring in the area. Replacing or rerouting the cable away from the noise source should solve the problem.

If poor cabling has been used throughout the network, errors may be reported by all stations. However, those with the longest cable runs will have the most problems. Poor-quality cable is very susceptible to electrical noise, and will typically present a variety of problems, usually intermittent. Use a tool such as the Fluke DSP-100 cable tester, or the LANMeter test tool's **Cable Scan** function to diagnose these problems.

Power problems

Bad ac power can cause hubs or concentrators to introduce noise into the cable system. The result is data corruption as it passes through the device.

Important: The power problem does not have to come from your office, your floor, or even your building—it could come from down the block or farther away, depending on what is connected between you and the substation.

If your UPS power supply gives an overload alarm, but is reporting a load less than its rating, it is likely a harmonics problem. A Fluke 41 Power Harmonics Analyzer will help identify problems related to potentially dangerous harmonics in your electrical distribution system.

Bad cable or connector

Coax cables using BNC connectors are frequently the source of problems because of abuse by users. If the connector can be pulled free of the cable with moderate tension, the connection should be reterminated. UTP cables are often constructed improperly. Typical problems include using wire pairs that are not twisted together, using stranded wire RJ-45 connectors for solid core wire (or the opposite), low-quality wire, punch-down blocks and patch panels (that do not meet even Category 3 requirements), etc. Use a tool such as the Fluke DSP-100 cable tester, or the LANMeter test tool's cable tests to diagnose these problems.

Cable too long

If a cable is too long, it may cause excessive loss of bandwidth to collisions, or in extreme cases late collisions. A too-long network is one in which the end-to-end signal propagation time is greater than the minimum legal-sized frame.

Note: It is unlikely that simply too much cable is the cause of late collisions, as it would require more than five kilometers of cable. Parameters such as attenuation and NEXT have a greater effect than simple length.

Station drop cables that exceed the specified maximums may result in dropped connections for the station that is attached to the network through that cable.

Grounding problems

The Ethernet standard describes how each thick coax segment should be grounded at one—and only one—point along the cable (grounding thin coax is only recommended). If the cable is not grounded, or if it becomes grounded at more than one point, then intermittent problems may result. The problem related to multiple ground points is a *ground loop* effect, where current flows along the cable—often causing data to be corrupted. The easiest way to create a potential ground loop is to allow the BNC "tee" connector on the back of a station to come in contact with the grounded metal shell of another connector.

Note: Both the center conductor and shield of a coax cable are electrically isolated in the PC by the NIC with greater than 250 kΩ at 50 and 60 Hz.

You can test for voltage on a cable shield with any good-quality multimeter (any of the Fluke digital multimeters would be suitable. See the discussion starting on page F-27 for more information on proper grounding.

Ground loops, other wiring problems, and violations of the standard are usually the cause of ghosting, though the problem is often discovered because a repeater has retransmitted the noise. When isolating grounding problems, remember that test results will vary depending upon where on the segment the measurement is made. Other possible problems include FCS errors, and collisions—and in some rare cases jabber. The LANMeter test tool **Network Stats** and **Error Stats** tests will detect these errors, often identifying the address of the station that sent the corrupted frame.

Faulty or misconfigured NIC

If a faulty NIC is suspected, it can be tested with the LANMeter test tool's **Expert-T** or **NIC Autotest**. These tests will also find configuration problems in a station. However, an NIC with an intermittent problem may pass this test, so if you strongly suspect the NIC is bad, you may wish to replace it even if it passes these tests.

A faulty NIC can be the source of virtually all types of Ethernet errors. In most cases though, the problem can be traced to improperly configured software driver files or cable problems. Errors such as short frames and FCS errors from a single station are most often configuration or corrupted-driver problems. Errors such as late collisions and jabber are often caused by marginal or failed hardware.

Hard fault

On coaxial networks the incidence of hard failures is substantially increased because users often do not understand that while there is no problem removing the "tee" connector from the back of their PC, removing either of the cables from the "tee" connector causes the network to fail. Similarly, the function and placement of termination resistance is not understood, nor is the reason for forbidding "stub" cables to be attached to the "tee" connector (which is sometimes done when a PC is moved. See Figure 2-1).

The LANMeter test tool's **Cable Scan** test can be specially configured to send a TDR pulse down a live coax cable, looking for opens, shorts, and other discontinuities of the cable while the network is in use. It can also check for the presence of one or both termination resistors by using the **DC Continuity** test. In 10BASE-T networks, the source of the cable fault is almost always quite obvious, as it will typically affect only a single user. The **Expert-T** test can be used in all cases to isolate a failure's cause with relation to the network, the NIC, or the cable.

Illegal hardware configuration

The common bus architecture and variety of cabling options permit users to construct Ethernet networks into a variety of interesting and creative designs. Unfortunately, this also means there are a variety of interesting and creative ways to violate the rules defined in the standard. Worse still, the protocol is robust enough to mask many minor—and some major—violations at low to moderate utilization rates. This means that when utilization increases significantly, typically at the worst possible times during the workday, performance of poorly designed or poorly installed networks will drop off rapidly, and the network may cease operating altogether. Refer to Appendix B for a summary of the more common Ethernet design rules. Correcting problems related to standards violations often requires long hours of physical inspection of all cables and connections. If this is necessary, it is strongly recommended that a complete set of network documentation (see Chapter 1) be developed at the same time. This will help avoid similar problems in the future, and will greatly facilitate troubleshooting when problems do occur.

Addressing/routing

When troubleshooting Ethernet problems, it is important to remember that Ethernet MAC addresses can cross hubs, switches, and bridged connections. But they will never cross routed connections. The "local" MAC address of the router is used when a message is retransmitted on a new segment, while the source and destination network-layer address is undisturbed.

Also, an Ethernet collision domain crosses hub and repeater connections, but stops at bridges and routers. That means that errors affect all stations on this side of a bridge or router. However, depending on the technology implemented in a switch, the collision domain may extend partly into the next segment. If the switch is using "store-and-forward" technology, it may be thought of as a bridge. But if the switch is using "cut-through" technology, then many errors are forwarded before the switch realizes that the frame has an error. If the first half of the frame is intact (at least 20 bytes good), then the switch will have already begun forwarding—regardless of what follows. More sophisticated switches will temporarily change from cut-through to store-and-forward if the error level on a port goes too high.

Token Ring Errors

Token Ring operates in the presence of soft, or intermittent, errors. The station that detects a soft (recoverable) error transmits the Report Soft Error frame two seconds after the event that caused the error. Each Report Soft Error frame contains the type of error and quantity of those errors detected during the preceding two-second period.

Soft errors are either isolating or non-isolating. Isolating error frames include information that limits the scope of the reported problem to two stations, their cables, and any equipment (MAUs, for example) between the two stations. The two stations in this "fault domain" are the station reporting the error and its Nearest Active Upstream Neighbor (NAUN). This "fault domain" information is invaluable in troubleshooting a ring. Remember, in the case of isolating errors, the fault may not rest with the reporting station—it could be the station shown as NAUN. (Don't shoot the messenger!) By definition, non-isolating errors do not provide reliable fault domain information, but are still useful in the troubleshooting process and often *do* pinpoint the failure.

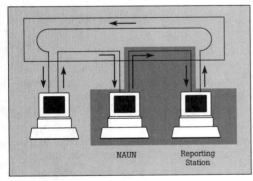

Figure A-1. *Token Ring fault domain.*

Diagnosing Token Ring problems

Token Ring's error frames can provide you with a valuable insight into solving network problems. Table A-2 gives a summary of errors reported on a ring and many of their most likely causes. The sections following the table describe the errors in detail and their causes and cures.

Note that beacons, claims and purges are ring management frames and not soft errors. They can, however, be used in much the same way as soft errors to diagnose problems. Information about these frames is displayed on the LANMeter test tool's **Network Stats** screen.

Description of error frames

Abort (abort delimiter transmitted error)
(isolating)

An abort error is reported by any ring station that either recovers from a transient error internal to the ring station, fails to recover from a hard error internal to the ring station and sends the error frame just prior to deinserting, or detects a corrupted token.

A/C (address recognized, frame copied)
(isolating)

A/C errors are also known as ARI/FCI errors. They are reported when an adapter receives more than one Active Monitor Present (AMP) or Standby Monitor Present (SMP) frame with A/C bits set to zero, without first receiving the intervening AMP frame. This error may occur as a result of other errors, or indicate a problem with the upstream neighbor, and is sometimes due to improper frame handling by a switch, bridge or router, or a marginal station improperly participating in the neighbor notification process.

Causes	Error Type												
	Abort	ARI/FCI	Beacon	Burst	Claim Token	Freq	Frame Copied	Internal	Line	Lost Frame	Purge	Rec Congest	Token
Insertion/Removal	•	•		•					•	•	•		•
Noisy Line	•	•		•					•	•	•		•
Faulty NIC	•			•		•		•	•	•	•		•
Active Monitor					•								
Hard Fault			•										
Congestion												•	
Bridge/Router							•						
Duplicate Address							•						

Table A-2. *Token Ring errors chart.*

Beacon frame (ring management)

A ring station that is detecting a hard error will immediately begin issuing beacon frames until the hard error is corrected, and if a claim token process fails to recover the ring, the ring station will escalate the problem and begin issuing beacon frames. During the initial phase of a beaconing state, both the ring station issuing the beacon frames and that station's NAUN will briefly deinsert from the ring and execute self-diagnostics. If either station detects the hard fault, that station will remain out of the ring, and the ring should recover on its own. If no fault is detected then manual intervention by the network support staff will be required to recover the ring. The beacon frame contains the address of the beaconing station and its NAUN.

Burst error (isolating)

Burst errors are reported by any ring station that detects the absence of any signal transitions for five half-bit times between the start and end delimiter of a frame or token.

Claim token (ring management)

A claim token frame is issued any time that:

- A standby monitor has a timer expire indicating that it has been too long since a token was last seen.

- A standby monitor has a timer expire indicating that it has been too long since the last neighbor notification process.

- The active monitor is unable to purge the ring.

- A new station inserts into the ring and does not detect an active monitor.

- A station detects a frequency error.

- A beaconing station receives one of its own beacon frames back.

- Any station detects an individual beacon frame the second time (the frame is starting to circulate around the ring a second time).

- Any station (not the source of the beacon) has been observing and repeating beacon frames, but then has a timer expire, indicating that no beacon frame has been seen for too long.

- Any station detects a signal loss condition.

If the claim token process fails to elect a new active monitor and restore the ring, the failure condition of the network will escalate to a Beaconing state.

Frame copy (non-isolating)

Frame copied errors are reported by any ring station that detects a frame containing its own destination address, but with the address-recognized bits already set, indicating a possible duplicate address.

Frequency error (non-isolating)

Frequency errors are reported by any ring station that receives a signal clocked at a frequency outside the acceptable range of variation.

Internal error (isolating)

Internal errors are reported by any ring station that detects an internal error (a self-diagnostic error of some type) that was recoverable. (The reporting card should always be replaced soon.)

Line error (isolating)

Line errors are reported by any ring station detecting a token or frame that contains either a Frame Check Sequence (FCS) error, or some type of protocol code violation between the starting and ending delimiters of the frame or token.

Lost frame (non-isolating)

Lost frames are reported by any ring station that fails to see a transmitted frame returned to it before a timer expires.

Purge (ring management)

Purge frames are issued by the active monitor if its timer expires before the token returns, to recover from an error condition, or immediately upon assuming the job of active monitor. If the purge frame makes it around the ring and is received without errors by the active monitor, the ring is assumed to be operational and a new token is issued. Multiple purge frames may be required before normal ring operation is restored. A ring purge frame causes all ring stations to reset themselves to default values for timers, etc.

If purging fails to restore normal ring operation the problem will escalate into the claim token process.

Receiver congestion (non-isolating)

Receiver congestion is reported by any ring station that sees a frame addressed to it, but has no buffer space available for the frame. Unless issued by an interconnect device (bridge, router, etc.) or a network resource (such as a file server), these errors are *usually* benign and do not adversely affect overall ring performance.

Token (non-isolating)

Token errors are reported by the active monitor when: 1) a token is received with the monitor bit of a normal token or priority token set; 2) the start delimiter of a message has an illegal code violation; or 3) if a timer expires indicating that it has been too long since a token was last seen.

Description of causes and cures

Knowing which errors are present and their associated fault domains can help you determine the causes of Token Ring network problems. Use Table A-2 to determine the most likely causes, then refer to the descriptions below to solve them.

Insertion/removal

The process of inserting or deinserting a station from the ring will cause a few errors. Most often these are token and burst errors. This is the normal result of the electro-mechanical relays used in the MAU connections. Stations may insert and deinsert themselves repeatedly in the case of some NIC failures. If errors occur when stations are not inserting or deinserting, the likely cause is induced noise or a faulty NIC. In most cases, it is alright to ignore errors generated when a station inserts or deinserts. However, if the topology is stable, there should be no errors—even with very high utilization (above 95%).

Cabling

The majority of LAN problems are cable-related. (Appendix F covers cabling issues in depth.) Cable problems can show up in many forms. These are explained below:

Noise source

If soft errors are limited to a specific domain, a source of electrical noise may be close to a cable. Common sources of this type of noise include fans, heaters, photocopiers, fluorescent lights, elevators, any type of electric motor, etc. In other cases, a cable not designed for LAN traffic or one that is poorly installed may be susceptible to background noise present in any office.

Testing suspect cables with a cable tester is the fastest way to isolate either problem. Both the cable on the reporting station and its upstream neighbor should be tested. If the problem is intermittent, some cable testers can be used to run a long-term (i.e., 24 hour) test. Any noise "spikes" that occur during that period will be identified, helping to determine the cause of the noise. Replacing or rerouting the cable away from the noise source should solve the problems.

Bad cable or connector

Bad cables or connectors will almost always show up as errors in a specific domain. Use a cable tester like the Fluke DSP-100 or the LANMeter test tool's **Cable Scan** function to diagnose these problems.

General noise or "environmental" problems

If soft errors are reported in many areas around the ring, it's likely that there is a general noise problem. If poor cabling has been used throughout the network, errors will be reported by all stations, but those with the longest cable runs will have the most problems. If a cable bundle leading to a wiring closet passes too close to a noise source, it will cause errors to intermittently appear on all stations using those cables.

Marginal MAUs can introduce noise into the system, resulting in errors being reported by many of the stations plugged into the MAU. Use your network documentation to determine if the stations identified in reported fault domains are connected to the same MAU, to MAUs in the same wiring closet, or even to rings in the same building. If the ac power in a wiring closet is marginal or bad, this can also cause errors to appear intermittently on all stations attached to that set of MAUs (see Power problems below).

The easiest way to determine if the ring is noisy is to measure phase jitter with a LANMeter test tool. (Note: For this specific test, phase jitter measurements are valid only on rings without "jitter busting" or other retiming circuitry.) The cause of a noise problem can be tracked down by removing individual stations or bypassing individual MAUs and watching the phase jitter measurement. If the problem cannot be isolated to a specific cause (MAU, punchdown block, cable), it may be necessary to test a sample of the cables using the **Cable Scan** or **Lobe Test** function. Also try using the **Traffic Generator** to send LLC traffic configured with each of the three available jitter patterns in the background while you watch for an increase in soft errors in the **Network Stats** screen. Use the soft error fault domains to isolate the suspect station. Repeat the test with the suspect station removed to verify that the station is truly the source of the problem.

Power problems

Bad ac power can cause MAUs or concentrators to introduce noise into the cable system, resulting in data being corrupted as it passes through the device.

Remember: The power problem does not have to come from your office, your floor, or even your building. It could come from down the block or farther away depending on what is connected between you and the power company substation.

Usually, if the errors appear to be coming from the entire ring, the network is often not at fault. The problem is most often an environmental problem. However, lightning damage can cause network adapter cards to become marginal and exhibit this type of behavior.

If your UPS power supply gives an overload alarm, but is reporting a load less than its rating, it is likely to be a harmonics problem. A Fluke 41B Power Harmonics Analyzer will help identify problems related to potentially dangerous harmonics in your electrical distribution system.

Cable too long

Cables that are too long can cause intermittent errors. Check them using a cable tester or a LANMeter test tool. Maximum cable lengths at 16 Mbps are 100 meters (330 feet) for Type 1 (150Ω shielded cable) and 45 meters (150 feet) for Type 3 (100Ω unshielded twisted pair cable). Maximums for 4 Mbps are 240 meters (780 feet) for Type 1 and 100 meters (330 feet) for Type 3. Consult the *IBM Token-Ring Network Introduction and Planning Guide* for an exhaustive discussion of how to calculate longer allowed lobe lengths.

NAUN too far away

This can be a problem where the ring and its MAUs are distributed over a wide area. Figure A-2 shows that when all stations on an in-between MAU are shut off, the signal may not be able to travel the distance between two distant stations. This problem can be solved temporarily by leaving an in-between station on at all times, by adding repeaters, or by reconfiguring your rings.

Too many stations

Having too many stations can cause excessive phase jitter, resulting in high soft error rates. Having too many stations can also cause Token Ring internal timers to expire and disrupt data flow, which may cause excessive purges, claim tokens and even intermittent beaconing. Table A-3 shows the suggested maximum number of stations per ring according to the IBM technical documentation. Count any repeaters (including active MAUs) as additional stations when calculating maximum station counts per ring. Some active or intelligent MAUs count for more than one station, depending on the number of active connections (i.e., each IBM 8220 counts as two stations and each IBM 8230 counts as three stations).

It is good practice to limit the number of stations per ring to 50 or less, in order to minimize the number of users affected by a serious error.

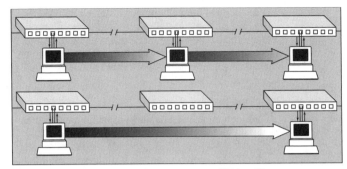

Figure A-2. Distance too far for an unrepeated Token Ring signal.

Ring Speed	Cable Type		
	Type 1	Type 3	Type 5
4 Mbps	260	72	132
16 Mbps	140	72	132

Table A-3. Guideline for maximum number of stations per ring, based on ring speed and cable type.

Faulty NIC

If a faulty NIC is suspected, it can be tested with the LANMeter test tool's **Expert-T** or **NIC Autotest**. These tests will also find configuration problems in a station. However, an NIC with an intermittent problem may pass this test, so if you strongly suspect the NIC is bad (as in the case of *frequency* or *internal* soft errors), you may wish to replace it even if it passes these tests.

Active monitor

When a station performing the job of active monitor leaves a ring, the claim-token process is used to elect a new active monitor. Occasionally, this will happen in a normally operating ring. However, if claim tokens are issued when there is no change in the ring topology (no stations joining or leaving the ring), it could indicate a problem with the active monitor. The **Ring Stations** test provides a history of which station has been the active monitor over the period of time the test was running. If the ring tends to have problems when a particular station is the active monitor, try removing that station to see if it solves the problem. With some NICs, running certain programs such as the IBM Ring Diagnostic Program on a dedicated station can help, as that station will tend to remain the active monitor. Some bridges and routers also have a configuration option that will cause them to attempt to obtain and keep the active monitor job.

Hard fault

Beacon conditions occur in cases of hard (permanent) faults. Hard faults include broken cables, stuck MAU ports, and bad NICs. See Chapter 2 for information on dealing with beaconing.

Receiver congestion

Data coming into a NIC is first stored in a buffer, then read into the card's logic. Simultaneously, the data is retransmitted by the NIC to the downstream neighbor. Congestion problems are serious if the reporting station is a server, bridge or router. Congestion can result when the ring station:

- Is overloaded, and the buffer becomes full
- Network drivers are not properly configured
- Network drivers are not loaded

A common cause of congestion errors is warm-booting a ring station. In some cases this will cause the station to remain in the ring, but if network drivers are not loaded, the card's buffer will fill up quickly and generate errors from that point forward. Unless the station is an important network resource (server, bridge, router, etc.), receiver congestion should be considered as a benign error that does not constitute an emergency.

Frame copy

The presence of frame copy errors can sometimes be traced to switch, bridge or router configuration problems, instead of duplicate addresses on other rings. If the network uses locally administered addresses, verify that there are no stations on the same or other rings within the network using the same address as the reporting station. Locally administered addresses are managed through special configuration files stored on the PC, and can be accidentally copied from one station to another with great ease. Since the file is created for a single PC, duplication of the file will cause duplicate addresses on the network.

When troubleshooting Token Ring problems, it is important to remember that Token Ring MAC addresses can cross hubs, switches and bridges. But they will never cross routed connections. The "local" MAC address of the router is used when a message is retransmitted on a new ring, while the source and destination network-layer address is undisturbed. Thus, almost all frame copy errors indicate the presence of a device on another ring with a duplicate address, since the protocol will not allow a duplicate on the same ring.

A station holding the same address as any other station on the same ring will abort the insertion process with minimal, and often cryptic, error messages. Use the LANMeter test tool's **Expert-T** test to quickly identify this problem.

Bridges and routers

Problems are sometimes caused by improperly configured bridges or routers, especially in source-routed networks. Again, divide-and-conquer is the best approach. First, check bridges and routers for misconfiguration, incomplete configuration, and especially for old software or firmware revisions. The default settings of all devices may not be appropriate for your network. Now, try disabling the feature in some bridges and routers to actively seek the job of active monitor, or to assume the job of Ring Parameter Server. Preventing a bridge or router from taking the Ring Parameter Server job will sometimes solve station-insertion failure problems too.

The relatively new category of switches represents nothing more than a multi-port bridge that has been optimized for certain performance characteristics. Treat switches like any other bridge. Also, the software controlling switches is relatively new, and often suffers from many of the problems that plagued bridges in the past. The two most common problems noticed recently are the Ring Parameter Server problem described in Chapter 2, and a tendency to improperly change the frame-copied bits—creating the symptom of a duplicate address in the bridged network.

Appendix B — Operation

Media Access Protocols

There are two fundamental ways in which stations are able to access a network: through token passing and contention. In contention networks, stations wishing to transmit are not required to wait their turn; instead they may transmit at any time they wish—providing the cable appears to be idle at that instant. This creates a situation where a certain number of stations transmit simultaneously with some regularity, causing corruption of data. An apparent data loss is to be expected, and the sending stations correct for these data collisions routinely. Ethernet is an example of a contention protocol.

In token-passing networks, each station is constrained from sending a message on the cable until it comes into possession of the electronic "token." By controlling the token, the station wishing to transmit a message is assured that no other station will attempt to transmit a message at the same time. This control avoids situations where data would be lost or destroyed because two or more stations transmitted at the same time. Token Ring is an example of a token-passing protocol.

Ethernet Operation

Note: *The descriptions that follow relate to 10 Mbps Ethernet. The frame structure is identical for all speeds (10/100/1000 Mbps), but some of the design rules, physical layer attributes, and frame handling are different at higher speeds.*

Introduction

Ethernet operates on a "bus" structure, which is a technical way to say that every station always hears all messages at almost the exact same time. The official designation is Carrier Sense Multiple Access with Collision Detection (CSMA/CD). CSMA/CD simply means that when two stations realize that they are talking at the same time, they are supposed to stop and wait a polite amount of time before trying again.

The rules and specifications for proper operation of the CSMA/CD protocol commonly known as IEEE 802.3, ISO/IEC 8802.3, or Ethernet are not particularly complicated. However, when a problem occurs in Ethernet, it is often quite difficult to isolate the source of the problem. Whereas, in the case of Token Ring, problems typically occur between one station on the ring and the next—and the addresses of the two suspect stations are reported! Because of the common bus architecture (which can be described as a *distributed single point of failure*), the domain of the problem is all stations within the collision domain. In situations where repeaters are used, this can include stations up to four segments away.

According to the rules, any station on an Ethernet network wishing to transmit a message first "listens" to ensure that no other station is currently using the cable. If the cable is quiet, the station will begin transmitting immediately using *Manchester* encoded data. But because the electrical signal takes a small amount of time to travel down the cable (called propagation delay), it is possible for more than one station to begin transmitting at—or near—the same time. When this happens, a collision will result. Normal transmission voltages measured on coax are between 0 and -1.025 volts (0 to -2.05 volts unloaded). For UTP cable the normal peak differential voltages are between 2.2 and 2.8 volts (from above +1 volt, to below -1 volt).

Assuming that a collision does not occur, the sending station will transmit 64 bits of timing information known collectively as the preamble, followed by: the addressing information, certain other header information, the actual data, and a checksum (FCS) used to ensure the received message was not corrupted along the way. A receiving station recalculates the FCS to determine if the incoming message is valid and hands good messages to the next higher layer in the NIC card.

The primary difference between the various Ethernet frame types is found in how the preamble is specified, the usage of the length/type field, and what is found in the first few octets of the data field. The terms "byte" and "octet" are used interchangeably in different sections of this document, and, in either case, will mean a group of eight binary bits. The term "octet" is a precise way to indicate units of eight bits, and is commonly used in technical networking discussions because many computers use "bytes" (or "words") composed of more than eight bits.

For all frame types, there is an eight-octet sequence of alternating 1's and 0's, concluding in a pattern of two consecutive 1's that is used for synchronization (1010...1011). The only difference between the frames described below is whether the timing information is specified as preamble and start frame delimiter (SFD), or if the two are combined into a longer preamble. In all, the binary information is the same.

Each receiving station will synchronize with the timing information, but not store it. All information *following* the binary "11" pattern at the end of the timing information will be retrieved from the cable and passed up to the MAC layer in the NIC card where a new checksum will be calculated and compared with the checksum at the end of the frame. If the frame is intact, it must then be interpreted according to the rules for whichever protocol it claims to contain.

There were a notable number of changes to the basic structure of Ethernet included in the 1998 version of the standard. One significant change was that two-byte addresses were explicitly excluded, though they were included in all prior versions. The maximum value for the 802.3 Length field was specified as 1536 (600 hex), where it was previously assumed to match the maximum data size of 1500 (5DC hex). The range between 1500 and 1536 is "unassigned" at present. At about the same time, the growing availability of virtual networks as described in IEEE 802.1Q caused the insertion of two new fields into the basic frame to support VLANs. These two fields added 4-bytes to the maximum frame length, when present. The size of an Ethernet frame has also undergone some changes over the years. Almost everyone is familiar with the minimum sized Ethernet frame being specified as 64 bytes, but the actual size on the wire has always been 72 bytes (64 bytes plus the preamble and SFD). The preamble and SFD are timing information that is discarded by the chipset and thus not included in the frame size. The largest Ethernet frame has also similarly been 1526 instead of 1518. If 802.1Q VLANs are present, this size now grows to 1530 (1522 bytes plus the preamble and SFD) bytes through the addition of 4 bytes of tag (see Figure B-2.) There

are other protocol extensions which have similar effects. For example, the ISL switch protocol that Cisco created adds 30 bytes to the frame size. If any VLAN protocol is present, but an intervening switch or bridge is not configured to participate in the VLAN, then the frame is likely to be discarded for being larger than 1518 (1526) bytes and thus is considered an illegal frame.

For all speeds of Ethernet transmission, the standard describes how a frame may be no smaller than "slot time." For 10 and 100 Mbps Ethernet slot time is 512 bit-times (64 bytes, not including the timing information). For 1000 Mbps Ethernet slot time is 4096 bit-times (including the extension). Slot time is just longer than the longest possible round-trip delay time when maximum cable lengths are used on the largest legal network and all hardware propagation delay times are at the legal maximum, plus the 32-bit jam signal used when collisions are detected. In other words, slot time is the time it can theoretically take on the largest legal Ethernet network for a signal to get to the far end, collide with another message at the last possible instant, and then have the collision fragments return to the first station and be detected. For the system to work the first station must learn about the collision before it finishes sending the smallest legal frame size. To allow versions of Ethernet that are faster than 100 Mbps to co-exist with the slower versions, another new field was introduced: the extension field (see Figure B-2.) This field is present only on the greater-than 100 Mbps links, and allows minimum sized frames to be stretched long enough to meet slot-time requirements for the 10 and 100 Mbps versions. For example, slot time for 1000 Mbps Ethernet is 4096 bit times (excluding the preamble and SFD). The extension is discarded when the frame is passed to a 10 or 100 Mbps segment.

When data on the bus is examined by a protocol analyzer, the frame formats and data structures below will be observed as described. However, if the signal is examined with an oscilloscope directly, then binary values will have to be manually reordered for each octet. This is because Ethernet transmits each octet in consecutive order from the preamble to the frame check

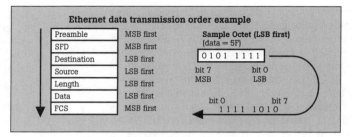

Figure B-1. *Ethernet bit transmission order.*

sequence (FCS), but the bit order is reversed so that the least significant bit (LSB) is transmitted first (*except* for the preamble, (SFD), and FCS—which is sent most significant bit (MSB) first). (See Figure B-1.)

Frame types

Among the many possible frame types, five different frame types are in common use on Ethernet. They are: IEEE 802.3, Novell 802.3 "Raw," IEEE 802.2, Ethernet II (or Ethernet v2.0) and Ethernet SNAP.

Within the category of widely supported Ethernet frame types is the 802.3 Raw frame to which all versions of Novell's NetWare up to version 3.11 default. Later versions of NetWare default to the 802.2 frame. In the 802.3 Raw frame, the first two bytes of the data field (which correlates to the IPX checksum) are filled with the default value "FFFF," since IPX relies on the MAC layer protocol for error checking. This data looks exactly like a global broadcast DSAP address in the 802.2 frame. Therefore, it has the potential to create problems on Ethernets that use the proper 802.2 frame—though most networking products are aware of the 802.3 Raw frame and are designed to avoid problems.

Other "almost-Ethernet" implementations that you might still encounter include LattisNet and StarLAN-10. LattisNet was developed by Synoptics, and StarLAN-10 was developed by AT&T. Both were developed before the 10BASE-T Standard was released and are not fully compatible with 10BASE-T, though traffic from both can coexist with other Ethernet traffic on the same cable. The most noticeable difference is the lack of a link-pulse, which is required by 10BASE-T.

Products developed by these companies after completion of the standard are now fully compliant.

In Figure B-2 there are two frame formats shown. The first format is the traditional Ethernet framing, while the second shows the new fields that are possible if VLANs are present, and/or if the frame is seen on a Gigabit Ethernet link. The remainder of this description will ignore the extra fields shown at the bottom of Figure B-2.

802.3 Frame (See Figure B-2.)

Octets	Description
7	Preamble
1	Start Frame Delimiter (SFD)
6	Destination MAC Address
6	Source MAC Address
2	802.1Q Tag Type [data=8100]
2	802.1Q Tag Control Information
2	Length/Type Field (Maximum 600 in hexadecimal, otherwise protocol type)
46 to 1500	Data (If less than 46 bytes, then a pad must be added to the end)
4	Frame Check Sequence (CRC Checksum)
*	Extension field (only used in greater than 100 Mbps Ethernet)

The size of the Extension field is (slotTime minus minFrameSize) bits, inclusive, and is made up of symbols that are readily distinguishable from data bits.

**The extra fields shown above are only present if 802.1Q VLANs are being used, or if the frame is seen on a Gigabit Ethernet link. They are equally possible in the other frame types described here, but are not shown.*

Novell 802.3 Raw Frame (See Figure B-3.)

This frame is actually a true and valid 802.3 frame, except that the first two octets of the data field are always filled with the Novell IPX checksum data. The remainder of the data field would be filled with other IPX header and data. Future versions of NetWare may begin using this checksum field as an actual checksum, but at present it is filled with a default value (FFFF), and NetWare relies on the FCS checksum in the Ethernet frame to ensure delivery of valid data. This frame type pre-dates the completion of the 802.3 Standard.

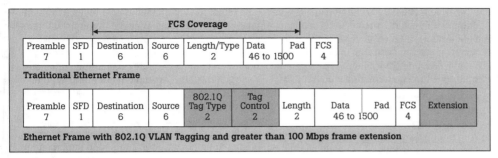

	FCS Coverage						
Preamble 7	SFD 1	Destination 6	Source 6	Length/Type 2	Data 46 to 1500	Pad	FCS 4

Traditional Ethernet Frame

Preamble 7	SFD 1	Destination 6	Source 6	802.1Q Tag Type 2	Tag Control 2	Length 2	Data 46 to 1500	Pad	FCS 4	Extension

Ethernet Frame with 802.1Q VLAN Tagging and greater than 100 Mbps frame extension

Figure B-2. Data fields for an Ethernet 802.3 frame.

Ethernet II Frame (See Figure B-4.) Also known as Ethernet v2.0 or DIX Ethernet.

Octets	Description
8	Preamble (ending in pattern 10101011, the 802.3 SFD)
6	Destination MAC Address
6	Source MAC Address
2	Type Field (Must be larger than 600 in hexadecimal or it is interpreted as an 802.2 frame)
46 to 1500	Data. (If less than 46 bytes, then a pad must be added to the end.)
4	Frame Check Sequence (CRC Checksum)

802.2 Frame (See Figure B-5.) 802.3 MAC frame plus Logical Link Control (LLC) data.

Octets	Description
7	Preamble
1	Start Frame Delimiter
6	Destination MAC Address
6	Source MAC Address
2	Length/Type Field (Maximum 600 in hexadecimal)
46 to 1500	Data. (If less than 46 bytes (including DSAP, SSAP, and Control), then a pad must be added to the end.)
1	802.2 LLC Destination Service Access Point (DSAP)
1	802.2 LLC Source Service Access Point (SSAP)
1 or 2	802.2 LLC Control Field (2 octets if sequencing is used)
4	Frame Check Sequence (CRC Checksum)

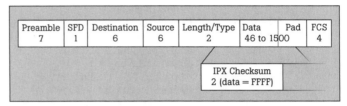

Preamble 7	SFD 1	Destination 6	Source 6	Length/Type 2	Data 46 to 1500	Pad	FCS 4

IPX Checksum 2 (data = FFFF)

Figure B-3. Data fields for an Novell 802.3 (Novell Raw) frame.

Preamble 8	Destination 6	Source 6	Type 2	Data 46 to 1500	Pad	FCS 4

Figure B-4. Data fields for an Ethernet II frame.

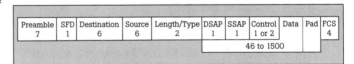

Preamble 7	SFD 1	Destination 6	Source 6	Length/Type 2	DSAP 1	SSAP 1	Control 1 or 2	Data	Pad	FCS 4
							46 to 1500			

Figure B-5. Data fields for an Ethernet 802.2 frame.

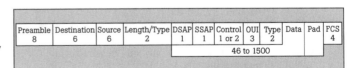

Preamble 8	Destination 6	Source 6	Length/Type 2	DSAP 1	SSAP 1	Control 1 or 2	OUI 3	Type 2	Data	Pad	FCS 4
								46 to 1500			

Figure B-6. Data fields for an Ethernet SNAP frame.

Ethernet SNAP Frame (See Figure B-6.)

The Sub-Network Access Protocol (SNAP) is an extension of the 802.2 LLC, offering support for more than the 127 unique protocols allowed by the two 8-bit Link Service Access Point (LSAP) fields (the DSAP and SSAP), and allowing vendors to create their own protocol sub-types. Because SNAP is itself a defined protocol code within the protocol types supported by the 802 Standard, the DSAP and SSAP are always set to the value AA, designating this to be a SNAP frame.

Octets	Description
8	Preamble, ending in pattern 10101011
6	Destination MAC Address
6	Source MAC Address
2	Length of Data Field (Maximum 5DC in hexadecimal)
46 to 1500	Data. (If less than 46 bytes (including DSAP, SSAP, Control, OUI, and Type), then a pad must be added to the end.)
1	802.2 LLC Destination Service Access Point (DSAP) [data = AA]
1	802.2 LLC Source Service Access Point (SSAP) [data = AA]
1 or 2	802.2 LLC Control Field (2 octets if sequencing is used)
3	SNAP Organizationally Unique Identifier (OUI)
2	SNAP Type Field
4	Frame Check Sequence (CRC Checksum)

Error handling

The most common (and usually benign) error condition on an Ethernet is the collision. Collisions are the mechanism for resolving contention for network access. A few collisions provide a smooth, simple, low-overhead way for network nodes to arbitrate contention for the network resource. When the network cannot work properly due to various problems, collisions can become a significant impediment to useful network operation. Collisions are only possible on half-duplex links.

Collisions waste time in two ways. First, network bandwidth loss is equal to the initial transmission and the collision jam signal. This is *consumption delay*, and it affects all network nodes. Consumption delay can significantly reduce network throughput. The second type of delay is due to the collision backoff algorithm, which causes the individual colliders to wait before retransmitting. *Backoff delays* are not usually significant until long after consumption delays are evident. Following each successful or failed transmission attempt is an enforced idle time for all stations of not less than 9.6 microseconds (interframe spacing) that further impacts throughput.

The considerable majority of collisions occur very early in the frame, often before the SFD. Collisions occurring before the SFD are usually not reported to the higher layers, as if the collision did not occur. As soon as a collision is detected, the sending station(s) are to transmit a 32-bit "jam" signal that will enforce the collision, so that all stations have a chance to detect it. It is the jam signal taking the place of the FCS checksum at the end of the collided message that allows stations to detect collisions on segments other than the local segment. The jam signal may be composed of any binary data so long as it does not form a proper checksum for the portion of the frame already sent. The corrupted, partially transmitted messages are often referred to as "collision fragments," and sometimes by the slang term "runts."

To create a collision on coax cable (10BASE2 and 10BASE5), the signal travels down the cable until it encounters a signal from the other station. The waveforms then overlap, canceling some parts of the signal out, and reinforcing (doubling) other parts. The doubling of the signal pushes the voltage level of the signal beyond the allowed maximum. This over-voltage condition is then sensed by all of the stations on the local cable segment as a collision. In most cases, the over-voltage threshold is between -1.404 and -1.581 volts on 10BASE2, and between -1.448 and -1.590 volts on 10BASE5.

On UTP cable (10BASE-T) a collision is detected on the local link only when a station detects a signal on the RX (receive) pair at the same time it is sending on the TX (transmit) pair.

There is no possibility remaining for a "legal" collision after the first 64 octets of data (plus preamble) have been transmitted by the sending station(s). The theoretical maximums for legal network propagation times are exceeded before then. Collisions occurring after the first 64 octets are called "late collisions." Late collisions result from improper installation of the network, physical damage to the network, or from failed network card(s) somewhere within the collision domain. The old attribution that a late collision is literally the result of a too-long cable is challenged by calculating the delay introduced by cable only—requiring a cable more than five kilometers long. While propagation delay introduced by the cable is a factor, it is much more likely that other factors such as cable impedance mismatches, signal attenuation along the cable, too many repeaters, and marginal interfaces result in situations where a shortened cable eliminates late collisions.

Other possible errors (FCS, jabber, etc.), will be handled by the MAC layer of the NIC—generally by discarding the frame and notifying the LLC layer of the error. Some types of errors (alignment, short frame, etc.) will cause the MAC layer to notify higher layers of the error, but will often be recoverable without having to discard the frame.

Be very careful when troubleshooting collision problems because the obvious answer is usually wrong. The addresses found in collision fragments belong to stations that transmitted legally. Most of the stations that collide with those legally transmitted frames are also operating legally (they did not "hear" anything on the wire, so they began to transmit). Also, in the event that there is a large enough fragment to have an address, the address is often corrupted and should never be used for troubleshooting. If there is a station that has gone "deaf" and is stepping on other transmissions because it does not hear them, it will likely never be discovered because it transmits into another transmission and it's data is corrupted. You will not obtain that deaf station's address from the fragment, though you may find the address of the properly transmitting station. If the segment is too long (too many repeaters) then you will see the adress of the near station, but not the far station. There are more examples, but the short answer is to troubleshoot the presence of too many collisions, but don't examine the fragments closely. Using collision fragments will just cause frustration.

Interframe spacing

After a frame has been sent, all stations on the Ethernet are required to wait a minimum of 9.6 microseconds before the next frame may legally be transmitted by any station. This delay time is called the interframe spacing, the interframe gap, or the interpacket gap, and is intended to allow slow stations time to process the previous frame, and to allow the cable to become quiet.

However, a repeater is expected to regenerate the full 64 bits of timing information (preamble and SFD) at the start of any frame, despite the potential loss of some of the beginning preamble bits to slow synchronization. Thus, because of this forced reintroduction of timing bits, some minor reduction of the inter-frame gap is not only possible but expected. Unfortunately, some chipsets are very sensitive to a shortening of the interframe gap, and will start failing to "see" frames as the gap is reduced. With the increase in processing power at the desktop, it is now very easy for a personal computer to saturate an Ethernet with traffic, and to begin transmitting again before the interframe spacing delay time is satisfied.

Ethernet switches present a special challenge here because they are totally optimized for forwarding of frames. It is quite common for a switch port to dominate a shared segment of Ethernet to the point that nearly all traffic is coming through the switch port, and the local shared media devices are unable to transmit more than an occasional frame. The instant each 9.6 microsecond gap has elapsed, a switch port is trying to deliver the next frame, and ordinary station interfaces have little chance of transmitting. (See Appendix G where switches are discussed in more detail.)

Retransmission

After a collision occurs and all stations allow the cable to become idle (each waits the full interframe gap), then the stations that collided must wait an additional—and progressively longer—period of time before attempting to retransmit the collided frame. The waiting period is intentionally designed to be semi-random, so that two stations are not in delay for the same amount of time before retransmitting. Otherwise, the result would be more collisions. This is accomplished by expanding the interval from which the random retransmission time is selected on each retransmission attempt. The waiting period is measured in increments of 51.2 microseconds (the time required to send 64 octets—512 bits—at 100 nanoseconds per bit, called "slot time"), and is controlled by the formula: $0 \leq r < 2^k$, where r is some random number of slot-times, and k is the number of backoff attempts (up to a maximum of 10 for the backoff value). The total maximum number of retransmission attempts is 16, though the backoff value remains at 10 for the last few attempts.

As an example, after the fifth consecutive collision without being able to transmit the current frame, the waiting time would be a random delay interval between zero and thirty-two slot-times ($0 \leq r < 2^5$). Restated, the delay would be a random number of 51.2 microsecond time units ranging from an immediate retry attempt up to 1638.4 microseconds later.

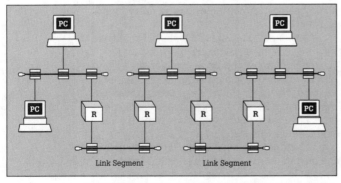

Figure B-7. *Collision domain configuration example for a 10BASE5 maximum end-to-end link between two devices.*

If the MAC layer is still unable to send the frame after sixteen attempts, it gives up and generates an error to the next layer up. Such an occurrence is very rare and would happen only under extremely heavy network loads, or when a physical problem exists on the network.

Ethernet implementation rules

Because of the possibility that network service could be interrupted by timing and electrical problems, the standard is very specific about numbers of stations per segment, maximum segment lengths, number of repeaters between stations, etc. Stations separated by repeaters are within the same collision domain. Stations separated by bridges or routers are in different collision domains.

Note: *Additional special rules apply for installations where fiber optic connections (such as Fiber Optic Inter-Repeater Links (FOIRL), 10BASE-F, 10BASE-FB, 10BASE-FL, and 10BASE-FP) are used. For example, when five segments are present then FOIRL segments should be limited to 500 meters; when four segments are present FOIRL segments can be the full 1000 meters.*

Ethernet switches, depending on whether they use "store-and-forward" or "cut-through" technology, can be thought of as either terminating a collision domain like a bridge, or partly extending the collision domain somewhat like a repeater, respectively. (See Appendix G where switches are discussed in more detail.)

Figure B-7 illustrates one maximum end-to-end configuration for an Ethernet collision domain (10BASE5 is shown). Between any two distant stations, only three repeated segments are permitted to have stations connected to them, with the other two repeated segments used exclusively as "link" segments to extend the network. However, repeaters do not count toward the maximum of 1024 stations on an Ethernet collision domain.

10BASE5

A 10BASE5 "thick" coax cable has a solid central conductor, a minimum nominal velocity of propagation (NVP) of 0.77c, 50Ω of impedance/termination resistance, and uses "N" style screw-on connections. Each of the maximum five segments of thick coax may be up to 500 meters long (1640 feet), and each station is connected to a transceiver on the coax via an Attachment Unit Interface (AUI) cable that may be up to 50 meters long (164 feet). Two types of transceiver connections are commonly used: the most common is a clamp-on style, where a small hole is drilled into the cable, through which the transceiver connects to the center conductor (often called a "vampire" tap). The other style requires the cable to be cut in order to screw the transceiver onto the two new ends.

There may be up to 100 stations on any individual 10BASE5 segment (including repeaters), with a maximum of 1024 stations connected by repeated segments (within one collision domain). Out of five consecutive segments (in series between any two distant stations), only three may have stations attached. As shown in Figure B-8, station connections to the coax should be separated by not less than 2.5 meters (8.2 feet) to avoid creating electrical "echoes" on the cable because of alignment with fractional wavelengths. Thick coax manufactured for Ethernet is marked every 2.5 meters to aid placement of taps, and to avoid this problem. For the same reason, if a segment cannot be constructed from a single piece of thick coax then each cable used on the segment should be made from lengths equal to 23.4, 70.2 or 117 meters, and these lengths may be mixed as needed to form the required overall length. As a last option, if these lengths are not possible, then the segment should be constructed from shorter cables built of cable from the same manufacturer and lot.

10BASE2

A 10BASE2 "thin" coax cable has a stranded central conductor. (Be sure that stranded coax is specified when new cable is ordered—many installers find it hard to work with, and will use solid-core coax where possible.) It has a minimum NVP of 0.65 c, has 50Ω of impedance/termination resistance, and uses BNC "tee" style connections. Each of the maximum five segments of thin coax may be up to 185 meters long (600 feet), and each station is connected directly to the BNC "tee" connector on the coax. The maximum length of a "stub" (the connection that attaches a 10BASE2 station to the primary thin coax center conductor)

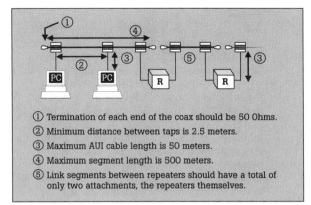

① Termination of each end of the coax should be 50 Ohms.

② Minimum distance between taps is 2.5 meters.

③ Maximum AUI cable length is 50 meters.

④ Maximum segment length is 500 meters.

⑤ Link segments between repeaters should have a total of only two attachments, the repeaters themselves.

Figure B-8. *10BASE5 network design limits.*

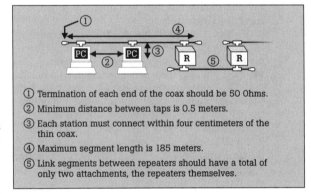

① Termination of each end of the coax should be 50 Ohms.

② Minimum distance between taps is 0.5 meters.

③ Each station must connect within four centimeters of the thin coax.

④ Maximum segment length is 185 meters.

⑤ Link segments between repeaters should have a total of only two attachments, the repeaters themselves.

Figure B-9. *10BASE2 network design limits.*

is 4 centimeters, or about 1.5 inches. (See Figure 2-1.) Effectively, no stubs are allowed. Stubs of any significant length will cause echoes on the cable, and will exhibit themselves as a variety of problems—which are very difficult to isolate.

There may be up to 30 stations on any individual 10BASE2 segment, with a maximum of 1024 stations connected by repeated segments (within one collision domain). Out of five consecutive segments (in series between any two distant stations), only three may have stations attached. As shown in Figure B-9, station connections to the coax should be separated by not less than 0.5 meters.

10BASE-T

A 10BASE-T unshielded twisted-pair (UTP) cable has a solid conductor for each wire, which should be 0.4 to 0.6 mm (26 to 22 AWG) diameter. (To keep from breaking the cable after repeated flexing, patch cables at the station end should be made from stranded wire—but they should be kept relatively short.) UTP has a minimum NVP of 0.585 c, has 100Ω of impedance, and uses eight-pin RJ-45 modular connectors. Cables between a station and a hub are generally described as between 0 and 100 meters long (328 feet), though the precise maximum length is determined by propagation delay through the link segment (any length that does not exceed 1000 ns of delay is acceptable). Usually, 0.5 millimeter (24 AWG) diameter unshielded twisted wire in a multipair cable will meet the requirements at 100 meters.

Though UTP cable meeting the TIA/EIA-568-A requirements for Category 3 is adequate for use on 10BASE-T networks, it is strongly recommended that any new cable installations be made with Category 5 materials and Category 5 wiring practices, using all four pairs, and meeting either the T568A or T568B (preferred) EIA pin-out arrangements. With this type of cable installation, it should be possible to operate many different media access protocols (i.e., Ethernet, Token Ring, and most of the new 100 Mbps or faster protocols) over the same cable plant, without rewiring.

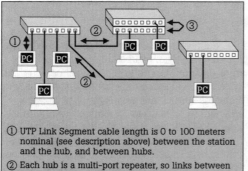

① UTP Link Segment cable length is 0 to 100 meters nominal (see description above) between the station and the hub, and between hubs.

② Each hub is a multi-port repeater, so links between hubs count toward the repeater limit.

③ These two "stackable" hubs with interconnected backplanes count as only one hub (repeater).

Figure B-10. 10BASE-T network design limits.

10BASE-T links generally consist of a connection between the station and a hub. Hubs should be thought of as multi-port repeaters, and count toward the limit on repeaters between distant stations.

Although hubs may be linked in series (sometimes called daisy-chaining, or cascading), it is best to avoid this arrangement where possible in order to keep from violating the limit for maximum delay between distant stations. The physical size of a 10BASE-T network is subject to the same rules as 10BASE5 and 10BASE2 concerning number of repeaters. As shown in Figure B-10, when multiple hubs are required, it is best to arrange them in hierarchical order so as to create a tree structure instead of a chain. Also, performance will be improved if stations are separated by fewer repeaters. "Stackable" hubs, or concentrators with common backplanes that will support several multi-port adapter cards permit large numbers of stations to be connected to a device that counts as a single hub (repeater).

Mixed-media networks

It is not only allowed, but it is expected, that an Ethernet network could contain multiple types of media. The standard goes out of its way to ensure that compatibility is maintained. However, when implementing a mixed-media network, it is important to pay particular attention to the overall architecture design. It becomes easier to violate maximum delay limits as the network grows and becomes more complex. The timing limits include: 1) cable length and its propagation delay, 2) delay of repeaters, 3) delay of transceivers (including NICs and hubs), 4) interframe gap shrinkage, and 5) delays within the station. A simple description of architecture limits is given below. If your network is implemented using new high-performance hardware—although it is strongly recommended that corners not be cut—it is possible that some of these limits can be exceeded. Refer to the technical timing descriptions detailed in Chapter 13 and Appendix A of the current ISO/IEC 8802-3 or ANSI/IEEE 802.3 Standard, and the technical information about your hardware performance.

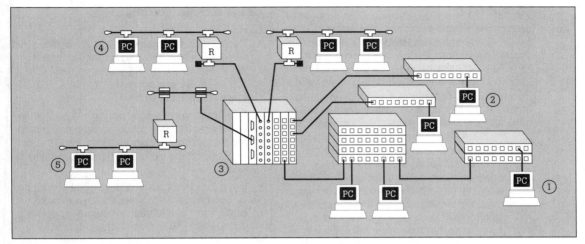

Figure B-11. *Example of a mixed-media Ethernet network configuration.*

An architectural example is shown in Figure B-11. All distances between stations are acceptable, though in one direction the architecture is at its limit. The most important aspect to consider is how to keep the delay between distant stations to a minimum—regardless of the architecture and media types involved. A shorter maximum delay will provide better overall performance.

- Figure B-11 can be redrawn (see Figure B-12) to show the logical path between stations. There are five segments and four repeaters from station ① to any other station in these paths. For 10BASE-T connections the maximum of three segments with stations does not apply, because no other stations are on the same cable. Each connection is described as a link segment.

- From any station (except station ①) to any other station in the diagram the path is only three repeaters. Since these alternate paths include 10BASE5 and 10BASE2 links, the other requirements still apply (such as only three segments with stations).

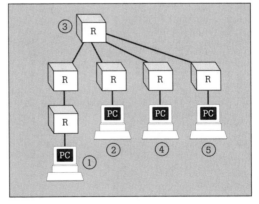

Figure B-12. *Logical diagram of Figure B-11.*

Grounding

Each coax segment (thick or thin) may be grounded at one point *anywhere* along the cable that is convenient. However, it is best to purchase termination resistors that have the ground connection (usually a short conductive chain with a tab at the end containing a screw hole). Using these special termination resistors ensures that you will always know where the segment s*hould* be grounded. Then, if you find any other suspicious connection, you will know to correct it.

The standard requires 10BASE5 to be grounded, and only recommends that 10BASE2 be grounded—though it's a good idea to connect the ground to avoid problems. If problems develop after you have grounded a segment, and it worked prior to that time, then the segment is probably shorted to ground somewhere already. Stating the obvious, this indicates a pre-existing problem on your network that should be corrected. (See Appendix F for more information on grounding.)

Some simple guidelines

Cable

- Don't install long cables. Make all runs as short as possible, and certainly no longer than is permitted by the media access protocol you are using. For example, never install UTP runs longer than 100 meters.

- Don't try to save money during a new installation by purchasing inferior cabling and materials. You will more than make up the difference troubleshooting cable and connector problems later.

- If you build your own cables or buy pre-made cables, be sure to test them with a reliable cable tester before you use them—*especially* if you are already in troubleshooting mode.

Network

- Limit the size of each collision domain. Use switches, bridges or routers where possible instead of repeaters.

- Limit the number of stations on each segment. Keep well within the legal maximum for your media type.

- Isolate high-traffic stations from the rest of the users with routers, bridges or switches. Group stations onto segments that are as close as possible to the most-used server. It is better to have slower response time from seldom-used resources than to degrade response time to resources used frequently.

- Document your network. (See Chapter 1.)

Token Ring Operation

Introduction

Token Ring operates at two speeds (4 Mbps and 16 Mbps), using a synchronous method of data transfer. Quite unlike Ethernet, there is *always* a signal being transmitted on a Token Ring. In fact, the absence of a signal for more than 2.5 bit-cell times will cause the station detecting this idle time to report an error. In order to extract data from the signal being retransmitted by each station in turn around the ring, each station implements a special circuit called a phase-locked loop (PLL). This PLL clock circuit compensates for minor variations in the frequency of the signal being passed to it from the previous station. According to the standard, only one station on the ring—which ever station is currently holding the job of active monitor—will transmit using a crystal oscillator.

The crystal oscillator in the active monitor station is then the source clock upon which all other stations on the ring will rely for the "correct" timing information. When the active monitor (re)transmits a message (its own, or passing along a message from another station), it "cleans up" a problem called "jitter" by sending the message based on the clock from the crystal instead of a PLL clock. Jitter is a mis-alignment of an incoming signal against the clock that is being used to sample it. If jitter becomes too great for the PLL to compensate for, some amount of the data will be read incorrectly and the message will become corrupted.

In practice, the industry has determined that having the signal for the entire ring controlled by a single crystal oscillator presents too much opportunity for failure. To compensate for jitter problems induced in this manner, many so-called "intelligent" products now offer retiming and other methods of reducing jitter. This usually means that they will also transmit using a crystal, not just the active monitor station. Additionally, each time the signal changes media (i.e., copper to fiber optic) the signal is retimed. Other implementations of token-passing (such as FDDI) require all stations to retime signals.

Since it is impossible to send complete messages constantly and at all times, the protocol defines how to terminate a message before it is fully sent (Abort Sequence), and how to hold the medium while preparing a message to be sent (by sending Fill). To distinguish between the beginning and end of messages, and to distinguish fill data from actual messages, the standard defines a special sequence of code violations to be used for this purpose. These violations of the *Differential Manchester* encoding, together with the PLL, allow a Token Ring station to synchronize data transfers with other stations.

Because of the variable number of stations in a given ring, the total ring circumference and the speed data is being transmitted, the beginning of a frame will usually have passed completely around a ring and back to the sending station before the end of the frame is sent. This means that the sending station must be able to simultaneously transmit a message, receive the same message, verify that it returned intact, verify that it was received by the destination station, and strip its message off the token before releasing the empty token.

Although it is not often implemented, Token Ring permits users to establish a priority system between themselves. Stations with a higher priority may set the reservation bits of a passing frame or token, thereby requesting that the next token be issued at a higher priority level, forcing lower-priority stations to wait until all higher-priority stations no longer wish to transmit. Up to eight levels of priority may be assigned.

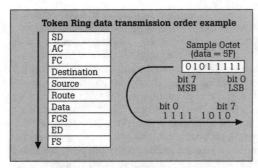

Figure B-13. *Token Ring bit transmission order, transmitted with the most significant bit (MSB) sent first.*

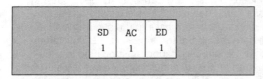

Figure B-14. *Data fields for a Token Ring 802.5 empty token.*

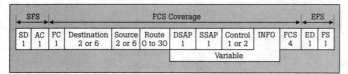

Figure B-15. *Data fields for a Token Ring 802.5 frame.*

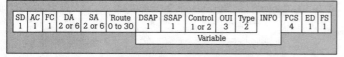

Figure B-16. *Data fields for a Token Ring SNAP frame.*

Token Ring transmits each octet of a message in order from the Start Delimiter (SD) through to the end of the message as shown in Figure B-13. All octets are transmitted with the most significant bit (MSB) sent first.

Frame format

There are only two different frame types in common use on Token Ring. They are: IEEE 802.5 and Token Ring SNAP. Regardless of which frame type is used to transport data, an empty "token" will be circulated whenever there is an idle time on the ring. Once a station wishes to transmit, it will capture a passing token and convert it to a frame by including all of the other fields required. As soon as the frame has passed completely around the ring and back to the sending station, it will strip the frame back to a token and pass the empty token along for another station to use. If the station has more to send, it must wait for the next empty token to arrive.

802.5 Token (See Figure B-14.)

Octets	Description
1	Start Delimiter (SD) [J K O J K OOO]
	J = non-data J (code violation)
	K = non-data K (code violation)
	O = zero bit
1	Access Control (AC) [PPP T M RRR]
	PPP = priority bits
	T = token bit
	M = monitor bit
	RRR = reservation bits
1	Ending Delimiter [J K 1 J K 1 I E]
	J = non-data J (code violation)
	K = non-data K (code violation)
	1 = one bit
	I = intermediate frame bit
	E = error-detected bit

802.5 Frame (See Figure B-15.)

Octets   Description

Start of Frame Sequence (SFS)

1   Start Delimiter (SD)

1   Access Control (AC)

Frame Check Sequence (FCS) Coverage

1   Frame Control (FC)
[FF ZZZZZ]
F = frame-type bits (00 = MAC, 01=LLC)
Z = control bits

2 or 6   Destination MAC Address

2 or 6   Source MAC Address

0 to 30   Routing Information (optional field)

Variable   Information Field (the standard
holds that this field may be from 0
octets up to the size permitted by
the maximum token hold time. No
specific number is identified. In
practice the maximum value is
approximately 4,500 octets on a
4 Mbps ring, or 18,000 octets on
a 16 Mbps ring)

1   802.2 LLC Destination Service
Access Point (DSAP)

1   802.2 LLC Source Service Access
Point (SSAP)

1 or 2   802.2 LLC Control Field
(2 octets if sequencing is used)

4   Frame Check Sequence
(CRC Checksum)

End of Frame Sequence (EFS)

1   Ending Delimiter (ED)

1   Frame Status (FS)
[A C r r A C r r]
A = address-recognized bit
C = frame-copied bit
r = reserved bit

Token Ring SNAP frame (See Figure B-16.)

The Sub–Network Access Protocol (SNAP) is an
extension of the 802.2 LLC that offers support for
more than the 127 unique protocols allowed by
the two 8–bit Link Service Access Point (LSAP)
fields (the DSAP and SSAP), allowing vendors to
create their own protocol sub-types. Because
SNAP is itself a defined protocol code within the
protocol types supported by the 802 Standard,
the DSAP and SSAP are always set to the value
AA, designating this to be a SNAP frame.

Octets   Description

1   Start Delimiter (SD)

1   Access Control (AC)

1   Frame Control (FC)

2 or 6   Destination MAC Address (DA)

2 or 6   Source MAC Address (SA)

0 to 30   Routing Information (optional field)

Variable   Information Field

1   802.2 LLC Destination Service
Access Point (DSAP) [data = AA]

1   802.2 LLC Source Service Access
Point (SSAP) [data = AA]

1 or 2   802.2 LLC Control Field
(2 octets if sequencing is used)

3   SNAP Organizationally Unique
Identifier (OUI)

2   SNAP Type Field

4   Frame Check Sequence
(CRC Checksum)

1   Ending Delimiter (ED)

1   Frame Status (FS)

Token Ring insertion process

When a Token Ring station connects to a local ring the following insertion process steps are taken (virtually all of which are transparent to a network user):

1. **Lobe Test:** The NIC performs self diagnostics, including a test of the lobe cable that attaches that station to the MAU. During the lobe test, the NIC transmits a large number of a specific message frame to the MAU and back, as a simple cable test. The transmitted data is compared to the received data to verify that this path is operational. If this test fails, the NIC will terminate the insertion process and report an error.

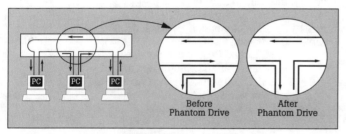

Figure B-17. *Application of Phantom Drive voltage to a Token Ring MAU port.*

2. **Apply Phantom Drive:** The NIC then applies a "phantom" voltage to the lobe cable, which causes a relay in the MAU port to change state. This causes the NIC's connection to change from a "loopback" condition to a direct connection with its upstream and downstream neighbors. (See Figure B-17.) When the phantom voltage reconfigures the MAU port, there is an interruption of the ring caused by the relatively slow relay. For about 20 milliseconds, the ring will be physically broken while the relay changes state. During this time, the NIC performing the additional job of active monitor will become aware that a problem has developed on the ring and will begin a ring recovery procedure.

3. **Active Monitor Check:** Once the new NIC is on the ring (the relay is again closed), the new NIC will begin listening for traffic on the ring. If other NIC(s) are already on the ring, the new NIC should begin receiving a special error recovery message sent to all NICs from the active monitor called a ring purge. The purge frame will cause all NICs to reset themselves to default values for certain parameters and wait for the active monitor to issue a new token. After the active monitor observes purge frames that have begun to make it completely around the ring and back, it will originate a new token and announce its presence by initiating the neighbor notification poll process. If no active monitor is detected, the new NIC will attempt to assume the job.

4. **Duplicate Address Test:** As soon as the new NIC is a participating member of the ring, it will check for the presence of another NIC using the same address. The new NIC will perform this test before participating in the neighbor notification process. The duplicate address test is accomplished by sending a message that is addressed to itself. If the message returns *without* being marked as having been received by another NIC, then the new NIC remains in the ring. Otherwise the new NIC immediately removes itself from the ring and reports an error.

Note: As a special case, it is possible to fail the duplicate address test if locally administered addresses are used and the address is different by only the first two octets.

5. **Neighbor Notification Process:** The new NIC will now participate in the neighbor notification process initiated by the active monitor. The NIC currently holding the active monitor job leads off by announcing itself. Each successive *active* station (the NIC must have phantom drive applied to its own MAU port)—in physical ring order—sends its own message announcing itself as a *standby monitor*. All NICs on the ring act as standby monitors and are prepared to take over if the active monitor fails. During this process, all other NICs on the ring become aware of the new NIC. When the active monitor receives a standby monitor

message from the last NIC, it finishes the process by sending a neighbor notification process complete message. (This process also occurs about every seven seconds on an error-free ring.) If the new NIC does not receive a neighbor notification process message that it can reply to, it will remove itself from the ring and report an error.

6. **Request Initialization:** After determining that no other NIC on the local ring is using the same address, the new NIC will make a request to the Ring Parameter Server, asking for any special non-default settings that are in use on the ring. The Ring Parameter Server is an optional job, and on most rings no NIC has been configured to perform this job. However, the address of this NIC is predefined by the protocol so all NICs know how to reach it. If the request returns to the new NIC *without* having been marked as received by an NIC performing the Ring Parameter Server job, the NIC will assume that no such NIC is present and will complete the insertion process.

If the initialization request returns to the new NIC and the message *is* marked as received, the new NIC will wait for a message containing the special parameters needed to operate on the ring from the Ring Parameter Server or a *change parameter* frame from the Configuration Report Server. Once the message is received, the NIC is fully inserted into the ring. When a Ring Parameter Server appears to be present, and no reply frame is received within two seconds, the new NIC will then repeat the request several times. If all requests time-out without a reply, the new NIC will remove itself from the ring and report an error.

Normal operation

After a station has inserted into the ring, and the ring is again operating smoothly, the following process is used to pass messages.

1. Each NIC will pass the token around until it is captured by one of the NICs and changed into a frame by adding a message. An empty token is 24-bits long (three octets). Once turned into

a frame, an empty token can grow to approximately 4500 octets on a 4–Mbps ring, or 18000 octets on a 16–Mbps ring—though the standard does not specify an exact largest size. Instead, the standard indicates that transmission of a single frame cannot exceed a token holding time of 10 milliseconds.

2. As the message travels around the ring, each NIC will examine the frame to determine whether the message is intended for it. Whether or not the message is addressed to a particular NIC, *all* NICs (except the one that sent the message) will forward *all* messages. As each NIC forwards the message, it will verify that the message is not corrupted. If any NIC detects a problem, it will set a marker bit at the end of the message to let all other NICs know the message is corrupted.

3. When the message reaches the intended destination NIC, that NIC will copy the message into a buffer while it passes it along. During the copy process, the destination NIC will change two other marker bits, the address recognized and frame copied bits.

4. When the message returns to the station that sent it, that NIC will remove the message from the frame—stripping the frame back into a token and passing it along for some other NIC to use. If that station wishes to send another message, it must wait until an empty token comes by (that is not reserved by a higher-priority station), so every station on the ring has an equal chance to send messages.

Beaconing

There are four types of beacon frame: type 1 is used only by stations implementing the Dual Ring protocol (see IEEE 802.5c), type 2 indicates a long-term loss of signal, type 3 indicates bit streaming (i.e., when the upstream neighbor is stuck transmitting fill), and type 4 indicates streaming claim token frames (i.e., when the upstream neighbor is stuck transmitting claim tokens). Regardless of the beacon type, beaconing constitutes a network emergency for Token Ring networks.

If an error is detected that meets the conditions required for beaconing, the following steps will be taken:

1. Any NIC detecting a severe error condition will begin sending beacon frames to all other NICs on the local ring. The address of the NIC originating the frame and the address of that NIC's nearest active upstream neighbor (NAUN) are included in the beacon frame.

2. The NAUN for the NIC originating the beacon frame recognizes its own address as being within the fault domain, and deinserts from the ring to run self diagnostics. If the diagnostics pass, it will reinsert into the ring without performing a normal insertion protocol handshake.

   If a failure is detected, the NAUN will remain off the ring, and the ring should recover itself. Normal diagnostic failures of this type include network adapter failures and lobe cable failures.

3. If the originating NIC is still detecting the hard error condition when a timer expires, it assumes that the NAUN has already run self diagnostics and returned to the ring. The originating NIC will then remove itself from the ring for diagnostics, to determine whether it might be the source of the error, since the NAUN was not. If no failure is detected during diagnostics, the originating NIC will reinsert, and resume sending beacon frames.

   Again, if a failure is detected by the originating NIC, it will remain off the ring and the ring should recover itself.

4. If neither NIC detects the failure, then the failure point is most likely located in the cable path between the MAU connections for both stations, possibly due to a failure of a MAU or RI/RO cable somewhere between those two connections. At this point, the ring can be recovered only through manual intervention.

Predefined Token Ring protocol addresses and functions

The Token Ring protocol defines several NIC addresses and functions as part of the specification. Each NIC on a ring will respond to messages sent to a specific NIC address, any general broadcast message, and messages sent to the functional address for any special ring job(s) the NIC may be performing at that time. Several of these special addresses and functions are listed below.

Active monitor

The active monitor can be any NIC on the ring. If no active monitor is present when a NIC inserts into a ring, the NIC will assume the job itself. The active monitor recovers lost tokens, maintains the master clock, ensures that a proper ring delay exists, purges the ring when errors are detected, monitors proper token and frame transmission, and initiates the neighbor notification process.

Standby monitor

All NICs on the ring act as standby monitor(s), prepared to take over for the active monitor in the event the current active monitor fails or is turned off. At that point, some NIC will issue a claim token and wait to see if another NIC has a higher address. The NIC with the highest address will become the active monitor. That NIC will then hold the job until it is turned off, or another claim token is issued by any NIC—which causes the election process to start over.

Additional ring functions

The following functions may or may not be present on the ring. NICs, however, will report to these addresses regardless of their presence or absence. The **Ring Parameter Server** maintains values such as timers, ring number, etc., and can also remove NICs if they threaten ring integrity. When soft errors occur, the reporting NIC sends a message to the **Ring Error Monitor** for collection and analysis. The **Configuration Report Server** controls individual ring NICs at the direction of the network manager. Network managers can use the **LAN Bridge Server** to analyze the performance of bridges and multi-ring networks. All NICs listen to the **LAN Bridge Server** and **Broadcast** addresses, which are typically used by the MAC layer and the upper layer protocols, respectively.

Appendix C — Troubleshooting

Troubleshooting: First Aid for a Healthy Network

The key to successful troubleshooting is for the technician to know how the network functions under normal conditions. This enables the technician to quickly recognize abnormal operation. Any other approach is little better than a shot in the dark.

Unfortunately, many LAN products are not delivered with adequate performance specifications, theory of operation, or condensed technical data to aid in troubleshooting. The successful technician will thoroughly study whatever data is available, as well as develop in-depth insight into the function of all components and how to operate them. Finally, he or she will remember that conditions appearing to be serious defects are often the result of improper usage or operator error.

The foundation of this insight is gained only with formal training. But the true troubleshooting master learns in the trenches, through trial and error, comparing notes with others, and discovering tried-and-true methods that are not taught in school. The following information can help shorten your learning curve and give you proven advice on how to isolate and solve network problems.

Two approaches to troubleshooting almost always result in disappointment, delay, or failure. On one extreme is the theorist, or "rocket scientist" approach. On the other is the practical, or "caveman" approach.

- The rocket scientist analyzes and re-analyzes the situation until the exact cause of the problem has been identified—rather than simply pinpointing the root of the problem and correcting it. This sometimes requires taking a high-end protocol analyzer and collecting a huge (megabytes) sample of the network traffic while the problem is present and inspecting it in minute detail. While this process is fairly reliable, few companies can afford to have their networks down for the hours—or days—it can take for proper analysis.

- The caveman's first instinct is to start swapping cards, cables, hardware and software until, miraculously, the network begins operating again. This does not mean it's working properly, just that it's operating. Unfortunately, the troubleshooting section in some manuals actually recommends caveman-style procedures as a way to avoid providing more technical information. While it may be faster, this approach is not very reliable, and the root cause of the problem may still be present. In fact, the parts used for swapping may include marginal or failed parts swapped out during prior troubleshooting episodes.

For the technician in search of the proper way to troubleshoot, the following approach makes the most sense:

Analyze the network as a whole rather than in a piecemeal fashion. One technician, following a logical sequence, will almost always be more successful than a gang of technicians, each with their own theories and methods for troubleshooting.

The logical technician asks the operator questions, runs diagnostics, and thoroughly collects information. In a short time, he or she can analyze and evaluate the symptoms, zero-in on the root source of problems, make one adjustment or change one part, and cure the problem. The key is to simply isolate the smallest failing element and replace it. *Complete understanding of the cause of the failure is not required.* After the network is again running, further analysis may be undertaken—preferably in a lab environment.

There are many technicians with years of experience who have not yet mastered the following basic concept: a few minutes spent evaluating symptoms can eliminate hours of time lost chasing the wrong problem. All information and reported symptoms must be evaluated in relation to each other, as well as how they relate to the overall operation of the network; only then can the technician gain a true understanding of what they indicate. Once you have collected data about the symptoms, you will then need to conduct tests to validate or eliminate what you think the problems could be. Perhaps they are mental and do not involve the network or physical testing at all. Once you think you understand the problem, you must then verify it. At this stage your efforts will be directed toward attempting to cause the problem to recur on demand.

Just as important, the logical technician always performs a checkout procedure on any repaired equipment or system, no matter how simple the repair. Far too often, the obvious problem is the symptom of another less-obvious problem, and until the source is eliminated, the situation will continue.

Five Key Steps to Successful Troubleshooting

1. Collect all available information, and analyze the symptoms of failure.
2. Localize the problem to within a single network segment, to a single complete functional unit or module, or to a single user.
3. Isolate the problem to specific hardware or software within the unit, module, or user's network account.
4. Locate and correct the specific problem.
5. Verify that the problem has been resolved.

Note: *To avoid unwanted repetition, and to make it possible to "back-out" any changes made, be sure to carefully and completely document all actions taken during the troubleshooting process.*

Step 1. Collect information

First, ask yourself if you understand the symptoms. Have the operator explain how normal operation appears, then demonstrate the problem. Verify the reported problem yourself, if possible. Is there any normal function missing, or is there an abnormal response?

Determine whether something was altered at that station or on the network just before the problem started. Often the operator does not realize that changing something unrelated can cause problems on the network, such as rearranging the location of a portable heater or photocopier, or installing a new piece of software or adapter card.

Note: *Check to be sure that you are not troubleshooting something that never worked before. Treat that situation like a new installation.*

Step 2. Localize the problem

Once the problem has been confirmed, all available information collected, and an analysis made of what is known, the next step is to reduce the problem to a single segment or functional unit. Based on the analysis, determine if the problem is related to a segment of the network, or localized to a single station. Reducing the scope of the problem in this way is where *divide-and-conquer* begins, and isolating the problem to the smallest unit in Step 3 is the goal.

Can the problem be duplicated from another station, or using other software applications at the same station? Identify whether the problem is limited to one station, or one network resource such as a printer.

If the problem affects more than one station try shortening the cable segment on a bus topology, or recabling a ring or star topology to create the smallest possible network for troubleshooting purposes. Try a different Hub or MAU for star topologies or for multi-segment networks.

Step 3. Isolate the problem

Step 3a. If the problem affects an entire network segment, isolate the problem by reducing the variables to the fewest possible number. Turn off or disconnect all but two stations. Once those two are communicating add more stations. If they are not communicating check the physical layer possibilities such as the termination of the cable, the cable itself, or the specific hub or MAU port.

Step 3b. If the problem can be isolated to a single station, try a different network adapter, a fresh copy of the network driver software (without using *any* of the network software or configuration files presently found on that station), or connect a new network cable to that station. If the network connection seems intact, determine if only one application exhibits the problem. Try other applications from the same drive or file system. Compare configurations with another workstation. Try a fresh copy of the application software (again using none of the existing software or configuration files).

Step 3c. If only one user experiences the problem, check the network security and permissions for that user. Find out if any changes have been made to the network security that might affect this user. Has another user account been deleted that this user was made security equivalent to? Has this user been deleted from a security grouping within the network? Has an application been moved to a new location on the network? Have there been any changes to the system login script, or the user's login script? Compare this user's account with another user's account that is able to perform the desired task.

Step 4. Correct the problem

Once a single operation, application or connection is localized as the source of the problem, identifying the specific fault should be simple. For network hardware, it is most expedient to simply replace a part, and attempt to repair the part later. Remember: The goal is to restore full operation of the network as soon as possible.

Two avenues exist for solving software problems. The first option is to reinstall the problem software, eliminating possibly corrupted files and ensuring that all required files are present. This is an excellent way to ensure that the second option—reconfiguring the software—works on the first try. Most new applications allow for a software switch that tells the configuration program to disregard any existing configuration files, which is a good way to avoid being misled by the error and duplicating it yet again.

If the problem is isolated to a single user account on the network, it is often easiest to delete the entire account and start over, or repeat the steps necessary to grant the user access to the problem application or operation as if the user had never been authorized before. By going through each of these steps in a logical order, you will probably locate the missing element faster than by spot-checking.

Step 5. Verify problem resolution

Ensure that the entire problem has been resolved by having the operator test for the problem. This can be done by simply operating the equipment in the "normal" way. Also, have the operator quickly try several other normal operations with the equipment. Sometimes a repair in one area causes other problems, and sometimes whatever was repaired turns out to be a symptom of another underlying problem.

Appendix D — TCP/IP

Preventing Problems

There are several steps that can be taken to prevent or reduce the likelihood of problems in a TCP/IP environment. The most important step is to have thorough documentation of the network itself. While it may seem that such careful documentation is not needed in a small network, hours of down-time and network troubleshooting can be avoided by attention to these issues. The most common problems in a TCP/IP environment relate to IP addresses and related configuration parameters, so a little proactive work in the beginning will go a long way toward avoiding problems in the future, as well as solving more quickly those that do occur.

IP address administration

IP addresses need to be administered in such a way that there are no duplicate addresses assigned, and that old addresses are made available if a machine is reassigned to a different network or permanently deactivated. Create a system for address assignments that is easy to administer and maintain. To keep users from coming up with their own addresses, they need to know whom to contact to get a new address. If you make the process easy to access and easy to use, it will encourage users to follow the rules for getting addresses. If possible, use a Dynamic Host Configuration Protocol (DHCP) server so that IP addresses are dynamically assigned from a pool of addresses—thereby avoiding the problem of duplicate addresses almost entirely. Creating a DHCP server with some of the more recent versions of network operating systems can take as little as five minutes.

If your network is connected "live" on the Internet, addressing issues take on even greater importance, as problems in your network can potentially affect other companies' networks too.

Document host configurations

Be sure to document the actual configuration of each host. This documentation should include information about IP addressing, subnet mask, default router configuration, the kind of machine it is, who the end user or contact is, and where the host is physically located. When problems occur, this information will be invaluable, and can eliminate hours of troubleshooting effort.

Sometimes hosts will appear to operate despite configuration problems. However, when changes to the network or the host take place, those hosts with incomplete or inaccurate configurations will suddenly stop operating. Verification of the host configuration is often the last area suspected in these situations because the host had been working until this "unrelated" change took place. Yet a glance at the configuration documentation for that host can solve a configuration problem, or eliminate very quickly the configuration as a likely source of the problem. Also, the process of documenting the host configuration will often highlight incomplete configurations.

Controlled-change processes

End-user hosts are not the only IP systems that have configuration problems. As changes are made to hubs, switches, bridges, and gateways, it is possible to introduce configuration problems. Control of the change environment will reduce the number of problems and will dramatically shorten troubleshooting time. And a change-log documents the time, specific changes and order of occurrence when possible configuration problems were introduced. If possible, the "before" and "after" configuration files should be copied or printed for inclusion in the network documentation. Knowing what was changed permits support staff to "back-out" unsuccessful changes and restore network operation quickly.

Solving Problems

Do not attempt to solve what appears to be an IP problem until you have verified that no other problems exist in lower layers of the protocol stack. Many hours of troubleshooting time have been wasted chasing symptoms, when the real problem was a bad cable or interface card.

Also, verify that the desired server or service has been operating successfully until now. The troubleshooting process is completely different if you are trying to solve a new installation problem instead of attempting to restore service to something that has been up and running.

Cannot connect problems

This assumes that 1) the server or service has been operating properly prior to this problem, and 2) you have already verified that the media access protocol is operating correctly with the troubleshooting steps described under **Cannot access server or service** in Chapter 2. It is important for you to check that you have:

- Cold-booted the host in question (a warm-boot does *not* reset all adapter cards).

- Verified that the host has not had any hardware failures.

- Verified that all required network cables are present and properly connected.

- Verified that all required network adapter software driver files were loaded, and that no errors were reported when they loaded.

- Verified that nothing has been changed on the problem host recently that may have caused this problem, such as reconfiguring or adding software or hardware.

- Verified that the attached MAC layer is not experiencing errors. (It is pointless to troubleshoot network layer problems if the MAC layer is marginal or failing.)

Check your documentation and determine the following: 1) that the host has been configured with the correct IP address; 2) that the assigned address is valid for that subnet; 3) whether there is another station using the same address; 4) that the default router or gateway address is correct and configured properly; and 5) that the DNS server address is correct and configured properly if you are using DNS (**local** problems). Also check that the DNS server itself is not down, and that the desired target host is accessible from this connection (**global** problems).

Is it a local problem?

Ask the affected user to attempt the *exact same network operation* from another nearby station that is operating correctly. This is the fastest way to isolate user-account problems from network problems. If the attempt is successful, then troubleshoot the first user's connection, equipment, and software configuration. If the attempt fails, use a different account to attempt the same operation. If the parallel attempt from a "good" but different account is successful, troubleshoot the first user's account on the target host.

IP configuration issues

The correct IP address for the network. If a host is using an invalid address for the subnet to which it is connected, it will be able to send packets out, but the reply will not come back (it may have gone somewhere else or been discarded by the router).

Check the configuration described in your documentation to ensure that the configured address falls within the range allowed by the local subnet, check the configuration of a nearby station in the same subnet to ensure that your documented subnet is accurate, or run the LANMeter test tool's TCP/IP **Top Senders** or **Top Receivers** test to see if most of the listed addresses match the subnet range you are expecting and if the assigned address is within that range.

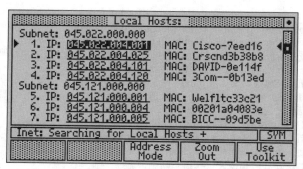

Figure D-1. *Fluke Enterprise LANMeter **Segment Discovery** test results, "zoomed" on Local Hosts screen.*

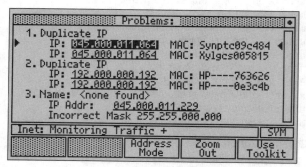

Figure D-2. *Fluke Enterprise LANMeter **Segment Discovery** test results, "zoomed" on Problems screen.*

The Enterprise LANMeter test tool's Internet TCP/IP **Segment Discovery** test will rapidly assemble a list of all active IP hosts on the local segment—regardless of whether they have the correct address for this subnet. The test will disregard any traffic from off the local segment, so that you get a list of only the local hosts. A quick glance through the sorted list will reveal whether there is a host with an IP address that does not match the subnet. (See Figure D-1.)

Duplicate IP addresses. A duplicate IP address is probably the most well-known problem in TCP/IP networks. Two stations with the same IP address will cause either intermittent connection problems for both stations, or severe problems with one station until one of the stations is turned off. Later, when both machines are active again at the same time, problems will reappear.

One method to discover stations with duplicate IP addresses is to send ARP packets to their IP address. All duplicated stations will respond to the ARP along with their MAC addresses.

The Enterprise LANMeter test tool's Internet TCP/IP **Segment Discovery** test will quickly identify any duplicate IP addresses on the local IP segment. (See Figure D-2.) Once detected, the duplicated address is shown together with each MAC address that is using the problem IP address. Further testing may be performed on any of the listed address pairs by using the Toolkit of SNMP queries.

The LANMeter test tool's **ICMP Ping** test can also be used to help isolate this problem. Each time the ping test is executed, an ARP packet is sent. If more than one station responds, or if the problem station is turned off and *any* station responds (except when routers are configured with proxy ARP enabled), then a duplicate address is likely. Use the MAC address identified by the ARP to track down the other station.

Note: *It is not uncommon for a single MAC address (network interface) to have more than one IP address assigned to it—especially router interfaces. However, it is absolutely forbidden for a single IP address to be used by more than one MAC address.*

Incorrect subnet mask. The subnet mask tells a host station how much of the 32-bit IP address is used for the network address, and how much is used for the host address. The most common subnet mask problem is created when "non-standard" subnets are used, or when an address range is further subnetted to allow for additional segments. If a host is using the wrong subnet mask, it may decide that it does not really exist on the same logical network segment as certain other local hosts, and the first host will not talk directly with them. In some cases, enabling proxy ARP on a local router will permit these incorrect configurations to operate normally.

The Enterprise LANMeter test tool's Internet TCP/IP **Segment Discovery** test will quickly identify hosts on the local IP segment with subnet masks that do not match other hosts. (See Figure D-3.) Further testing may be performed on any of the listed hosts by using the **Toolkit** of SNMP queries.

Incorrect default routers. If a host does not have a default router configured (sometimes shown as default gateway), all off-net communications will fail. More often, problems occur when the configured router is not actually a router or is a sub-optimal router. If a non-router is sent packets to forward, it may return the ICMP message, "Destination unreachable: Network unreachable." Other host implementations may actually forward those packets to their own default router, consuming valuable CPU and memory resources. Some UNIX workstations and other IP hosts permit routing protocols to be enabled, and will look like routers to the local subnet.

Hosts may also be unable to communicate with other hosts on the same physical segment when multiple subnets are configured to exist on the same network segment. A local router configured to support multiple subnets on a single port, or configured to support "proxy ARP" enables you to create a work-around for this situation, allowing all stations to talk to each other. If a router supports proxy ARP, it will respond to ARP requests in cases where the router knows a route to the ARP destination IP address—even if that destination IP address is on the same local segment. With proxy ARP enabled, many nodes that have incomplete or incorrect configurations will still be able to operate. The primary issue with proxy ARP is that it allows sloppy configurations to still function. It also dramatically increases the sizes of ARP caches, and in some cases causes confusing results. Depending on the quality of the operating software, if a router has proxy ARP enabled it may respond to all ARP requests—even if those networks do not exist. It will either forward requests to its default route (a default route is often shown as an IP network of "0.0.0.0" in the router's routing tables), or it may discard them. Many network managers choose to disable proxy ARP to enforce correct configurations. Proxy ARP is often enabled by default, and must be explicitly disabled.

Use the Enterprise LANMeter test tool's Internet TCP/IP **Segment Discovery** test to identify routers that are configured with proxy ARP enabled. (See Figure D-4.) The **ICMP Monitor** test offered by all models can be used to look for potential problems on the local IP segment. (See Figure D-5.) If an ICMP error is detected, use the "Zoom In" softkey to obtain the address of the problem station(s).

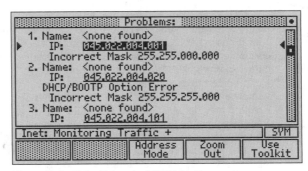

Figure D-3. *Fluke Enterprise LANMeter **Segment Discovery** test results, "zoomed" on Problems screen.*

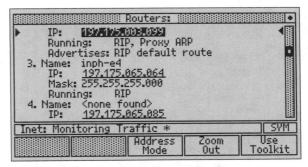

Figure D-4. *Fluke Enterprise LANMeter **Segment Discovery** test results, "zoomed" on Routers screen.*

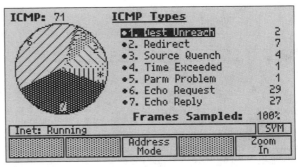

Figure D-5. *Fluke LANMeter **ICMP Monitor** test results screen.*

The Enterprise LANMeter test tool's Internet TCP/IP **Segment Discovery** test will identify all local hosts that are sending routing protocols—whether or not they are actually routers. Usually, the associated MAC address will supply enough information to determine whether the host is really a router or not (see Figure D-6). Further testing may be performed on any of the listed address pairs by using the Toolkit of SNMP queries.

If a particular host is suspect, run the Enterprise LANMeter test tool's Internet TCP/IP **Scan Host** test to quickly determine how the host is configured using a variety of SNMP queries and Ping tests. (See Figures D-6 and D-7.)

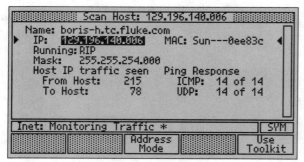

Figure D-6. *Fluke Enterprise LANMeter Scan Host test results screen, showing a workstation improperly configured to send the routing protocol RIP.*

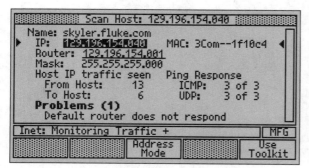

Figure D-7. *Fluke Enterprise LANMeter Scan Host test results screen, showing a host with an incorrect default router configuration.*

Incorrect DNS server(s). If possible, hosts should have more than one DNS server configured. DNS allows secondary servers to keep current from primary servers. If a host is configured for at least two DNS servers that can be connected over different paths, the probability of applications failing due to no access to DNS will be lower.

A number of tests can be run to help identify this problem. First, the LANMeter test tool's **ICMP Ping** can be used to verify that the configured DNS server is reachable. If it cannot be reached, the **Trace Route** test can be used to locate where the communications failure is occurring. Also, the Enterprise LANMeter test tool's Internet TCP/IP **Toolkit** can be used to query the configured DNS server—thus verifying valid configurations. And the Enterprise LANMeter test tool's Internet TCP/IP **Segment Discovery** can be used to identify that or other DNS servers available from this segment.

Encapsulation issues

Most IP packets on Ethernet networks use Ethernet II MAC frames. In some cases, however, IP may be seen as it exists on Token Ring and FDDI networks: over 802.2 and SNAP. Problems may exist if IP hosts need to be specially configured to handle 802.2 and SNAP encapsulations. This issue is most common when there are Ethernet-to-Token Ring source-routed transparent bridges.

Is it a global problem?

If other users on the same segment (or subnet) also have problems, it is unlikely that the problem relates to an individual station. Determine what path the connection uses through your network, move one "hop" closer (go to a station on the other side of the nearest router or to another station on a different subnet or segment), and attempt the *exact same network operation* again. Also try the same operation from another user's account. If the attempt works from this distant network connection point, troubleshoot the addressing, router, or gateway that provides services off the local subnet. If the attempt still fails, check to ensure that the target server or service is actually online, that the DNS server is still operating, and that the target server or service can be reached from some other station.

The LANMeter test tool's **Trace Route** or **Path Discovery** test can be used to both verify connectivity to a target host, and to simultaneously identify marginal or failed routers or segments between this connection and the target host. (See Figure D-8.) If a communications failure exists in the path, it should be detected with this test. Also, if the Enterprise LANMeter is used to perform the traceroute function, then there is a hyperlink from this test to the Internet TCP/IP **Toolkit** where SNMP queries may be made to the highlighted router in the path. From the Toolkit you can check the routing tables, determine whether or not the required router interface is up, and see if the interface is experiencing errors on the attached segment.

Physical problems

No response to ARP (host or router not there). If a host ARPs for the target host (or the next hop if that host is on another subnet) and there is no response, most likely there is no host on that network receiving that ARP frame. Most likely, one of the following reasons apply: 1) the requested IP address is incorrect; 2) there is a physical problem on the LAN; or 3) the requested host (or the router) is down. (See Figure D-7.)

The LANMeter test tool's **ICMP Ping** test can be used to verify this process. (See Figure D-9.) It will show you both the response time for any replies received, as well as the MAC address of the device attached to the local segment that the reply frame came from (either the target, or the router leading to the target). It also shows whether or not there was a reply to the ARP frame issued before the Ping was sent.

Routers not connected to next hop. When an "ICMP Destination Unreachable: Network Unreachable" message is returned to the host, a traceroute test will show which router is having the problem. (See Figure D-8.) One common cause, assuming that the IP addresses are correct, is a physical problem such as a failed WAN or LAN segment attached to that router. While many IP networks can handle one or more path failures, there may not always be a mesh topology that can route around failed segments.

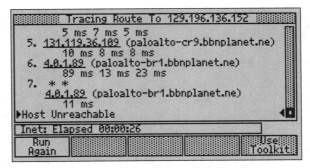

Figure D-8. *Fluke Enterprise LANMeter **Path Discovery** test results screen. An asterisk (*) indicates a missing response.*

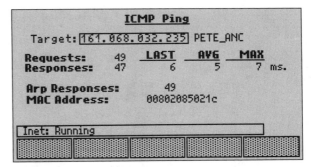

Figure D-9. *Fluke LANMeter **ICMP Ping** test results screen.*

Interface Table
1. 3Com_NETBuilderFDDI/1-1
I/F: Up, FDDI (100 Mbps)
FDDI: Wrap_B
State: Ring_Op
MAC: 080002030ac2
MTU: 4500
IP: 45.0.28.2
Mask: 255.255.252.0
2. 3Com_NETBuilder
I/F: Down, Other (0 bps)
MAC: None
MTU: 0
Inet: Target: 45.0.12.2
Refresh View
Copy To Log
Leave View
Display Stats

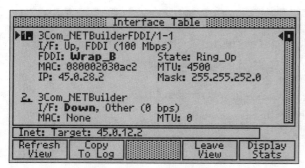

Figure D-10. *Fluke Enterprise LANMeter* ***Toolkit, Interface Table*** *test results screen.*

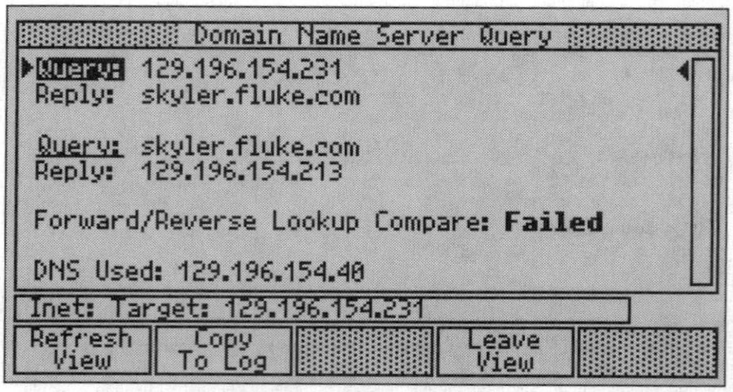

Domain Name Server Query
Query: 129.196.154.231
Reply: skyler.fluke.com
Query: skyler.fluke.com
Reply: 129.196.154.213
Forward/Reverse Lookup Compare: Failed
DNS Used: 129.196.154.40
Inet: Target: 129.196.154.231
Refresh View
Copy To Log
Leave View

Figure D-11. *Fluke Enterprise LANMeter* ***Toolkit, Domain Namer Server Query*** *test results screen, showing DNS server database problem.*

The LANMeter test tool's **Trace Route** or the Enterprise LANMeter test tool's **Path Discovery** tests will help locate path failures.

Use the Enterprise LANMeter test tool's hyperlink from the Path Discovery test to the **Toolkit** where SNMP queries may be made to the highlighted router address in the path. From the Toolkit you can check the routing tables, whether or not the required router interface is up, and if the interface is experiencing errors on the attached segment. (See Figure D-10.)

DNS issues

One of the most common problems with hosts obtaining requested information from DNS is basic communications difficulty in contacting the DNS server. DNS requests typically use IP/UDP and need to go through the same process as any other IP host-to-host communication. Many IP host implementations allow more than one DNS server to be configured. It is a good idea to configure the address of a backup DNS server where possible. To increase the odds of reaching a server, many installations will have the two DNS servers separated onto different networks.

One of the most frustrating problems for network professionals to troubleshoot is when information within the DNS database is incorrect or inconsistent. While DNS can be used for information other than host names and addresses, such as electronic mail information, most problems encountered by hosts are with name-address resolution. The basic problem is that a name-to-address lookup is not consistent with the information returned from an address-to-name lookup. A typical DNS database consists of two separate files: one containing the name-to-address lookup table, and a second containing the address-to-name lookup table. It is quite easy for these two files to be out of synchronization because of a typographical error. UNIX system tools such as NSLOOKUP, DIG or HOST can be used to diagnose these problems.

The Enterprise LANMeter test tool's Internet TCP/IP **Toolkit** offers a single test to verify an entry from both directions. (See Figure D-11.) If the address is supplied, the test obtains a name. Then the resulting name is used to obtain an address. If the two do not match, then the test fails.

Routing problems

Assuming that both hosts are properly configured, a variety of routing problems can prevent connections from becoming established. The routers that make up an IP network must share routing information. When there is a problem with this process, inconsistent information in the routing tables may prevent end-to-end connectivity.

The most common causes of inconsistent information in routing tables are physical link problems and incorrect router configuration information. When physical LAN or WAN links are going up and down, routers send routing updates to each other when a link status change is discovered. Until this new information can propagate throughout the network, various routers may not have the correct view of the network. Connection attempts made during this intermediate time period may fail because portions of the network are temporarily unreachable. These routing problems will typically represent themselves as no response at all, or with "ICMP Destination Unreachable: Network Unreachable" messages.

The Enterprise LANMeter test tool can be used to view the routing tables of all routers that separate two hosts. Routing table entries will show where routes are unstable. In Figure D-12 the invalidated entry was caused by an entry in the router's routing table that had expired, but as yet had not been removed from the table or updated. The LANMeter test tool can also be used to monitor the ICMP errors.

Traceroute is a very effective tool to locate the routers that are affected with these problems. Remember: Don't shoot the messenger. Just because a router is not handling the data correctly does not mean that it is the source of the problem. Often, another router is the culprit and *it* is sending bad information out over the network.

If a router port or the attached LAN or WAN segment is having problems, the Traceroute results will be affected too. If all hops up to a certain point are solid, and then frames begin to be dropped after that point, examine the routing tables of the routers identified from that point onward. If another path exists, try increasing the RIP "cost" for the problem connection. This will force the routers to seek a different path to the destination host.

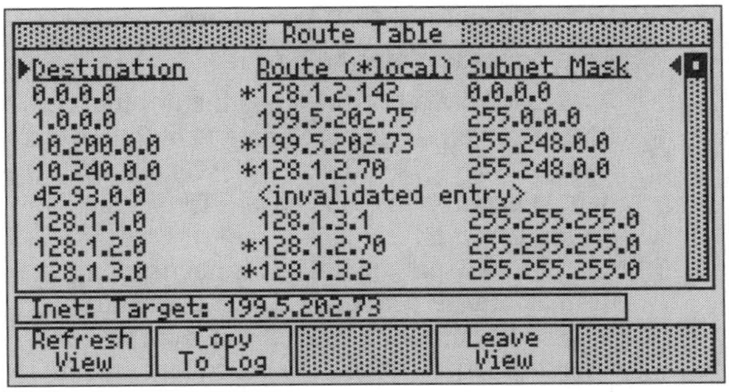

Figure D-12. *Fluke Enterprise LANMeter* **Toolkit, Route Table** *test results screen.*

Another problem that can adversely affect routers is inaccurate data in the ARP tables. Each router builds a table showing which IP address is associated with which MAC address. If a host attempts to join a local segment with a duplicate IP address, it causes the table to replace the correct MAC address with the MAC address from the misconfigured host. Traffic that was destined for the original host is then sent to the second (misconfigured) host instead.

To fix this problem temporarily (so you can get the network running until a proper correction is possible), have the router delete its existing ARP table and build a new one. If the ARP table continues to have problems, try shortening the ARP cache timeout. The ARP cache timeout parameter determines how long the router will "trust" information in the ARP table, and causes the router to discard entries that have been in the table for more than a configured period of time. In order for this fix to last, the problem station must be located and reconfigured quite soon.

The Enterprise LANMeter test tool can be used to quickly locate hosts with duplicate IP addresses, using the Internet TCP/IP **Segment Discovery** test.

Server configuration problems

No process listening to port

After an IP packet has reached the destination host or server, IP offers the data to higher layers such as TCP or UDP. TCP or UDP will also offer the data to applications such as an FTP or TELNET server, or to NFS.

If the network application is not listening to the TCP or UDP port, an "ICMP Destination Unreachable: Port Unreachable" message will be returned. Troubleshooting applications such as Traceroute use these messages; however, these ICMP errors are not expected from a server that should be offering these services. If they are being returned, it often means the server's networking processes have failed and either the networking processes or the entire server will need to be restarted.

Access security issues

Just as broken or failed segments or devices can prevent IP packets from arriving at the destination host, router and server configurations can be used to prevent connectivity. Usually in the name of security (which probably needs to be enhanced anyway), many network managers are installing a variety of filters or "firewalls" to prevent unauthorized use of the network. Of course, these security features may sometimes prevent the authorized user from accessing the network too.

Router filtering

Most dedicated routers have filtering capabilities. These filters may be based upon IP addresses, or even on the higher-layer protocol and service ports. Router filtering is probably the first place to implement security controls in a network. It is important, however, that they are not used to replace computer system or application security controls. One of the most common mistakes in setting up filters is not fully understanding the hierarchy of the filters and the bit masking that is often required. Careful design and testing of filters are required to avoid network service disruptions.

Traceroute and ping are effective methods to detect if routers have security filtering turned on. Traceroute will show if a router is discarding packets. Ping is useful to bounce packets off of different interfaces on a router to see where the filter is activated.

A problem more common than security controls preventing *authorized* use of resources is when controls put into place fail to prevent *unauthorized* use. Tools such as ping and traceroute are effective methods of testing IP-level filtering in routers to see if the proper controls are working.

Server filtering

Just as routers can filter packets, many servers (particularly UNIX servers) can filter as well. Data filtering, in combination with other controls, can effectively control who has access to the system and its applications. However, to ensure that these controls are constantly in place, continuous monitoring and intervention may be needed.

IP address

Address filters simply offer a list showing which hosts or which IP networks are allowed. These lists may also indicate which network applications (FTP for example) are allowed. Just as in dedicated routers, the most common mistakes come from a lack of understanding as to how to properly configure the filters.

Logon or password security

After the IP packet arrives and is passed to the network operating system, most network operating systems require a password or some other sort of user identification and authentication before access is given. In fact, many applications offer similar password protection. This simple problem is often overlooked and is easily verified. Be sure to check a connection to a similar service, preferably on the same segment as the target server.

Many network operating systems permit the network administrator to lock out users when too many bad passwords have been tried. It's a good idea to set a low number for the alert so you quickly discover when someone's account is being hacked. Before you suspect foul play, be sure to verify that a user is experiencing problems logging in, that the user's account is valid, and that the user's account is not locked out.

Intermittently dropped connections

This assumes that the host has been operating properly prior to this problem, and you have already verified that the media access protocol is operating correctly with the troubleshooting steps described under **Connections that drop** in Chapter 2. Especially ensure that you have:

- Cold-booted the host in question (a warm-boot does *not* reset all adapter cards).

- Verified that the host has not had any hardware failures.

- Verified that all required network cables are present and properly connected.

- Verified that all required network adapter software driver files were loaded, and that no errors were reported when they loaded.

- Verified that nothing has been changed on the problem host recently that may have caused this problem, such as reconfiguring or adding software or hardware.

- Verified that the attached MAC layer is not experiencing errors. (It is pointless to troubleshoot network layer problems if the MAC layer is marginal or failing.)

Lost packets

When packets are lost, higher layers will repeatedly attempt to get packets through to the other host. Modern TCP implementations will even delay these retransmissions to allow any network congestion to clear up. However, if communication cannot be reestablished, the connection will be dropped.

Use a continuous ping test to see if there is significant packet loss. It is not uncommon for an IP host to fail to respond to the first ping, but all subsequent pings should receive a reply. Any significant discrepancy indicates a problem.

If the host is on the local physical network, try using the Enterprise LANMeter test tool's Internet TCP/IP Scan Host test. This test sends a variety of pings and SNMP queries to the target host.

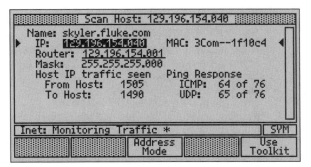

Figure D-13. Fluke Enterprise LANMeter **Scan Host** *test results screen, showing lost ping responses.*

Route flapping

When LAN or WAN links have serious problems, they will often cycle up and down every several seconds. Whenever one of these links changes state, it may trigger routing protocol updates. Whenever these networking protocols indicate a changed route, routers may make changes in their routing information that creates "black holes." These "black holes" are parts of the network that, for several seconds, may not be accessible by all or part of the network. After additional time, routing protocol updates have had time to traverse the network, bringing the network back into a stable state. If network segments (WAN or LAN) are cycling every several seconds, the network as a whole is unstable and the routing information will be constantly inconsistent. This "route flapping" will also waste a router's CPU resources.

The Enterprise LANMeter test tool can be used to view the routing tables of all routers that separate two hosts. (See Figure D-12.) If routes are unstable, the routing table entries will reflect the instability. Another way to find this problem is to conduct a Traceroute test to a variety of target stations on distant LAN segments.

Slow or poor performance

A note about performance

Performance bottlenecks are a fact of network life. At times these bottlenecks can be addressed, for example, when moving from a 64-kbps link to 1.5 or 2.8-Mbps dedicated circuit. In a healthy network, the primary bottlenecks will be the throughput of the WAN links and the performance of the computer systems. It is a common error to immediately assume that poor performance on a network is due to a slow local connection (Ethernet or Token Ring), and that increasing the speed of the local connection or installing a switch will solve the problem. In fact, the most common causes of poor performance are a computer at either end, and slow WAN links.

There are two issues to consider when addressing performance: 1) throughput and 2) latency. Throughput is the measurement of bits flowing through a link. A 10-Mbps Ethernet has more throughput than a 64-kbps WAN link. Latency is the delay of data through the components and the entire system. Dedicated resources such as point-to-point WAN links have an unchanging latency. However, shared resources such as LANs, computer systems, routers and shared WAN services such as frame relay networks have a variable latency. When shared resources become loaded, the latency of data going through will increase as packets have to wait to be transmitted or to go through the system.

It is important to understand if performance problems are throughput-related or latency-related before making changes.

Important: Making performance changes without understanding the cause can become very expensive or have no performance impact, and may actually worsen the user's performance. This is not uncommon when installing switches.

Routing protocol decisions

IP Routers use various routing protocols to communicate with each other so that IP packets can traverse the network in the fastest possible method. How the routing protocols interpret the network topology may often significantly impact performance.

Routing protocols such as RIP use a method called Distance-Vector routing. Distance-Vector routing assumes that the best path to a destination network is via the shortest path (least number of hops). At times, protocols such as RIP will make a poor decision such as when packets are sent over a single slow, congested WAN link instead of a series of two idle high-speed WAN links.

Other protocols such as OSPF, and Cisco's IGRP and EIGRP take into account the connection speed or other attributes such as the load of the LAN and WAN segments. OSPF even considers variables like reliability, delay and throughput. These protocols will typically make better routing decisions in complex networks.

Traceroute will show the path IP packets take through the network. Comparing the Traceroute path with the link speeds may help identify routing problems that incorrectly make use of slow-speed links.

Slow WAN connections

Low-throughput WAN links

In many installations, LANs or WANs that are experiencing intermittent physical problems can create performance problems by destroying packets or by creating router congestion as the routers queue traffic waiting for the link. A lost packet will result in a retransmission.

Intermittent physical problems can also create a routing issue, which is called "route flapping." As the links cycle from up to down and up again, the routing protocols send updates regarding the changing status of the link and the impact on the available routes. These routing updates can negatively impact router performance throughout the network as they spend processor time recalculating routes.

Network topology

Understanding the topology of the network and the path that IP packets take from one network to another is very useful in discerning performance-related problems.

Many networks will begin the process of interconnecting LANs using low-speed links. These slow links may be enough for the initial applications and for a small number of users. However, as more critical applications are deployed and as more users add traffic, WAN links are often the most obvious place to look for improved performance. These slow links not only add latency when there is sufficient bandwidth for the offered traffic loads, but they are often the primary source of congestion as more traffic is added.

Tools such as traceroute can help identify slow, congested links as the test displays the round-trip response time for each hop through the path to the target node.

The impact of congested links

As long as the offered traffic going through a network segment is less than the available throughput, the system should be able to handle the load with no problems. When the offered load is greater than the available bandwidth, the routers will start to queue the data, and then transmit it when the link is available. Packets will be discarded as the router's buffer fill with queued data. Additionally, higher-level applications such as NFS or TCP will time-out and will attempt to retransmit the data, which, in some cases, will make the problem worse as even more data is sent. Advanced algorithms with TCP implementations will slow down retransmissions to prevent additional congestion.

Slow routers

Servers as routers

LAN and WAN routers are an important part of a TCP/IP network. It is relatively easy to add IP routing to a PC or server as a low-cost, short-term solution. However, as IP routing becomes more important, most networks utilize stand-alone dedicated routers. It's important to note that the task of moving IP packets from one interface to another consumes both memory and CPU resources. Performance will suffer if those resources are also needed for other applications.

Congested routers

Some people are very concerned about routers failing to keep up with data. This is rarely the case. When only a few LAN and/or WAN links are involved, dedicated, stand-alone routers will almost always have enough CPU and memory resources to handle the traffic. In cases where there are many high-speed LAN interfaces on one router with a lot of traffic, the central processor or memory of a router may become overloaded. Much of this problem can be corrected by using multi-interface cards that can route traffic without placing any load on the router's central processing unit.

An indication of router or link congestion is ICMP Source Quench packets. The router will send these packets to a host, indicating that the host should slow down its transmission rate. Note that many TCP/IP implementations ignore these packets when they are received.

ICMP echo packets from a ping application are often useful to see if packets are being discarded due to congested links or routers.

Slow hosts

Not all hosts are created equally

No matter how fast the LAN speeds are and how large or fast the server is, actual performance will still not exceed the performance capabilities of a slow host. Make sure that the entire link's performance is understood, including the capabilities of the hosts.

Old, tired interfaces and drivers

Many performance improvements have been made lately in LAN interfaces and in the corresponding software drivers. Periodically, check the manufacturer's specifications to see if there have been significant performance improvements in newer software. Of course, being on the leading edge of technology is not for everybody. Still, do not become too far behind on current hardware and software revisions.

Overloaded server

Everything else being equal, servers with higher-speed CPUs, more memory and faster disks can perform more work than slower systems. However, it's important to keep in mind that not all applications are the same and may place different demands on systems and networks. Do not forget that any slow portion of a system will create a performance bottleneck for the entire system, and that there is always another bottleneck. At times, components such as faster LAN interface cards or faster I/O sub-systems such as SCSI may help much more than a faster CPU.

Networked applications to look out for

Watch for applications that many people can easily access, and which place a larger load on the system than local applications.

X-windows

X-windows applications allow users to start a session on the server, then send graphics windows back to the end-users' system. Typically, X-windows applications are much more CPU- and memory-intensive than ordinary virtual terminal sessions from TELNET. Of course, CPU and memory consumption also depends upon which applications are being run.

NFS

As more and more people connect via NFS to a server and access files, more memory and disk I/O resources will be called upon. Typically, disk reads place less of a load on a system than disk writes, as many systems post every write to the disk while reads are cached. Balancing applications on different disk spindles so that disk writes are spread out will minimize this affect.

Operation

The TCP/IP protocol was developed by a large number of organizations starting with research funded by the Defense Advanced Research Projects Agency (DARPA). It is commonly refered to as TCP/IP, though this is only one combination of the basic protocol, Internet Protocol (IP), together with one of the several OSI Layer 5 protocols, Transport Control Protocol (TCP), that commonly run on top of it. As the IP protocol was developed essentially by a committee (and is still being added to), this summary cannot address each of the possibilities in that suite of protocols. To obtain specific information about the different clarifications and add-on's to the basic IP protocol suites, you are advised to obtain copies of the published Request for Comment documents (RFCs). To start with, obtain *rfc-index.txt*, which offers a short description about each document. RFCs are the nearest equivalent to a published "Standard" for TCP/IP. To start with, obtain rfc_index.txt, which offers a short description about each document. RFCs are the nearest equivalent to a published "Standard" for TCP/IP. RFCs may be obtained from many sources, one of which is **http://www.rfc-editor.org/rfc.html**. Most of the RFCs are text documents ending in ".TXT," though some are postscript and end in ".PS."

Note: *To learn about registering a Domain Name, go to* **http://www.internic.net/**.

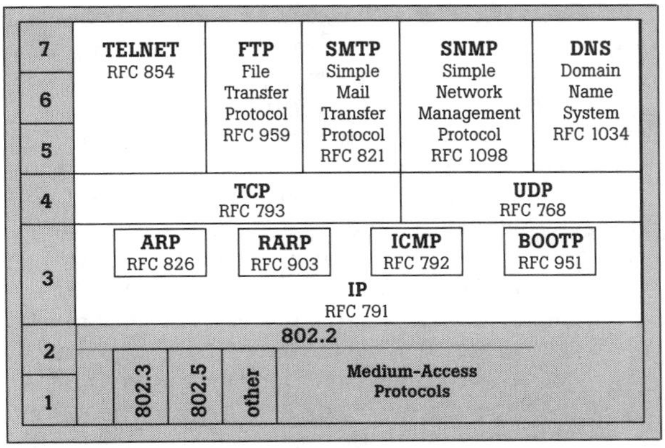

7	TELNET RFC 854	FTP File Transfer Protocol RFC 959	SMTP Simple Mail Transfer Protocol RFC 821	SNMP Simple Network Management Protocol RFC 1098	DNS Domain Name System RFC 1034
6					
5					
4	TCP RFC 793			UDP RFC 768	
3	ARP RFC 826 RARP RFC 903 ICMP RFC 792 BOOTP RFC 951 IP RFC 791				
2	802.2				
1	802.3 802.5 other	Medium-Access Protocols			

Figure D-14. *Partial list of TCP/IP protocols shown in relation to the OSI 7 Layer model.*

Figure D-14 shows several of the common protocols that operate on top of the IP protocol, and their dependencies. One of the first reference RFCs is shown with some of the more common protocols, though there are usually several for each. IP itself is a connectionless datagram protocol that relies on higher layers to guarantee delivery of data. As a generality, the IP protocol provides "best effort" or "connectionless" delivery of data, User Datagram Protocol (UDP) provides "semi-reliable" delivery of data, and TCP provides "reliable" delivery of data. IP itself will operate on top of just about any medium access protocol, though the most common are Ethernet (802.3) and Token Ring (802.5).

It should be noted that the dependencies implied by Figure D-14 are somewhat indistinct. For instance, an Address Resolution Protocol (ARP) frame contains some of the fields required by IP, but not all of them. DNS services often run over UDP, but can also run over TCP if a more reliable connection is appropriate for the application. IP is usually transmitted over local area network connections such as Ethernet and Token Ring, but may also be sent over dial-up telecommunications links such as Point-to-Point Protocol (PPP).

Each protocol layer places additional overhead that will measurably reduce network throughput. The amount of overhead depends on each specific protocol. Out of a fairly standard sized TCP datagram encapsulated in an IP frame (576 octets) and an Ethernet 802.2 frame, only 88.6% represents the actual OSI Layer 5 information (which includes still more overhead!). If the frame size gets smaller, the amount of actual throughput (once the overhead is removed) drops considerably. (See Figure D-15.) It is best to configure all equipment to utilize the largest frame size that will cross all interconnected LAN segments. This will optimize the bandwidth usage. Probably the most common maximum transmission unit (MTU) is 1500 octets.

Basic addressing

IP addresses are globally controlled and assigned in set ranges for most networks. To obtain a unique IP network address, contact Network Solutions, InterNIC Registration Services at (703) 742-4777, or via electronic mail at HOSTMASTER@INTERNIC.NET. Since the purpose of the Internet is to connect many networks into a single world-wide virtual network, there must be a single entity managing the address assignments. Anyone wishing to connect to the Internet must obtain an assigned address range

from this organization. Though, in actual practice, it is often best to obtain an address through the Internet Service Provider that you will obtain your direct connection from. If there are no plans for your network to be connected to the Internet, then it is not necessary to obtain an official address range. However, even though your network may not be connected now, if it becomes connected in the future, the network manager will probably have to change the configuration of every single host in your network prior to going "live" if you do not use an officially assigned block of addresses. (See RFC 1918.)

Growing popularity of the Internet will exhaust the available addresses in the near future, and the best method for increasing the available addresses is being debated now. The next generation of IP addressing will likely be IP version 6 (IPv6). For most users, any increase will have little or no impact, but most network managers will find this change causes serious consequences. Countless software applications, routers, gateways, DNS servers, and many other parts of a network's infrastructure will have to be upgraded to take advantage of an explosion of available new services outside currently configurable maximum address ranges. As a network professional you should begin planning now for upcoming changes to the new address scheme.

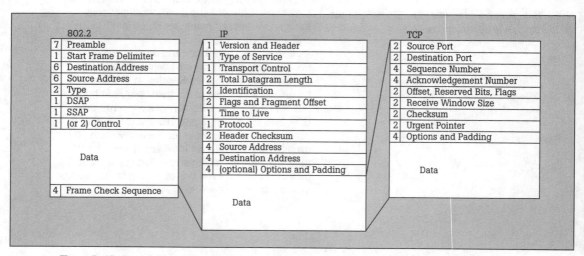

Figure D-15. Data fields for IP and TCP frames running over an 802.2 Ethernet encapsulation.

An IP version 4 (IPv4) address is a field of 32 binary bits. To make that string of 1's and 0's more readable, it is common practice to represent that address in four groups of eight bits (four octets), and then to convert each octet to decimal. Once the number is represented in decimal format, a period is used to separate each octet. The period is inserted to ensure that the separation is obvious. The resulting number is in a format known as *dotted-decimal*.

If you are looking at an IPv4 address with a protocol analyzer or other network diagnostic tool, you will see the address in either hexadecimal or dotted-decimal notation. Using an example address of 196.220.5.130, the different formats are shown in Table D-1. If you will be dealing with IP addresses regularly, you will want to learn to make these conversions.

The present 32-bit IPv4 address range is divided into five classes of addresses. Class A offers the largest number of available hosts, Class B offers a smaller number, and Class C offers the smallest. All Class A addresses were assigned long ago; it is all but impossible to get a Class B address at this time; and the supply of Class C addresses is shrinking rapidly. Class D is reserved for a special user-definable and limited form of broadcasting, and Class E is reserved.

In the Table D-2, the *Address Range* column specifies part of the first octet of the address, and is commonly used as a quick check of the address class.

Note: *There are actually two fewer hosts than the table shows for each class of address, since you are not allowed to assign broadcast addresses (all 1's, or all 0's in the host field) to individual hosts. To calculate the numbers yourself, convert the number in the Address Range column back to binary and match it against what is shown as the left-most binary numbers in Figure D-16.*

binary	1100 0100	1101 1100	0000 0101	1000 0010
hexadecimal	C 4	D C	0 5	8 2
dotted-decimal	196	220	5	130

Table D-1. *Example IP address numbering system conversion table.*

IP Address Class	Address Range (first octet)	Default Subnet Mask	Maximum Hosts Possible
Class A	0-127	255.0.0.0	16,777,216
Class B	128-191	255.255.0.0	65,536
Class C	192-223	255.255.255.0	256

Table D-2. *Formal IPv4 address class ranges.*

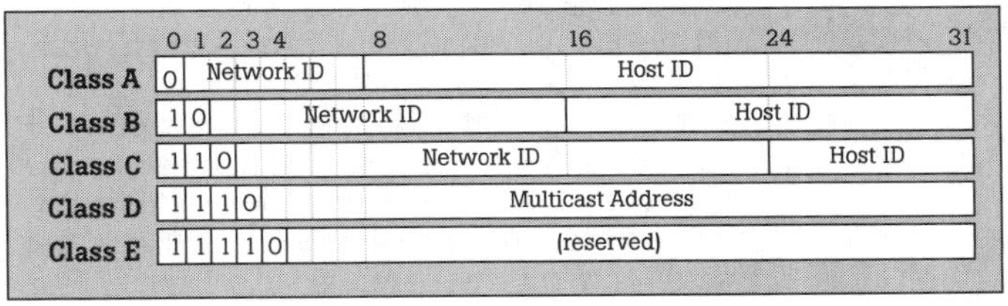

Figure D-16. *IPv4 address class ranges.*

Figure D-16 shows how the first bits determine the class of an IPv4 address. By locating the first binary zero value (reading left to right), you can determine what class of address is being used. Since binary numbering is not user-friendly, most people quickly learn the decimal number ranges that correspond to each class. (See Table D-2.) Theoretically, by determining the address class you can then learn the network address. The remaining binary digits represent the host address within the specified network.

Each IPv4 address is divided into two logical fields: a network identifier field, and a host identifier field. For simple networks, the address class defines where the logical division of the 32-bit field is made in order to separate the address into these two fields. (See Figure D-16.)

Subnet mask

When it comes to subnet masks, forget everything you have ever learned about classes of IPv4 addresses. It will only confuse you. In practice, you will *never* need to know what class of address you are dealing with, except when requesting a new block of addresses. If a network is connected to the Internet, it will have routers in it (each router port connects a physical network to the larger network), and each router port will require an internationally unique address. If it is *not* connected to the Internet, it is entirely possible that the IP addresses in use are arbitrarily chosen, and therefore do not follow *any* of the normal conventions, except the requirement that a unique address range be used for each physical network.

It is not prudent to construct a single physical network with more than several hundred hosts, because a network failure will prevent too many people from performing their work. This one reason is why routers are used to separate physical networks.

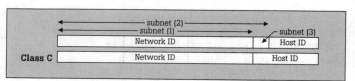

Figure D-17. IP "subnet" descriptions.

binary	1100 0100	1101 1100	0000 0101	10xx xxxx
hexadecimal	C 4	D C	0 5	8 0
dotted-decimal	196	220	5	128

Table D-3. Example IP address conversion table. (The "x" characters indicate the host address bits, and zeros were substituted to convert the hexadecimal and dotted-decimal examples.)

binary	1111 1111	1111 1111	1111 1111	1100 0000
hexadecimal	F F	F F	F F	C 0
dotted-decimal	255	255	255	192

Table D-4. Example IP address numbering system conversion table.

And since all networks connected to the Internet include routers, it has become common practice for network managers to take several bits from the host field to create additional network addresses and fewer host addresses. This is called "subnetting," and serves to sub-partition a network.

"Subnet" is a poor choice in terms of description. Subnet can refer to: 1) the network identifier indicated by the address class, 2) the complete network identifier—including any subnet, and 3) the further inclusion into the network address of some number of the binary bits from those allotted to the host identifier. Each port on a router requires a unique network address range, and this is a simple method of obtaining the necessary addresses. In Figure D-17, two bits were taken from the host field and included as part of the network address using the process of subnetting.

Combining both examples above—and using the same subnetting—the network identifier for the example address would be as shown in Table D-3.

These confusing examples highlight the need for some way to tell all network devices how to read the 32-bit address. The mechanism used to describe how to split the address into network identifier and host identifier is called the "subnet mask." It is precisely because of this process that address classes become meaningless in an operating network environment. All that matters is the full 32-bit address and the subnet mask.

The subnet mask tells each host how much of the 32-bit address is used to identify which IP network the host "lives" on, and how much is used to uniquely identify each host. This can be compared loosely to the postal system, where a city name is used for the network address, and the house number is used for the host address. This allows the postman (the router) to quickly sort and deliver the messages.

To calculate a subnet mask, set all network address bits to "1" (in this example use the first 26 bits—the left-most three octets plus two more bits from the right-most octet), and the host address bits to "0" (the right-most six bits). The string of 1s and 0s is then converted to dotted-decimal, and the resulting number is the subnet mask. In this example the result is as shown in Table D-4.

All IPv4 addresses are logical-ANDed with a subnet mask in order to derive the physical (logical) network being identified. Returning to the postal system comparison, we can now equate the full subnet (network identifier and any additional subnet bits) as both the city and street address, still leaving the host field as roughly equal to the house number.

Some software applications do not accept the standard dotted-decimal format for a subnet mask. However, as long as you can convert between the three types of addressing formats, you should be able to satisfy any requirement.

Be careful when creating and configuring the subnet and subnet mask. It is possible to create and use a non-contiguous mask where some bits are skipped-over, such as:

1111 1111 1111 1111 1111 1111 0100 0000

This is not only a bad idea, but you will not find much software that supports it. You would also be constantly troubleshooting the resulting addressing problems—not to mention what would be required to administer the addresses themselves and explain them to anyone else.

It is worthwhile to note that routers not attached to the local segment often use different subnet masks than local hosts will use, because they only need to know enough to forward a message to the next router along the way. Example: If a company is connected to the Internet, and has a Class B address, then the router that provides the connection from the Internet to that company will use a Class B subnet mask. Inside the company, the router probably uses a subnet mask that is closer to a Class C mask. This is because, to the Internet router, everything within that Class B range goes to only one router connection. Inside the company, the network manager will have further divided the address range, and will assign more restrictive subnet masks (fewer host bits) in order to have each router port support a unique block of addresses.

Exercise:
Take the following address block and subnet mask and find two details that fail to follow the "default" standards. Then calculate the range of host addresses that can be assigned using this information.

IPv4 Address: 197.78.165.0
Subnet Mask: 255.255.253.0

Answers:

1. The first octet shows the address to be a Class C address. By definition, that would mean that the first three octets are fixed. Yet the subnet mask shows that the host field extends into the "fixed" part of a Class C address, thus the network manager has changed some of the "fixed" part of the address.

2. The subnet mask is not contiguous. One of the binary bits was skipped over in deciding which bits were network address and which were host address.

3. The range of host addresses possible with this set of data is: 197.78.165.0 through 197.78.165.255, and 197.78.167.0 through 197.78.167.255—though you will probably have to convert all to binary to see this.

Host address

The remaining host bits in an address may be used for any connection to the physical network. However, there are two exceptions. The host bits should never be set to all "1" or all "0." These two addresses are reserved for special use. Therefore, a Class C address has only 254 available host addresses out of the available 256 unique addresses.

Other special addresses

- The Class A address of 127.0.0.0 is reserved for testing. If a host uses this address to send data, the protocol stack will return the data back to the sending application without actually having sent it out on the network. Also, *if* a frame is observed on a network bearing a 127 network address, it should never be forwarded by any host (including routers and gateways). The value found in the host portion of the address does not matter.

- The address of 32 0's is sometimes used by a host as it joins the network during initialization. It is never permitted to form a valid destination address. This address also appears often in routing tables as 0.0.0.0, and means the "default route." For a short time an address of 32 0's was also used as the broadcast address, but this has since fallen into disuse.

- The address of 32 1's is often used as a broadcast address for the local logical *network*. It is never permitted to form a valid source address.

- If the *host field* of an IPv4 address is set to all 1's, then the message is intended for all hosts on the local logical *subnet*. It is never permitted as a valid source address.

- If the *host field* of an IPv4 address is set to all 0's, then the message is intended for the local logical subnet itself. It is never permitted as a valid source address.

Host configuration

The host (any IP device on the network) configuration is critical to proper IP network operation. Depending upon the network and the configuration parameter(s), incorrect configurations can appear to function properly for a time. But, the network may be changed slightly later and the host will stop operating, or operate intermittently for no apparent reason.

The basic configuration parameters are:

- **IPv4 address**: A unique dotted-decimal address that is within the attached IP network's address range.
  Example: 192.5.202.25

- **Subnet mask**: The bit mask that is used to identify the separation point between the network portion of the host's IPv4 address and the host portion. If not specified in the node's configuration, the IP software will often use the default subnet mask for the IPv4 class.
  Example: 255.255.255.0

- **Default router**: Most IPv4 implementations rely upon being told the IP address of a single default router. If this router fails or becomes inaccessible, communication off the host's local IP segment is not possible.

- **DNS Server(s)**: Hosts use Domain Name System servers (DNS) primarily to resolve ASCII names into dotted-decimal addresses. Where possible, hosts should have more than one DNS server in its configuration to increase the chances of reaching one.

The Internet Control Message Protocol (ICMP)

Part of the IP protocol

The ICMP is an integral part of IP. Technically, ICMP packets are a protocol on top of IP, but many ICMP functions are required in IP implementation. ICMP packets can be requested by an application (such as ping) or are generated due to an error condition in a host or a router. It is not enough to know the source and destination of ICMP packets. Those ICMP messages created due to an error also contain the IP header of the offending IP packet. Analysis of these packets and of the original IP header offer a wealth of information in a troubleshooting scenario.

Most useful ICMP messages

Echo request and echo response

When a host receives an ICMP echo request message, it will respond with an echo response. Usually generated by the ping utility or by network management applications, ping is the most used diagnostic tool, testing for both reachability and response times.

Time exceeded

When a router detects an IP packet with the Time-To-Live (TTL) field equal to one (1), it will not forward the packet to the destination, and instead return an ICMP time exceeded message to the original sender. Each router will decrement the TTL field so that routing loops will eventually clear of data. Time exceeded messages are integral to the function of traceroute.

Destination unreachable: network unreachable

Destination unreachable messages are returned when an IP router is unable to deliver a packet to the destination IP network. The Network Unreachable message indicates that a host or router did not know how to reach the destination IP network. Network or routing problems are a common cause of this message type. Mistyped IP addresses are another common cause.

Destination unreachable: host unreachable

A Host Unreachable is sent by a router when it is unable to forward the IP packet to the destination host, though the correct logical network was reached. Usually, the host is either down or not reachable due to some LAN problem. Host unreachables are also caused by mistyped addresses.

Destination unreachable: port unreachable

After the IP packet arrives at the destination host, IP will forward the attached data to higher layers. If there is no process listening to the indicated TCP or UDP port, the Port Unreachable message is sent back. Attempting to connect to an unsupported service is a common cause—for example, trying to FTP to a machine that does not have an FTP server running.

Tools that use ICMP

PING

Probably the most used diagnostic tool, the Packet Internet Groper (PING), is able to test connectivity and, to some extent, response times to a destination host. The acronym *ping* has become a generic term, indicating a simple query and response process. The actual IP ping test is formed from ICMP Echo Request and Echo Reply frames. A minimal ping test only requires a destination IP address. Note that the *first* ping packet may fail. This seems to be common when the destination host needs to ARP before replying.

Advanced ping analysis includes continuous testing to monitor for intermittent failures. For the most part, each ping request should get a response back from the target host. All IP hosts should support IP Echo packets.

Traceroute

Traceroute is an advanced tool that takes advantage of the ICMP error messages sent by routers and hosts. Traceroute is used to discover the one-way path that an IP packet takes through a network.

Traceroute sends UDP packets to the destination using an unused UDP port number. When the packet reaches the target, a "Destination Unreachable: Port Unreachable" message is sent back to the source. In the meantime, the packets are sent with very low TTL values. When the first router encounters the packet, it will discard the packet and send an ICMP "Time Exceeded" message. Then the traceroute application will increment the TTL value so that the next packet will pass through the first router (which decrements the TTL value) and the second router will send back a "Time Exceeded" message.

This methodology allows the entire path to be discovered, assuming all of the following assumptions are true:

- All of the routers in the packet path support sending back ICMP "Time Exceeded" messages. Some network managers will disable ICMP messages sent from routers to reduce CPU requirements.

- There is an actual path through the network to the target host.

- The target host supports UDP and ICMP. If UDP or ICMP is not supported, the host will not send back a "Port Unreachable" message when it receives the test packets.

- The target host really is not running the assumed "unused" UDP port. If it is using that port then no reply will be given when the message finally reaches that host.

Appendix E — IPX (Novell)

Solving Problems

Cannot connect problems

Wrong frame type

One of the most common problems in a NetWare environment is the station using a frame type other than the one being used by the server. A client and server must be configured with the same frame type to communicate. On a station using ODI or VLM drivers, this frame type is controlled by the **NET.CFG** file. On a server, the frame type is specified in the **AUTOEXEC.NCF** file with the LOAD command, as in this example:

```
LOAD NE2000 FRAME=ETHERNET_802.3
BIND IPX TO NE2000 NET=4B823CF7
```

In NetWare version 4.x, there is an application that runs on the file server, **INETCFG.NLM**, which permits changes to the configuration files in a more user-friendly manner. The changes may also be implemented immediately, without rebooting the server, by issuing the *Reinitialize System* command at the server console prompt.

One of the easiest ways to verify network connectivity to a server is by using the LANMeter test tool's **Server List** test. (See Figure E-1.) The best use of Server List is to verify network and link connectivity from a given connection to the server. If the LANMeter test tool can display a list of servers, and a suspect PC cannot connect to a server in that list from the same cable connection, then you can be fairly confident the problem is with the software or adapter card in the PC. Another way to isolate this problem is to run the LANMeter test tool's **Expert-T** test between the suspect PC and the network. This test will identify which encapsulation the suspect PC is using and whether or not it will respond to a NetWare ping, in addition to a range of other problems.

Driver/adapter card problems

Driver and adapter card problems range from the simplistic "cannot connect" to intermittent hard-to-troubleshoot "dropped-connection" problems. The LANMeter test tool tests ensure that basic communications are operational, though they may pass an adapter card with poor-quality drivers if basic communication is established up through OSI Layer 3 between that station and the server. Verification of basic communications ability substantially reduces the necessary troubleshooting activity, and directs your efforts to the problem area quickly—in this case, the station software. Remember to have the affected user log into the server in the exact same way from another nearby—fully operational—PC in order to ensure that the problem does not reside in that user's login scripts.

It is always a good idea to use the most current and supported drivers from Novell. You can download the most current drivers from the NETWIRE forum on Compuserve. If you have Internet access, download them from Novell's anonymous ftp site: **ftp.novell.com**.

Physical problems

The dreaded "File Server Not Found" error message is often a result of a poor or non-existent connection to the network. Check the cables and verify you have a good connection to the hub. In 10BASE-T networks checking the link state LEDs on the hub and adapter card may not be sufficient—especially since many LEDs are now being driven by software instead of hardware control. A split pair cable can cause connection problems, even though the link state LEDs are correctly lit.

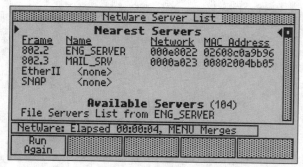

Figure E-1. *Fluke LANMeter* **NetWare,** *Server List test results screen.*

Not enough environment space

This can be an especially tricky problem because there is basic connectivity to the server, but the PC fails to complete a login—and possibly locks-up—during the login process. This occurs during execution of the login script if there is not enough DOS environment space. As an experiment try increasing the environment space by adding the following line to a DOS station's **CONFIG.SYS**:

```
shell=c:\command.com /E:2048 /P
```

This command allocates extra environment space (a total of 2048 bytes) to DOS during boot-up, and should permit NetWare to insert additional information resulting from your MAP commands.

Not enough license connections

When you run **NETx.EXE**, a workstation performs a "get-nearest-server" request, attaches to the first server to respond, and by doing so consumes one of the license connections. If you have a 10-user license, this uses up one license. If eleven people connect their stations to that server, the eleventh user will be unable to connect—even if the first ten did not actually login. If the workstation can change default drives to the network drive (usually F:), that consumes a connection. This process is the same even when the *preferred server* command is used in the **NET.CFG** file. The workstation must first establish a connection with the nearest server before getting directions to attach to the preferred server.

On the server console, the **MONITOR.NLM** screen offers a selection for connection information. This screen shows how many, and which, users are connected (and using a license connection).

If a station attempts to attach to a server that already has all of the license connections in use, the error message will be similar to when the server is turned off.

Note: *There is no indication that the problem is with the number of license connections.*

On one version of NetWare, the message was "A File Server Could Not Be Found." Another gave no message at all, it just refused to change defaults to the network drive **f:**.

Slow or poor performance

Slow or poor performance is one of the most common user complaints. The causes of poor performance are often solved by optimizing the network or server configuration, or by upgrading the server or PC hardware. However, it is important to thoroughly analyze the network topology and server configuration before throwing money at the problem. You can often achieve dramatic improvements in performance by a simple network reconfiguration.

Overloaded segment

When a network is experiencing slow performance, the natural tendency is to blame the LAN capacity. This sometimes results in needless and expensive upgrades to higher-speed network topologies. More often than not, this does not solve the problem, because the cause is more fundamental. In most networks (granted there are exceptions) the media speed is not the network bottleneck. Check the network utilization and error rates at the time that users are complaining. Don't be surprised if network utilization has short duration peaks of greater than 50% utilization; what is important is the average utilization level. However, if you *do* see average Ethernet utilization levels in excess of 40% (60% for Token Ring), then consider segmenting the network with routers, bridges or a switched hub.

Network topology

The network topology is one of the most over-looked areas in considering the sources of slow network performance. First, draw a diagram of how the traffic flows from the server to stations where users are having performance problems. Then, try to answer these questions.

- Is the traffic going through a router? Through a WAN link?
- What is the maximum packet rate through the path?
- What is the maximum packet size through the path?
- Do any bottlenecks appear in the path (such as a slow WAN link)?
- Can I move the logical or physical location of any network devices to make the traffic patterns more efficient?

Server configuration

Memory

NetWare servers need lots of RAM to work efficiently. Low RAM configurations are a common cause of poor performance. It is easy to detect this problem and the solution is simple. Load **MONITOR.NLM**, then check the Server Memory Statistics screen (for example; look under the Cache Utilization choice for NetWare 4.x; under the Tracked Resources choice for NetWare 3.12). This screen displays the percentage of system memory allocated to cache buffers. Ideally, you should install enough RAM to keep this value at least as high as 75%. Another memory statistic to monitor is the number of dirty cache buffers. If this number is consistently more than 70% of the total cache buffers, add more system memory; or you may need to upgrade the disk channel and/or controller.

It's important to remember that, as more disk space is consumed by files, the server's memory requirements also go up. NetWare servers keep critical disk information in memory to speed file read and write requests, which consumes memory space. Try freeing space on the disk to reduce memory requirements

The incremental addition of utility NLMs such as tape backup, software metering, UPS management, TCP/IP routing, CD-ROM sharing and anti-virus software causes reductions in available memory. If you are running low on memory, consider temporarily removing non-essential NLMs.

Adapter card bottlenecks

It's best to put the fastest adapter card possible in the server because the improved performance will benefit all users. At a *minimum* you should use a 32-bit ISA card. If your server supports a fast bus standard like PCI, consider upgrading the adapter card to the highest performance card type your server can utilize. A useful benchmarking program to characterize the relative performance of Server-to-Station interactions is PERFORM3.EXE. PERFORM3 does memory-to-adapter card transfers so the disk access time is not a consideration. This program is available on NETWIRE, on the Internet at *ftp.novell.com,* or *http://www.novell.com.*

Disk I/O channel

IDE drives are not recommended by Novell in NetWare servers. SCSI drives are generally faster. You can improve the performance of your disk I/O system, as well as increase its reliability, when disk mirroring using SCSI technology.

Slow WAN connections

WAN links can substantially slow down NetWare traffic. A relatively high-speed T1 link is more than six-times slower than a 10-Mbps Ethernet! That means if an application loads in 5 seconds over the LAN it will take about 30 seconds over the T1 link. This simplistic calculation does not even consider the effect of packet latency though the bridges and routers that adds even more delay. So, avoid loading large files over WAN links, especially program files that could be loaded locally. WAN links benefit the most from using larger packet sizes and Novell's packet-burst protocol. The packet-burst protocol boosts overall network performance by transferring multiple NCP replies for a single client request. Novell's new routing protocol, NetWare Link Services Protocol (NLSP) increases the maximum packet size, and lets servers and clients negotiate for the largest packet size communication. Before NLSP (and its predecessor LIP), all routed packets would automatically be set to 576 bytes. Using packet-burst mode and NLSP can increase performance up to 80%.

Overloaded server

In some cases, your server may be too busy to handle the demands placed on it. The most reliable indicator of this problem is to check for "Request Being Processed" (referred to as "delay") packets being sent by the server. (See Figure E-2.) Delay packets are sent by a server to inform the client that it cannot immediately process a request. Occasional delay packets are normal during peak times, but should not exceed more that 5% of all replies. Excessive numbers of delay packets are an indication of an overloaded server. If your server is overloaded, it is important to find out why.

Assuming there are no major configuration problems and there is adequate memory, NetWare servers are typically overloaded by excessive file requests or excessive routing. Remember, server utilization is not the same as network utilization.

Excessive file requests

Determine which users are placing the greatest demands of the server. To do this, use NetWare **Top Senders** or **File Stats**. Characterize the applications they are using and verify their PC configuration. Check for loading of large applications from the network, network-based temporary Windows swap files, and non-optimal path statements.

- Loading modern Windows-based applications over the network is very attractive from a version and software license perspective, but often puts a tremendous load on the server. As an example, it takes a transfer of about 1.4 Mbytes of data to download Word for Windows 6.0 over the network.

- When Windows is configured to load from the network, the default location of the temporary swap file is the network drive. Network-based swap files have two negative consequences. First, every time Windows is started, the client requests that the server create a large temporary swap file. Initializing this file, which can be greater than 10 Mbytes in size, is a server-intensive task. It will slow the Windows boot time and can affect the response time for all users. Additionally, the "swapping" of a client PC's processor memory to the network drive creates a large volume of traffic. Whenever possible, use a local hard disk for a swapfile. If you must use a network swapfile, minimize the effect on the network by adding as much memory to the PC as is practical, and avoid large swapfiles (greater than 5 megabytes). (This parameter is set in the Windows virtual memory configuration screen.)

- Poorly constructed path statements will create an unnecessary number of disk requests. You can significantly reduce the number of disk requests by fine-tuning a PC's path statement. Whenever possible, especially in batch files, explicitly state paths for network drive commands. Be sure that the local drive directories are in the path statement before the network drives, and that the path itself does not include multiple references to the same logical drive even though the drive letters are different.

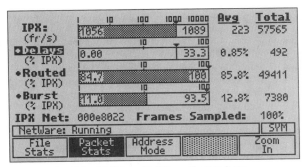

Figure E-2. *Fluke LANMeter **NetWare, Packet Stats** test results screen.*

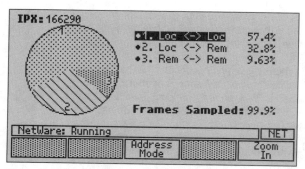

Figure E-3. *Fluke LANMeter* **NetWare, Routing Analysis** *test results screen.*

Excessive routing by a server

The primary job of a NetWare server is to provide file and printing services. Anything else you ask the server to do diverts system resources and processor time from its primary mission. Any NetWare file server with two or more adapter cards automatically becomes a router. It's tempting to take advantage of this "free" routing function to build complex networks, forcing file servers to do double duty. If you are experiencing performance problems with file servers also acting as routers, use the LANMeter test tool's Routing Analysis test to determine the percentage of routed traffic on your network and assess the load on these routing servers. (See Figure E-3.) If the percentage of *remote to local* and/or *remote to remote* traffic is greater than 30%, consider 1) adding dedicated routers to off-load the overloaded file servers or 2) relocating the servers closer to the clients.

Connections that drop

Watchdog time-outs

Intermittent dropped connections are one of most frustrating problems you will encounter. As a first step, verify that you are using the most current drivers from Novell. (See the discussion on driver/adapter cards.) Once you have eliminated this as the cause, you can suspect a more complex cause. Dropped connections, especially from idle stations, are often caused by a failure of the server to maintain contact with the workstation through the watchdog timer frames.

A server sends these "keep-alive" watchdog requests at periodic intervals to see if a logged in station is still alive. One way a server conserves valuable resources is by disconnecting powered-down stations. So, if a logged-in station fails to respond within a set number of requests, the server will disconnect the station.

One simple way to test for the watchdog time-out condition is to increase the number of watchdog requests, and the time interval between them. The following commands at the NetWare console prompt alter the watchdog packet parameters.

```
SET NUMBER OF WATCHDOG PACKETS
SET DELAY BETWEEN WATCHDOG PACKETS
SET DELAY BEFORE FIRST WATCHDOG PACKET
```

If this reduces or eliminates the dropped connection problem, it's likely you have a watchdog time-out problem. Unfortunately, there are many network conditions that can prevent a station from responding to a watchdog request even though that station is alive and well. Here are some things to look for.

Check for excessive broadcast traffic—that is, greater than 100 frames per second. Excessive broadcast traffic can sidetrack stations and prevent them from responding to the watchdog requests. Identify the broadcasting stations and see if you can reconfigure them to prevent excessive broadcasting. In large NetWare networks, the periodic service advertising requests and routing updates from servers can cause large amounts of background broadcast traffic. Consider blocking these packets on your routers.

Look for high collision rates. Ethernet packets are sent on as "best effort" delivery. In other words, the sending station assumes that the destination station has received the packet. High collision rates can interfere with this process.

In Token-Ring networks, look for congested receiver soft errors from devices along the path from the server to the station (server, bridge, router or end-node). Congested receiver soft errors are an indication of an overloaded device. This overload condition can prevent the watchdog request or response from being received, causing the connection to drop.

Operation

This section relates technical information primarily about NetWare versions from 3.x to 4.0x. Specific details have not been verified on older or newer versions of NetWare, so some differences may exist.

As shown in Figure E-4, NetWare begins at OSI Layer 3 with the Internetwork Packet Exchange (IPX) protocol. NetWare will operate on top of just about any medium-access protocol, though the most common are Ethernet (802.3) and Token Ring (802.5). IPX itself is a connectionless datagram protocol that relies on higher layers to guarantee delivery of data. Sequenced Packet Exchange (SPX) provides for reliable data transfer. When the **IPX.COM** or **IPXODI.COM** programs are executed, they also implement SPX.

Each protocol layer places additional overhead in each frame sent that will measurably reduce network throughput. The amount of overhead depends on each specific protocol. Out of a 500-octet sample NCP frame, only 440 octets (or 86%) represent the actual reply from a file server. Obviously, if the frame size gets smaller, the amount of actual throughput (once the overhead is removed) drops considerably. (See Figure E-5.)

In more recent versions of NetWare a new burst-mode protocol is available. When burst-mode is enabled, NetWare permits up to 64K bytes of data to be transmitted before requiring a reply, instead of requiring a reply for each frame sent. By using this feature, the amount of bandwidth required for a large data transfer is significantly reduced, despite the large header that is used in each frame. (See Figure E-6.) This is particularly helpful in large routed and WAN networks where frame sizes may be limited.

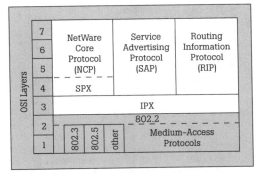

Figure E-4. *NetWare protocols shown in relation to the OSI 7-Layer model.*

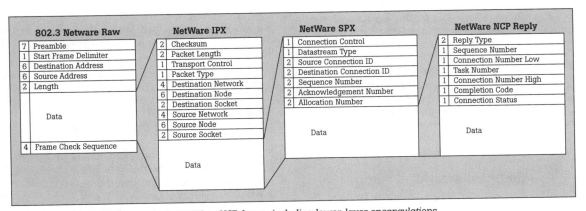

Figure E-5. *Data fields for a sample NetWare NCP frame, including lower-layer encapsulations.*

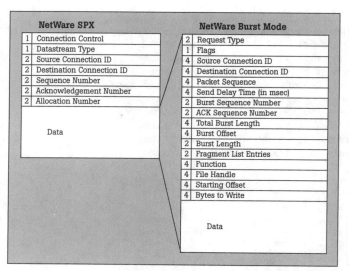

NetWare SPX	
1	Connection Control
1	Datastream Type
2	Source Connection ID
2	Destination Connection ID
2	Sequence Number
2	Acknowledgement Number
2	Allocation Number

NetWare Burst Mode	
2	Request Type
1	Flags
4	Source Connection ID
4	Destination Connection ID
4	Packet Sequence
4	Send Delay Time (in msec)
2	Burst Sequence Number
2	ACK Sequence Number
4	Total Burst Length
4	Burst Offset
2	Burst Length
2	Fragment List Entries
4	Function
4	File Handle
4	Starting Offset
4	Bytes to Write

Figure E-6. *Data fields for a sample NetWare burst mode frame, including an SPX encapsulation.*

Except for burst-mode, all requests must be replied to before another request is permitted. Since IPX, SPX and NCP are only aware of activities taking place at Layers 3 and above (respectively) in the OSI model, there is an extensive set of software timers used to determine if and when a frame is lost or discarded along the way between source and destination stations. If a timer expires without hearing from the other station, the request is retransmitted or an error is generated for a higher layer to handle. When media access protocols are experiencing large numbers of errors, the results range from very slow response times to dropped connections. If delay-related problems are suspected between stations, try temporarily increasing the watchdog timer and retry values. If this helps, the cause of the delay should be investigated and corrected.

Routed networks

Unlike IP, IPX does not provide for the fragmentation of an individual message along the way. If a large IP message originates on a LAN segment that permits large frames, but is addressed to a station on a distant segment that has a smaller

maximum frame size—or must cross a link with a smaller maximum frame size—the protocol rules permit the message to be repackaged into smaller units. Each sub-portion of the message will include the original header information, along with a note indicating which numbered piece it represents. The destination station is able to reassemble the original message from the parts without generating an error. If this were to happen to an IPX frame, each sub-portion of the message would be tested for completeness as if each were the whole original message.

To circumvent this problem in routed environments, each IPX frame is limited to a size that will cross all required connections without being fragmented into multiple pieces. A typical largest IPX frame size of 576 bytes is a fairly common solution to this problem. Since this again reduces throughput by forcing large transfers to be sent in many small frames, a new Large Internet Packet (LIP) protocol was developed to permit larger IPX frame sizes to be routed. LIP was a short-lived interim step, which was then quickly replaced with NetWare Link Services Protocol (NLSP). NLSP should also reduce the amount of "housekeeping" traffic on your network, unlike RIP and SAP protocols that update regularly whether or not there has been a change in available paths.

IPX addressing

A NetWare address consists of two parts: the network number (4 octets), and node address (6 octets). The network address is typically represented as network_number:node_address (example: 00003456:02608C000102). The IPX workstation address is automatically assigned as it logs into the server. The network number portion comes from the IPX network number associated with the frame type bound to the server's adapter card. All devices using that frame type on that segment must use the same network number. The node portion comes from the workstation's adapter card hardware MAC address. (The **NET.CFG** file allows users to assign a MAC address of their choosing, which will supersede the hardware address. A user-assigned address is known as a *locally administered address* (LAA).)

It should be noted—and emphasized—that IPX network addresses are entirely arbitrary and are chosen by the person configuring the file server. The only common convention in selecting these addresses seems to be in environments where IPX and IP are used together on the same network. In these situations, the assigned IP address of the file server is converted from decimal to hex and used as the IPX address. For example, the IP address 45.220.0.130 would convert to an IPX address of 2DDC0082 (45 converts to 2D, 220 converts to DC, 0 is 00, and 130 converts to 82). The advantage to this convention is the ease in which the general location of a particular device can be determined by simply checking the network diagram for where a specific IP subnet is used.

The network portion of a file server's NetWare address comes from the internal IPX network number set by the command IPX INTERNAL NET in the **AUTOEXEC.NCF** file (example: IPX INTERNAL NET 2DDC0082). The server's IPX node address is almost always the default value of 000000000001. An example file server's complete OSI Layer 3 IPX address appears as: 2DDC0082:000000000001.

Encapsulation of IPX

When data is transmitted by the file server or a workstation, it will be encapsulated within an OSI Layer 2 frame type. There are four standard Ethernet frame types defined by Novell: *ETHERNET_802.3* (often referred to as "NetWare Raw"), *ETHERNET_802.2, ETHERNET_II*, and *ETHERNET_SNAP*. In practice, Ethernet_802.3 is the most common, followed by Ethernet_II. However, as NetWare 4.x becomes more popular, Ethernet_802.2 will become more common. Ethernet_SNAP is often used when communicating with Apple computers. There are two standard Token Ring frame types defined by Novell: *TOKEN-RING* and *TOKEN-RING_SNAP* though the SNAP frame type is almost never seen. (See Appendix B for more information on frame encapsulation types.)

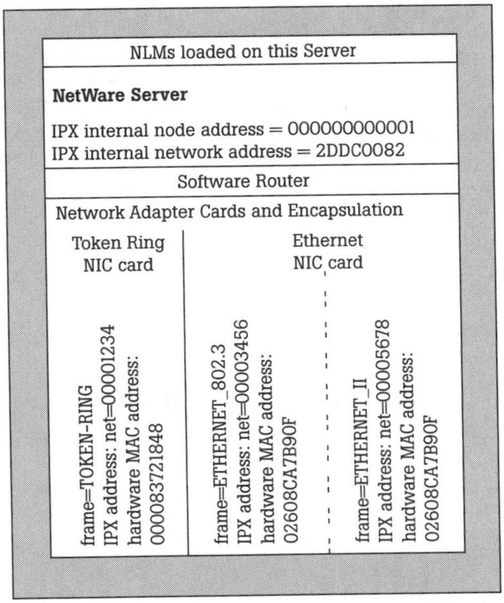

Figure E-7. *Logical diagram of a file server supporting three MAC layer encapsulations.*

The default frame type used by servers changed from 802.3 (raw) in versions of NetWare up to 3.11, to 802.2 in NetWare 3.12 and 4.x. This change caused many interoperability problems for networks migrating to newer versions of NetWare.

For each frame type used, there must be an IPX network address, so that routers have a complete IPX address to which they can refer. In Figure E-7 there are two NIC cards installed in the server supporting three encapsulations. Two frame types are bound to the Ethernet card. Note that there is a software router isolating the actual server software from the network interface cards, and isolating each frame type from all other frame types.

When a new workstation joins the network, it will send a broadcast message looking for any file servers. In the subsequent discussion with the "nearest" file server, the workstation will learn which IPX network address to use. The address assignment is made based on which frame type the workstation used to ask for a file server—the server responds with the IPX network address assigned to that frame type.

IPX routing

Since each NetWare file server has a simple software router built into the core operating system, the installation of two or more network adapters causes the file server to become a router in addition to its other duties. This configuration is a simple and inexpensive solution for networks that need a basic router but cannot afford one. Unfortunately, this causes a considerable reduction in the performance of the file server.

If a file server on a local segment is sent a ping request, the expectation is to receive a reply with zero "hops"—after all, it is on the local segment. With NetWare, because of the software router between the network and the server itself, even a local server will be at least one hop away. Figure E-8 shows a diagram of a simple network configuration, along with the results of two ping requests. In both cases, the result is one hop to the destination. Also, in both cases, the ping request crosses one software router to reach the destination.

A second situation that can be somewhat confusing also relates to the software router in each file server. When a station issues a Server List command, the response that is returned is from the perspective of the responding file server. If Figure E-8 had two file servers and only one station—and all three were on a single segment—the Server List response would show the responding server as being one hop away, and the other file server as being two hops away as in Figure E-9. This is because from the perspective of the first server, there are two software routers between itself and the other file server—thus two hops.

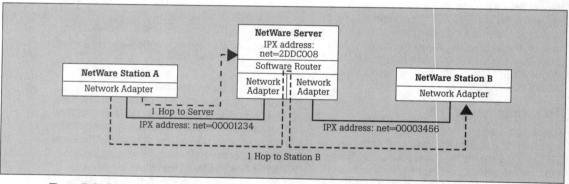

Figure E-8. Diagram of how router "hops" are counted, from a workstation perspective.

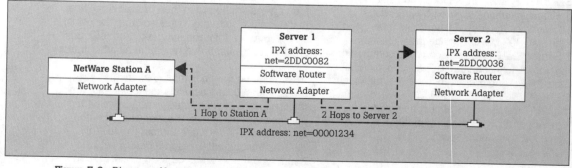

Figure E-9. Diagram of how router "hops" are counted, from a fileserver perspective.

Appendix F — Cable Testing

Until recently, there were no standards for testing the performance of *installed* UTP LAN cabling up to 100 MHz. All of the older standards (prior to TIA/EIA-568-A, TSB67, which was approved in late 1995) were designed to verify either raw cable or connecting hardware—but did not apply to a cable with connectors and other interconnect hardware attached. This appendix provides information about links in general, with some specific information derived from TSB67 for testing UTP links for performance up to 100 MHz. Note that the term "link" is used to describe installed assemblies of cabling components, i.e., connectors and cable.

Introduction

It is important to know the fundamental differences between power, telephone and LAN links. Power cables carry low frequency signals (typically 50 or 60 Hz) and are designed to minimize power loss. Standard telephone cable does not carry much power, but it uses up to 4 kHz of bandwidth. LAN cables carry high-bandwidth signals (the most common protocols use bandwidths of 4 MHz and higher), and are designed to allow correct decoding of signals that are transmitted over the cabling. There are several new LAN standards under development that will carry 100 Mbps and higher data rates across two or four pairs of conductors (and typically use bandwidths between 16 and 80 MHz). The actual bandwidth required by the LAN Standard being installed (FDDI, Fast Ethernet, etc.) determines the minimum parameters for selecting, installing, testing and operating UTP links for networking—not the raw throughput bit-rate.

Many network managers are unaware that the data-carrying capacity of the protocol rarely corresponds directly to bandwidth of the link (MHz is not the same as Mbps!). As an example, several popular protocols are shown in Table F-1 by the raw data rate, the bandwidth of the link after encoding and compression, and the grade of link required. The numbers shown are dependent upon the media access implementation (i.e., which encoding scheme is used, whether data is sent in half- or full-duplex, and how many pairs are required).

In anticipation of higher-speed protocols, new installations should always be made with the best available Category 5 cable, connectors, and interconnect devices (punchdown blocks, patch panels, etc.). In addition, all four pairs should be run when new UTP installations are made because some of the new protocols transmit on multiple pairs—unlike Ethernet and Token Ring, which use a single transmit and a single receive pair. For existing installations, it may be possible to extend their useful life by carefully selecting the media access method that will be used, and by using a TSB67 "Accuracy Level II" cable tester to verify the performance of your link in the channel configuration (see *Importance of Field Tester Accuracy* at the end of this appendix). Considering the significant installed base of Category 5 cabling, it is unlikely that even higher-speed LANs (e.g., 1 Gbps Ethernet, which is proposed to operate using 4 pairs of Category 5 wire) will be designed to require cabling that is rated for more than 100 MHz performance. Instead, more encoding and compression will be used. Also, twisted pair cable is only effective for current technologies up to about 115 MHz, at which point noise becomes louder than the data signal. (See Figure F-12.)

Protocol	Raw Data Rate	Fundamental Frequency	Cable Test Requirement	Required Cable Grade
10BASE-T	10 Mbps	10 MHz	10 MHz	Cat 3
100BASE-T4	100 Mbps	12.5 MHz	12.5 MHz	Cat 3
802.12 (VG)	100 Mbps	15 MHz	15 MHz	Cat 3
100BASE-TX	100 Mbps	31.25 MHz	80 MHz	Cat 5
FDDI (over copper)	100 Mbps	31.25 MHz	80 MHz	Cat 5
ATM	155 Mbps	77.5 MHz	100 MHz	Cat 5
1000BASE-T	1000 Mbps	~30 MHz*	100 MHz	Cat 5

*Expected outcome of the final Gigabit Ethernet standard (802.3ab).

Table F-1. Most high-speed protocols offer little relationship between the data rate (Mbps) and the signaling speed on the cable (MHz). The table shows the fundamental frequency for several common media access protocols. However, due to the accompanying harmonic frequencies, good performance requires additional available bandwidth. (See the Cable Test Requirements column.) The various network protocol standards specify cable test requirements (100BASE-TX requires testing to 80 MHz, the ATM Forum specifies 100 MHz for ATM, etc.), however, cables should always be tested to their highest frequency rating (Category 5 should always be tested to 100 MHz).

Test Parameters

Many of the measurements are reported in decibels (dB), and are calculated using the following formulas:

$$dB = 20 * \log\left(\frac{Voltage\_Out}{Voltage\_In}\right) \text{ or } dB = 10 * \log\left(\frac{Power\_Out}{Power\_In}\right)$$

The standard unit for the gain or loss of signals is the decibel (dB). When measuring cables, the voltage out is always less than the voltage in, so the dB in the above equations is negative, though by common convention the minus sign is generally left off in discussion.

Note: *The practice of using a mix of negative and unsigned numbers creates confusion, but has become widespread.*

The following paragraphs provide a basic introduction to a number of important LAN link characteristics. Understanding this information can help assure the proper operation of your LAN installation. Note also that some of the test parameters only apply to testing twisted pair cable, such as Near-end Crosstalk (NEXT).

Test parameters are grouped based on their practical usefulness.

Signal transmission

Before qualitative testing is possible, a link must be verified for simple pin-to-pin continuity, according to a specific wiring standard. TIA/EIA-568-A describes two pairing diagrams intended for use with standard networking protocols. (See Figures F-2 and F-3.) TSB67 further requires that a split pair test be performed as part of a wiremap test.

Wiremap

A wiremap test begins with a simple continuity test to assure that each connector pin from one end of the link is connected to the corresponding pin at the far end, and is not connected to any other conductor or the shield. While this is enough for telephone and other low-frequency applications, simple continuity between pins from one end of the link to the other is not sufficient for LAN applications.

Correct pairing

A number of vendors and organizations supply their own pairing diagrams. However, the TIA/EIA-568-A, T568A and T568B pairing diagrams are the most widely supported and specified. Although the T568B arrangement is somewhat more widely installed, the standard lists T568A as the preferred arrangement.

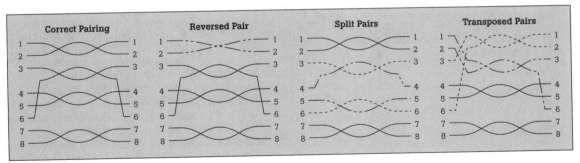

Figure F-1. *Common link wiring faults.*

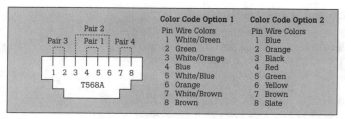

Figure F-2. *TIA/EIA-568-A pinout for T568A.*

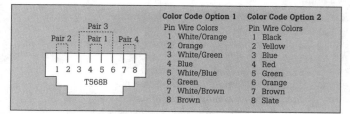

Figure F-3. *TIA/EIA-568-A pinout for T568B.*

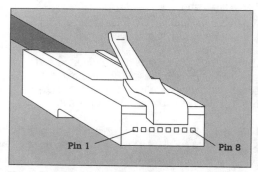

Figure F-4. *Position of pins in the 8-pin modular plug.*

With the practice of pairing by wire colors, mixed use of T568A and T568B is likely to cause link faults. If a mix of cable pairing and interconnect hardware is used, it is fairly certain that wiring faults will result through inattention to detail. Be sure to use the same wiring plan throughout the network.

In Figures F-2 and F-3, note that the actual pair positioning is the same—only the wire color pairs and pair numbering change. Figure F-4 shows how to count pin numbers on the modular connector.

Reversed pairs

The reversed-pair cable fault is perhaps the simplest wiring fault. A pair reversal occurs when a twisted pair is not connected with straight-through pin-to-pin continuity. For example, if one wire of a twisted pair was connected to pin 1 at one end and pin 2 at the other, and from pin 2 to pin 1 for the second wire (see example in Figure F-1), then the pair is said to be reversed.

Pair reversals can occur at any cable connection point, although they are most common at punchdown blocks.

Split pairs

Using individual wires from two different twisted pairs to form a transmit or receive pair is called a split pair (the two wire pairs will also begin acting as an antenna, broadcasting your data and receiving noise). Because the two wires are not twisted together as intended, the crosstalk cancellation effects are lost. While a link constructed this way exhibits correct pin-to-pin continuity, it will cause errors in data transmission.

Split pairs occur most frequently in two places: 1) at punchdown blocks or at cable connectors where not enough care was taken during cable installation or assembly, and 2) from technicians not understanding the importance of the twisting of the wire pairs. The second problem is usually because the technician has taken the first twisted pair and used it for pins 1 and 2, the second twisted pair for pins 3 and 4, etc. The result is shown in Figure F-1, where the wires used to form a wire pair (3 and 6) come from two different twisted pairs. To someone not accustomed to building network cables, splitting apart a twisted pair in order to straddle the middle two pins might seem completely wrong.

Cable testers cannot literally test for a split pair by using ac signal tests. DC ohms tests by digital multimeters (DMMs) do not find split-pair problems either. There are several methods that cable testers use to infer that a split pair is present. One of the most common methods is to infer the presence of a split pair when the NEXT measurement fails badly. If a wire pair is split, or if a link is assembled with wire that is untwisted (such as ribbon cable or untwisted telephone cable), it will have a large NEXT problem. As a result, whenever a NEXT test fails significantly it is assumed that a split pair may exist.

Transposed pairs

Transposed pairs occur when a twisted pair is connected to completely different pin pairs at both ends. In the case of reversed pairs, the same pairs of pins are used at both ends.

Transposed pairs commonly occur as the result of counting pin numbers from different sides of the connector or punchdown block at either end of the cable. This results in pin 1 connecting to pin 8, pin 2 to pin 7, etc.

The cable shown in Figure F-1 is transposed, but in a special way. When two Ethernet hubs are connected together in series (cascading them), the transmit and receive pairs must be transposed. Otherwise, receive will be listening to receive, and transmit talking to transmit. This special cable is often called a "Crossover Cable," and in this specific instance the transposition is done on purpose.

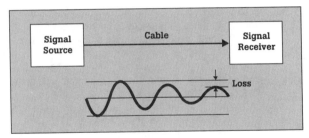

Figure F-5. *Attenuation loss illustration.*

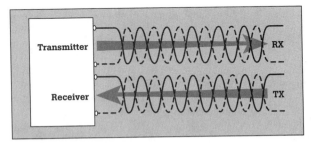

Figure F-6. *Attenuation results from the resistance of the transmission medium to the transmitted signal.*

Signal detection and decoding

Attenuation

Attenuation is the decrease in signal amplitude over the length of a link. (See Figure F-5.) The longer the link, and the higher the signal's frequency, the greater the attenuation (or loss) will be. Therefore, measure attenuation using the highest frequencies for the medium access protocol you are installing (or ever expect to use).

Attenuation needs to be measured only from one direction on the link (on all pairs), since attenuation of a specific wire pair is the same when measured in opposite directions. (See Figure F-6.)

Attenuation is caused by a loss of electrical energy in the resistance of the wire and when energy leaks through the cable's insulating material. This loss of energy (attenuation or insertion loss) is expressed in decibels (dB). Lower attenuation values are an indication of better link performance. For example, when comparing the performance of two links at a particular frequency, a link with an attenuation of 10 dB (a factor of 3.16) performs better than a link with an attenuation of 20 dB (a factor of 10). If there are faults on the link (such as impedance discontinuities), an additional amount of energy will be reflected and will be included in the test results for attenuation loss. However, the main impact is additional jitter during decoding of the signal at the receiver, which will result in corrupted data, and in turn, will result in more errors occurring on the network.

Link attenuation is determined by the cable's construction, length, and the frequencies of the signals sent through the link. In the 1 to 100 MHz frequency range, the attenuation is dominated by the "skin effect," and is proportional to the square root of frequency.

TSB67 defines the formulas in order to calculate the allowable attenuation for an installed UTP link for both link configurations: the Basic Link and the Channel. In addition, the TSB67 shows a table of allowable values for these links. The allowable values of attenuation apply to an environment at 20°C. Attenuation increases as temperature increases: typically 1.5% per degree Celsius for Category 3 links and 0.4% per degree Celsius for Category 4 and 5 links. In addition, the link attenuation may increase 2% to 3% if the cabling is installed in metal conduit. The network technician should remember to take temperature into consideration for both installation and testing purposes. TSB67 specifically permits adjustment of allowable attenuation for temperature. Such allowance is *not* permitted for the use of conduit.

Field testers are required to report the attenuation value and the frequency at the point of failure, or at the frequency where the greatest attenuation value was measured for a Pass condition. The testers are only required to use attenuation results greater than 3 dB for Pass/Fail purposes.

Figure F-7 shows a typical attenuation result from the Fluke DSP-100. The top curve is the TSB67 limit for attenuation, and the bottom curve is the result for this test. The cursor is positioned at the frequency where the worst-case attenuation was detected. The large type immediately below the graph shows the margin relative to the test limit. In this example the cursor is showing the worst attenuation result (+16.0 dB away from the limit) at the highest frequency measured (100 MHz).

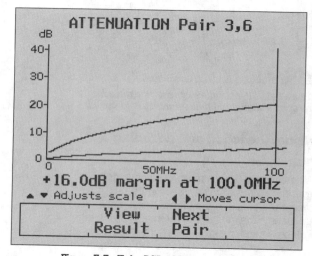

Figure F-7. Fluke DSP-100 attenuation test results.

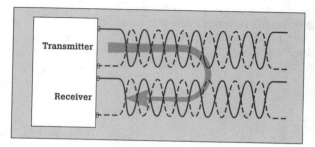

Figure F-8. NEXT is a measure of how much of the transmitted signal "leaks" onto an adjacent wire pair.

Near-End Crosstalk (NEXT)

When it comes to overall LAN link operation, crosstalk has the greatest effect on link performance. Crosstalk is the undesirable signal transmission from one wire pair to another nearby pair. (See Figure F-8.) Unwanted crosstalk signals are generally caused by the capacitive and inductive coupling between adjacent pairs. At higher frequencies, crosstalk increases and is more destructive to data. Most high-speed LAN protocols need two pairs of twisted–pair cable, one pair for each direction of traffic.

Test devices measure crosstalk by applying a test signal to one wire pair and measuring the amplitude of the crosstalk signals received by other wire pairs. Crosstalk is computed as the ratio in amplitude (in volts) between the test signal and the crosstalk signal when measured from the same end of the link. This difference is called near-end crosstalk (NEXT) and is generally expressed in decibels (dB). Higher NEXT values correspond to less crosstalk and better link performance. The NEXT test is also the most common test technology used to infer the presence of split pairs on UTP links.

While NEXT is a critical performance factor for UTP links it is also the most difficult to measure accurately, especially at lower frequencies where most of the common LAN protocols operate today. TSB67 specifies that NEXT be measured at not greater than the maximum frequency step increments shown in Table F-2. For improved accuracy, a smaller step size is better, though this may take longer to measure. A Category 3 link needs to be tested only to 16 MHz, and Category 4 link to 20 MHz, since that is their maximum frequency rating.

Frequency range	Maximum allowed step size
1-31.25 MHz	150 kHz (or 0.15 MHz)
>31.25-100 MHz	250 kHz (or 0.25 MHz)

Table F-2. Maximum frequency step sizes allowed for compliance with TSB67.

NEXT loss needs to be measured from every pair to every other pair in a UTP link, and from both ends of the link. This equates to twelve pair combinations for the typical four-pair cabling link. Many test equipment vendors allow the user to select larger frequency step sizes to shorten the time required to test the NEXT performance of a link. The resulting distance between measurements may not comply with TSB67, and may overlook link faults (especially NEXT faults).

All signals transmitted through a link are affected by attenuation. Because of attenuation, crosstalk occurring further down the link contributes less to NEXT than crosstalk occurring at the near end of the link—thus, the near-end crosstalk is most important, and is also the reason why it is measured closest to a transmission source. To verify proper link performance, you should measure NEXT from both ends of the link; this is also a requirement for complete compliance with TSB67.

Crosstalk can be minimized by twisting wire pairs, so that the signal coupling is "evened out." Twisted-pair wiring for LANs have more twists per unit length than telephone wiring. LANs use TIA/EIA Category 3, 4 or 5 wiring. Telephone wiring is typically Category 1, and may not seem to be twisted at all. The higher the category, the more twists per unit length in the cable are required, and the higher the frequency rating will be. To ensure reliable LAN communications, unshielded cable pairs must not be left untwisted—even for short distances. For this same reason, cables with parallel conductors (ribbon type or "silver satin" type cables) should never be used in LAN applications.

Signals from twisted-pair wiring may "leak" to the outside world. The principle behind twisted-pair cables is that, at every location along the cable, the voltage in one wire of a wire pair is equal in amplitude, but opposite in phase, to the voltage in the other wire of the wire pair. Of course there is a limit on this. In addition to some

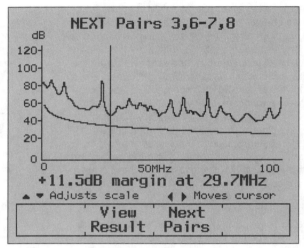

Figure F-9. *Fluke DSP-100 Near-end Crosstalk (NEXT) test results.*

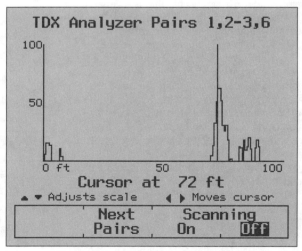

Figure F-10. *Fluke DSP-100 Time-Domain Crosstalk (TDX) test results.*

other undesirable side effects, imbalance creates the effect of an antenna (and thereby causes electromagnetic interference or "EMI"). To minimize the antenna effect, shielding the cable is a possible solution. However, when shielded cabling is used, a new set of potential problems is introduced: ground loops at power-line frequencies. The ground-loop problem is often more serious than the EMI problem. Substantial improvements have recently been made to cabling components—connectors in particular—which has had a positive impact, since the majority of link problems occur at connectors, and the new connectors reduce these effects.

Generally, the problem of NEXT is worse in shielded cabling. The reason for this is that crimping the plugs to the shield of the cable enhances capacitive imbalance, one of the sources of NEXT. Also, shielded twisted-pair wiring is harder to install correctly, making it more prone to this sort of problem. Shielded twisted-pair cable comes in two basic types; 1) *shielded twisted-pair (STP)* which has a shield around each individual pair, as well as around the whole cable, and is usually 150Ω cabling, and 2) *foil-screened UTP (FTP)* or *screened UTP (ScTP)*, which has a shield around the outside of the whole cable only, and can be either 100Ω or 120Ω cabling. The term ScTP is more widespread than FTP, although both are in common use. Proper grounding procedures must be followed when using these cable types. (See page F-27 for information on grounding.) ScTP is in wide usage in Europe because of strict laws intended to limit EMI emissions, and (as a side effect) also reduces external noise from interfering with the signals on the link. If balance can be maintained, however, UTP cabling can provide EMI performance levels that will also satisfy the European requirements.

Figure F-9 shows a typical NEXT test result from the Fluke DSP-100. The bottom curve is the TSB67 limit for NEXT, and the top curve is the result for this test. When a reported margin is positive, this indicates that the worst-case return loss is better than the limit, while a negative margin indicates that the result exceeds the limit. The cursor is positioned at the frequency where the worst-case margin was detected. The irregular shape of the top curve demonstrates that unless NEXT is measured at many points along the frequency range, low points (points of worst case NEXT loss) could easily go undetected. Therefore, TSB67 defines a maximum frequency step size for NEXT measurements, as shown in Table F-2. The DSP-100 always takes more samples than TSB67 requires, and *cannot* be configured to test at fewer points than TSB67 requires.

If a NEXT failure is detected, the DSP-100 series also offers a unique Time-Domain Crosstalk (TDX) test that pinpoints where along the length of the link the failure is occurring. The TDX test is displayed in the same graphic format as the Time-Domain Reflectometry (TDR) test. The cursor is positioned at the worst case NEXT measurement for the pair combination. The difference between TDR and TDX is that, in the case of a TDR, the signal is applied at one wire pair, and the reflections are measured on the same wire pair. TDR reflections occur because of impedance anomalies. TDX applies a signal to one wire pair and measures the coupled signal on an adjacent wire pair. TDX measurements are necessarily more sensitive than TDR measurements because of how little coupling there is (the amplitude of the signal is *much* smaller). TDR measurements cannot be made more sensitive than about 15% of the signal that is applied, since the characteristic impedance can vary by 15Ω around a nominal value of 100Ω.

Figure F-10 shows a typical TDX test result from the Fluke DSP-100. The peaks rising from the X-axis represent point-sources of crosstalk. The cursor is positioned at the distance where the worst-case point-source of crosstalk was detected. The link being tested exhibited a small amount of crosstalk at either end of the two meter patch cord, lots of crosstalk from poor workmanship at a cross-connect in a wiring closet 72 feet from where the DSP-100 was connected, and again a small amount of crosstalk at either end of the patch cord at the end of the link. A NEXT test only showed that crosstalk was slightly worse than allowed for the link.

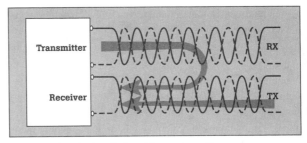

Figure F-11. ACR is calculated from attenuation and NEXT measurements.

Attenuation to Crosstalk Ratio (ACR)

ACR is calculated in an attempt to answer the question: While sending on the transmit pair, how much does the noise from crosstalk disrupt the (attenuated) signal I am listening to?

The attenuation-to-crosstalk ratio affects the bit-error rate (BER) directly and thereby the need for re-transmissions. The noise consists of both externally induced noise, and self-induced noise (which is NEXT). Normally, self-induced noise dominates externally induced noise. The ACR is the same as the signal-to-noise ratio when you deem that external noise is insignificant. The two factors considered in the calculation are NEXT and attenuation, as indicated in the name of the parameter. To obtain the ratio, the formula is: Insertion loss over (divided by) NEXT loss. After the math is worked out, you find that you can simply subtract the NEXT measurement from the attenuation measurement (when expressed in dB). The closer the ACR result comes to zero dB, the less likely your link is going to work. (See Figure F-12.)

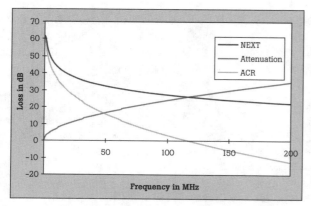

Figure F-12. *ACR graph. The graph is improperly based on calculations for a 100 meter Category 5 "channel" configuration listed in TSB67. TSB67 only offers verified performance calculation formulas out to 100 MHz, and the formulas are not accurate beyond that point. However, for the purpose of illustration this graph is extended beyond 100 MHz using the same formulas. The graph shows calculated worst-case limits and plots three values; NEXT, attenuation and the derived ACR.*

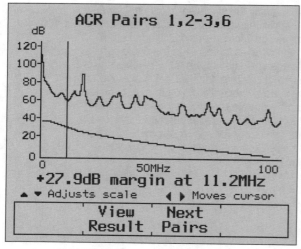

Figure F-13. *Fluke DSP-100 attenuation-to-crosstalk (ACR) test results.*

The measurement can also be viewed as the difference between the two measurements when plotted. Figure F-12 is derived from worst-case limit values for a Category 5 channel configuration listed in TSB67, and extended beyond 100 MHz using the same formulas.

In Figure F-12, at the point where the plot lines for attenuation and NEXT intersect, the desired data signal will be exactly equal to the amount of undesired crosstalk (where ACR crosses the zero mark). Notice that the crosstalk will begin to be louder than the data signal at around 115 MHz. To transfer data reliably, links used in LAN applications typically must perform at least 6 dB better than the limit.

Figure F-13 shows a typical ACR test result from the Fluke DSP-100. The bottom curve is the TSB67 limit for NEXT, and the top curve is the result for this test. The cursor is positioned at the frequency where the worst-case margin was detected. When a reported margin is positive, this indicates that the worst-case return loss is better than the limit, while a negative margin indicates that the result exceeds the limit. The DSP-100 permits results to be viewed for all cable pair combinations.

Signal-to-Noise Ratio (SNR)

The signal-to-noise ratio is almost the same as the ACR measurement. (See Figure F-14.) The primary difference is that the ACR measurement assumes (with reasonable justification) that external noise is not a significant factor, and will not greatly affect link performance. The SNR allows for external noise in the calculation by adding its effect to the NEXT.

An example of external noise might include the residual noise floor of the measuring instrument itself (for example, when you turn the volume on your stereo up very loud, but don't press "play"—the hissing, crackly noise you hear is noise from the circuits themselves). The only problem with this measurement is being certain that you have included all of the possible noise sources.

Return loss

Return loss is a measure of reflections that are caused by the impedance mismatches at all locations along the link and is measured in decibels (dB). Mismatches predominantly occur at locations where connectors are present, but can also occur in cable where variations in characteristic impedance along the length of the cable are present. The main impact of return loss is *not* on loss of signal strength (there is some, but generally it is not that much of a problem), but rather the introduction of signal jitter.

A simplified description of this type of jitter is that the edge of a signal representing a data bit is shifted slightly in time, such that, when the receiver circuit samples the signal, it incorrectly classifies the signal as either a binary 1 or 0 when it should have been the other value. (See Figure 1-10.) This jitter can vary the leading edge of the signal presented to the decoder in the receiver, or add to or subtract from the signal amplitude, and thereby cause decoding errors. The closer to a perfect match of characteristic impedance of the cabling to the output impedance of the transmit output, and to the input impedance of the receiver input, the better the return loss measurement will be. A lab test called the "eye-pattern" is typically used to evaluate the degree of jitter present in a network, and the corresponding loss of signal strength (the amount of energy that fails to transfer from the signal source to the receiver due to impedance mismatches).

At the time of this writing only the ISO/IEC 11801 Standard has suggestions for testing return loss on an installed link as part of the performance verification test and even this proposal has undergone large changes. (See Table F-3.)

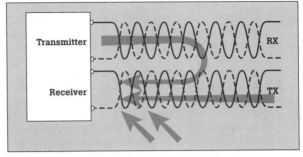

Figure F-14. *SNR is the same as ACR plus external noise influences.*

The return loss measurement varies significantly with frequency. One source of return loss is from the characteristic impedance of the cable. Another source is reflections from inside the link, mainly from connectors. At low frequencies, characteristic impedance of the cable tends to be high (up to 115Ω at 1 MHz), and at high frequency it tends to be low (down to 85Ω at 100 MHz). This means that a test device must allow for a 15% deviation from the 100Ω expected of UTP cable, or false warnings would be reported.

Frequency range	Upper limit return loss
1–20 MHz	15 dB
20–100 MHz	$15 - 10 * \log\left(\dfrac{\text{frequency (MHz)}}{20}\right)$

Table F-3. *ISO/IEC 11801 proposed limits for return loss on an installed 100 meter Class D channel link.*

In a typical return loss test result from the Fluke DSP-100 the bottom curve is the proposed ISO/IEC 11801 limit for return loss, and the top curve is the measured result for this test. (See Figure F-15.) The cursor is positioned at the frequency where the worst-case margin was detected. When a reported margin is positive, this indicates that the worst-case return loss is better than the limit, while a negative margin indicates that the result exceeds the limit. The DSP-100 will also show the wire pair and frequency where the worst-case return loss margin was measured.

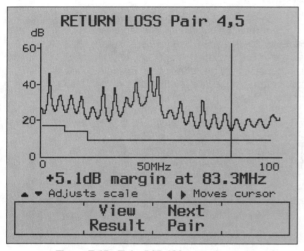

Figure F-15. Fluke DSP-100 return loss test results.

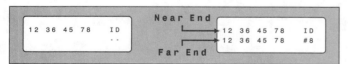

Figure F-16. Fluke 620 Wiremap test results without wiremap adapter at far end (left), and with wiremap adapter at far end (right).

Other commonly referenced test parameters

Capacitance

The TIA/EIA-568-A Standard, paragraph 10.2.4.3, states "Mutual capacitance value is provided for engineering design purposes only and is not a requirement for performance testing." If mutual-capacitance is out of specification, then both characteristic impedance and nominal velocity of propagation (NVP) will be impacted directly. Measurement of capacitance is not required at this time, and it is unlikely that requirements will be specified in future versions of TSB67.

From a troubleshooting perspective (not an engineering perspective), the goal of testing for mutual-capacitance problems is to identify the location of a link or installation fault. Rather than testing for a mutual-capacitance problem, it is far simpler and more accurate to use a TDR test to find the location of the problem.

Capacitance is also one of the test technologies used to infer the presence of split pairs in a UTP cable. The Fluke 620 takes advantage of capacitance (together with several other measurements) to allow technicians to learn link pairing from only one end of a link—a remote adapter is not required. (See left screen in Figure F-16.) If a remote adapter is present at the far end, the 620 will indicate pairing at both ends, and it will highlight any deviation from the chosen link standard. (See right screen in Figure F-16.)

Characteristic impedance

When a high-frequency electrical signal is applied to a cable, the signal source experiences an impedance. Impedance is a type of resistance that opposes the flow of alternating current (ac)— and network data is a type of high-frequency ac. A cable's characteristic impedance is a complex property, resulting from the combined effects of the cable's inductive, capacitive and resistive values. These values are determined by physical parameters such as the size of the conductors, the distance between conductors, and the properties of the cable's insulation material.

Proper network operation depends on a constant characteristic impedance throughout the system's cables and connectors. Abrupt changes in characteristic impedance (which are called impedance discontinuities or impedance anomalies) will cause signal reflections. The result can be disrupted signals transmitted through LAN links, and these will cause network faults.

The impact of incorrect characteristic impedance is more practically represented by the quantity called return loss (see description of return loss above). Return loss tells you directly how bad the total effect of all reflections is.

Termination resistance present at the link ends must be equal to the characteristic impedance. Frequently, this resistance is included in the interface of equipment to be connected to the LAN. A good match between characteristic impedance and termination resistance provides for a good transfer of power to and from the link and minimizes reflections.

Future high-speed LANs will be even more sensitive to changes in characteristic impedance. Lengths of untwisted wires must be kept to the absolute minimum and lengths of cable with different characteristic impedance should never be mixed. If the characteristic impedance seen by a signal suddenly changes as it travels along a link, a reflection occurs that causes the signal (or a portion thereof) to bounce back toward the source. This potentially causes problems when the signal is decoded at the receiver (it creates signal jitter). The characteristic impedance is almost always disturbed at terminations. A LAN can tolerate some disturbance. However, it is vitally important for the installer to untwist a UTP cable to the minimum extent possible, particularly when installing links for high-speed LANs. In fact, for Category 5 cable, a link is permitted to have a maximum of 13 millimeters (about half an inch) of untwisted wire at each interconnection (per TIA/EIA-568-A, paragraph 10.6.3.1). Installing an adapter (barrel connector) to connect two 8-pin modular jack (RJ-45) cables together exceeds this limit. Barrel connectors often have particularly bad NEXT performance and should never be used in a Category 5 installation.

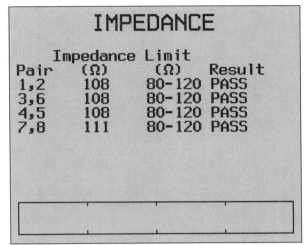

Figure F-17. Fluke DSP-100 characteristic impedance test results.

Reflected signals are attenuated as they travel back, so interference is reduced. Sharp bends or kinks in LAN cable can also alter the cable's characteristic impedance. Poor electrical contacts, improper cable terminations, improper cable pairing, and mismatched cable types (cables with different characteristic impedance values) will all cause impedance discontinuities, resulting in degraded link performance.

Characteristic impedance is a test technology that is sometimes used to infer the presence of split pairs in UTP cable. When there is a split pair, the characteristic impedance measurement is generally disturbed as well.

A typical characteristic-impedance test result from the Fluke DSP-100 offers numeric results, and shows the wire pair, the test result value, and the range permitted by the configured standard. (See Figure F-17.)

Margin

There are two issues related to margins: the accuracy of the tester, and the margin between the measured test results and the standards limits.

TSB67 requires that if the measured result is closer to the Pass/Fail limit than the measurement accuracy of the tester, then the instrument should indicate that there is some doubt about the Pass/Fail outcome. For example, if the accuracy of an instrument is 2 dB, and the measured margin is 1 dB, then it is quite possible that either the tester could fail a good link or pass a bad link. When this situation is possible, the tester is now required to qualify the Pass/Fail judgment with an asterisk (*), indicating this possible error. (See the section at the end of this appendix on *Importance of Field Tester Accuracy*.)

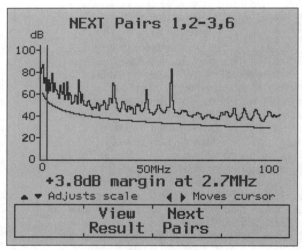

Figure F-18. *Fluke DSP-100 near-end crosstalk (NEXT) test results.*

When making Pass/Fail judgments during link tests, the margin between the Standards limits and the measured result must now be taken into consideration. Unfortunately, TSB67 does not require that the worst-case margin be reported for NEXT. Instead the TSB67 requires that *either* the worst-case NEXT *or* worst-case NEXT margin be reported, along with the margin at that frequency. The two results have generally no relation to each other. The worst-case NEXT typically happens at high frequencies; the worst-case NEXT margin (where the distance to the limit line is minimal) can happen anywhere in the frequency range, but most often occurs at the middle to lower frequencies where the most common network signals typically reside. Worst-case NEXT margin tells you how close you are to the limit; worst-case NEXT does not.

It is considerably more difficult to have accurate reporting of NEXT margin, because of dynamic range. Near 1 MHz, the test limit for NEXT is approximately 60 dB. For troubleshooting and link performance purposes, the worst-case margin is far more important than the comparatively useless worst-case measurement. The situation is like reporting that, under optimum conditions, a certain model of automobile is capable of exceptionally good fuel economy, when what you want to know is how efficient that particular vehicle is for in-city driving.

A tester must be able to make extremely sensitive measurements (as much as 80 to 90 dB), and that is not easy to do. In Figure F-18, the worst-case margin occurs at 2.7 MHz. Signals transmitted at low frequencies on this link are less likely to be successfully received than higher frequencies.

Figure F-18 shows a typical NEXT test result from the Fluke DSP-100. The bottom curve is the TSB67 limit for return loss, and the top curve is the result for this test. The cursor is positioned at the frequency where the worst-case margin was detected.

Noise

Noise problems on a LAN link include impulse noise and continuous wideband noise. Noise does not include signals from other wire pairs, which are measured as NEXT.

Impulse noise is measured by counting the number of voltage spikes that exceed a certain threshold. A low impulse count is desirable for good network performance. However, an impulse-noise test is not always sensitive enough for LANs that use higher levels of encoding than the common 10BASE-T networks. Wideband noise is a continuous- or longer-duration signal that is measured on the network link, yet is not a part of the data transmission signal. The lower the wideband noise voltage, the better the LAN performance will be. In order to resolve problems related to noise, it may be necessary to use other categories of tools, such as high-speed digitizing sampling oscilloscopes and spectrum analyzers with variable measurement bandwidths.

As mentioned under NEXT, due to "imbalance," LAN links also act as antennas. They can pick up noise signals from fluorescent lights, electric motors, photocopiers, and other similar devices that are located in proximity to the LAN cable. Also, when a transmitter of a radio or TV station is in the area, significant noise can be picked up. Remember that the lower FM and TV bands are within the 1 MHz to 100 MHz range at which nearly all LAN protocols operate. Be sure to consider these external noise signal influences when you are planning your installation, and route links as far away as possible or use shielded cable.

The LAN is a wideband system, meaning that all frequencies between 1 MHz and 100 MHz may be used in the transmission "in parallel" or "at the same time." Field testers limit the measurement bandwidth in order to reduce the impact of noise and measure the link properties with higher accuracy. Therefore, an analog field tester may never see any externally induced noise because of how narrowly the input signal is filtered.

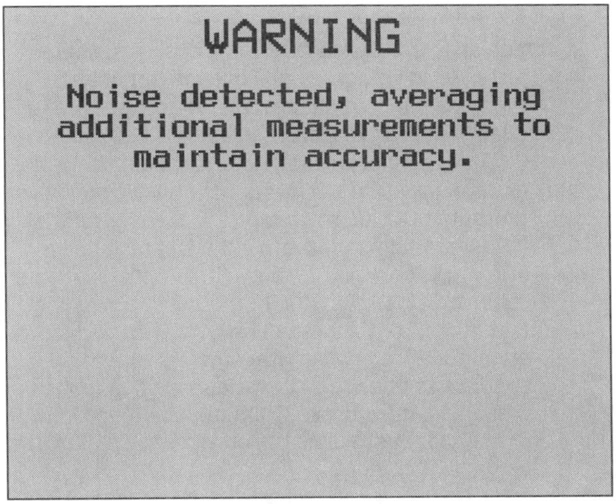

Figure F-19. *Fluke DSP-100 pop-up external noise warning.*

In a digital tester, bandwidth is reduced by averaging more samples of the NEXT response. Noise can easily be detected by comparing the results of multiple samples. However, even in the presence of substantial noise, an accurate performance indication of the link can be obtained by simply doing more averaging. Knowing that external noise is present is of significant value for the LAN owner when he has problems. It is entirely possible that the effects of a local broadcast station will either not be detected by a swept-frequency analog tester, or, if detected, the effects will be included as part of the NEXT results.

The Fluke DSP-100 will display the pop-up warning message if substantial external noise is detected during a test. (See Figure F-19.) It will then make some number of additional test samples in an effort to average-out the effects of the external noise, and provide an accurate result for the link being tested. No filtering is applied during testing, thus a problem at any frequency between 1 MHz and 100 MHz should be detected.

Resistance

The dc loop resistance test is a basic resistance test used to detect the presence of termination resistor(s) on coax cable and to detect poor-quality connections on UTP links.

A simple coax resistance test should show one of three expected results: open (no termination present), 50Ω (one terminator present), or 25Ω (two terminators present). If the test result deviates much from one of those three options, then a cable fault is likely. 802.3 Ethernet specifies that termination resistors shall be 50Ω with variations of only ±1%. However, the network will *usually* continue to operate with variations of up to several ohms, though this will introduce reflections of the data and reduce the effective maximum link length accordingly.

If the center conductor is shorted to the shield at the far end, then thick coax should measure around 5Ω at 500 meters, and thin coax should measure around 2Ω at 185 meters (maximum lengths for Ethernet). If there are poor-quality connections along the path, then each additional poor connection will add some amount of resistance.

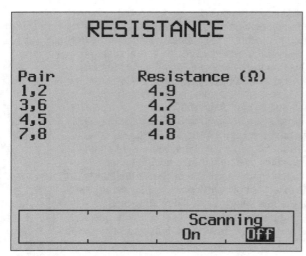

Figure F-20. *Fluke DSP-100 loop resistance test results.*

For UTP the dc loop resistance test is more significantly affected by link length. A typical dc loop resistance test on a 100-meter cable should provide results in the range of 9Ω to 12Ω. STP cable is slightly better at 100 meters, measuring around 6Ω to 7Ω. The test on UTP is performed by shorting the two wires from a twisted pair together at the far end, then measuring the resistance of the entire wire path. The quickest way to tell if there is a problem is to compare the results from all four pairs. If one pair shows 25Ω, and the other three are between 11Ω and 14Ω, it is highly probable that the 25Ω pair has a link fault.

For testing and verification, the Fluke LANMeter test tool and the DSP-100 both offer resistance tests for coax, and the DSP-100 offers a dc loop resistance test for twisted-pair cable.

Any problems with dc resistance show up as attenuation problems as well. Therefore dc resistance is not very important.

Figure F-20 shows a typical resistance test result from the Fluke DSP-100. The results are numeric, and show the wire pair and test result value measured.

TDR (Time Domain Reflectometry)

The TDR test is used to determine link length, as well as to identify the distance to link faults such as shorts and opens. When a cable tester makes a TDR measurement, it sends a pulse signal down a wire pair in a link and measures the amount of time in nanoseconds for the pulse to return on the same wire pair. Based on either published tables of typical cable delay values or upon a calibrated value, the tester then calculates the approximate length measurement.

If a returning echo is larger than a preset threshold (the minimum typically must be greater than approximately 15% of the transmitted pulse), it will display the calculated distance to the echo source. These small echoes are called anomalies and are caused by the faults described below. Most testers will display more than one distance: the distance to the end of the link, as well as one or two anomalies along the way. Some of the faults that will cause an echo reflection include poor connections, mixed-impedance cable segments, cable stubs, crushed cable, and severe kinks or over-tight tie-wraps.

The delay value used is called the Nominal Velocity of Propagation (NVP). NVP determines the speed at which a signal travels through a cable relative to the speed of light, and is expressed as a percentage.

An electrical signal travels at fairly uniform speed through a link. The actual speed of the electrical signal in a LAN cable is between 60% and 80% of the speed of light, or roughly eight inches (20 cm) per nanosecond. Signal speed is mainly affected by the composition of the cable insulation material (its relative permittivity). Periodic shortages of the insulating material "Teflon" have caused wire manufacturers to experiment with different insulating compounds for LAN wire. These different compounds will have varying degrees of effect on the NVP by changing the signal speed on different wire pairs.

Length measurements depend directly on knowing the NVP of the cable being tested. This is because the measurement is determined by the travel time of the test pulses through the cable. Most cable tester configuration screens allow users to choose from a range of cable types. The primary purpose of choosing the cable type is to tell the tester what the approximate NVP value is for the cable being tested. For maintenance testing you *could* leave the selection set at any cable type of the same impedance value as the cables you were testing all of the time—providing you understood that the length measurement was not going to be precise. It is almost always sufficient to learn that the problem is "a third of the way back from the end." With that information, you then look for a connection point (punch-down block, wall jack, etc.) in that general area. Almost all problems are found either at known connection points, or in the user's workspace.

The choices for cable types are prepared using NVP values obtained from published specifications from each cable manufacturer. The variation in NVP from lot-to-lot of the same cable type from a specific manufacturer can be 5% or more, and may reach 10% between different manufacturers. Therefore, if length accuracy is critical to your situation, you must determine the true NVP of each cable batch installed in your network. Verify the tester's length measurement by testing a known-length sample (longer than 50 feet, or 15 meters) of the same cable you will be installing or testing. All testers have a "calibrate" function that will allow you to adjust the NVP value to match this cable sample.

Note: *There are two common misconceptions with regard to the type of cable chosen when configuring a field tester. First, that you must pick the correct brand of cable in order to perform the test. Second, that if you choose a Category 5 cable, the test will always be performed over the frequency range 1 MHz to 100 MHz.*

When a cable-type selection is made, two parameters are usually configured: the NVP value, and (in most newer testers) the frequency range to be tested. If the category of cable is the same, such as Category 5 Belden *xxxx* and Category 5 AT&T *yyyy*, there is rarely any difference in the parameters offered—the actual NVP value supplied with the selection is almost always the same nominal value. Recognizing this fact, some newer testers are simply offering selections for Category 3, 4 and 5 cable, rather than making the user scroll through dozens of brand selections.

Most older field cable testers offered selections for cable that was rated for 100 MHz use, or even selections for Category 5 cable, but the tester performed tests only up to the frequency rating it was designed for—often a maximum of 10 or 20 MHz. A Category 5 cable type selection does not indicate that the test will be performed at up to 100 MHz. If you purchased a low-cost cable tester, or you purchased any cable tester prior to 1996, be sure to check the specifications of that tester to ensure that it is actually testing to the frequency you expect, and if it *is* able to test to 100 MHz that it complies with all of TSB67.

Length measurements of individual wire pairs inside a link may appear to be slightly longer than the measured length of the link being tested. This apparent discrepancy results from the twisting of the wire within the cable, which changes the overall cable length. Another reason is that wire pairs may have different insulation material, which affects the velocity of the signal on that wire pair. TSB67 specifies that the NVP must be calibrated using the wire pair with the shortest electrical delay and that the length of the cable shall also be based on the wire pair with the shortest electrical delay. Testers measure the length of the wire (based on the electrical delay as measured by the TDR function), not the length of the cable jacket.

Figure F-21 shows a typical TDR test result from the Fluke DSP-100. The line starting at zero on the Y-axis represents a graphical image of the amplitude and polarity of any signal reflected back toward the tester after a test pulse was sent. Any deviations from the zero position indicate the source of a signal reflection and are displayed along the X-axis in time. Based on the configured NVP value, the delay between the transmitted test pulse and any reflected signal (spike on the Y-axis) is converted to distance. The cursor is positioned at the graph position where the worst-case reflection was detected (usually the end of the link). Signals with positive polarity represent reflections from "opens," while signals with negative polarity represent reflections from "shorts." Both the DSP-100 and the LANMeter test tools offer TDR accuracy up to the connector on the instrument (zero dead-zone).

100 MHz UTP Testing Issues (Category 5)

The requirements for troubleshooting a link are generally far less stringent than the tests required for verifying a new installation for high-speed use. If the link operated successfully at any time recently, then only a few tests are generally needed to isolate a fault. However, upgrading the service provided on a particular link may require testing similar to a new installation.

It is very important that all parties involved are able to verify that a new or upgraded Category 5 cabling plant will meet network transmission requirements for the foreseeable future. End-user organizations want to make sure that their investment in the cabling plant will perform to expectation for a future implementation of a "fast" or 100 Mbps network standard. The installer wants to assure himself and his client that he will be able to deliver a high-quality installation. To certify a cabling installation, a generally accepted standard is required which defines the minimum level of performance, the method of measuring, and the performance requirements for the measurement tools.

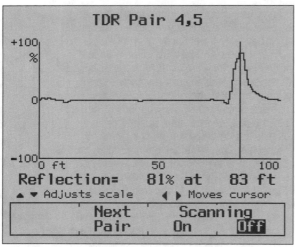

Figure F-21. Fluke DSP-100 time-domain reflectometry (TDR) test results.

End-users and installers waited many years for the publication of a standard for installed UTP cabling systems, primarily for Category 5 installations. In late 1995, the American National Standards Institute/Telecommunications Industry Association/Electronics Industry Association (ANSI/TIA/EIA) approved and published TSB67 to fill this need. The other documents (incorrectly) referenced in this same context were most often written for manufacturers of LAN cabling components (such as wire, connectors, punch-down blocks, etc.) to verify that their product performs properly at the indicated frequency range under laboratory conditions.

TSB67 has addressed all of the main issues related to field-testing the performance of an installed cabling system. TSB67 specifically addresses: 1) the parameters that must be tested, 2) the limits for each of these test parameters, and 3) the minimum accuracy and test execution requirements for field test equipment. TSB67 establishes a performance level for the physical cabling system using the UTP copper transmission medium that is independent of a network standard. It is expected that the European International Organization for Standards (ISO) will leverage off the research done for TSB67 to update the ISO/IEC 11801 Standard.

Field tester accuracy

Two accuracy levels

The crucial property of Near-end Crosstalk (NEXT) Loss must be measured accurately to assure that the Pass/Fail decision for a link is made with a very high degree of confidence. Much research leading to the formulation of TSB67 has focused on issues surrounding the NEXT measurement. TSB67 establishes two levels of performance for field testers. The criteria for these levels consist of performance factors that influence the accuracy of attenuation and NEXT measurement. They are: Random Noise Floor, Residual NEXT, Output Signal Balance, Common Mode Rejection, and Dynamic Accuracy. Requirements for each of these factors for each of the two accuracy levels are defined in the region from 1 MHz to 100 MHz (TSB67 Appendix A, Section 1) and translate into a computed measurement accuracy.

Actually, the measurement accuracy is more a figure of merit than a true measurement accuracy, because numerous assumptions are made that may or may not always be true. Annex B of TSB67 specifies in detail how Network Analyzer comparisons are conducted and the level of agreement that must be obtained between a reading by the field tester and the results measured by the Network Analyzer. TSB67 requires that the calculated measurement accuracy be in harmony with the results of Network Analyzer comparison.

Hardware is key

It is important to note that performance characteristics are not a function of the software features of a tester but are instead at the core of the hardware design, the selected electronic components, and the circuit board lay-out.

It is quite *unlikely* that 100 MHz field cable testers that were shipped prior to TSB67 can be adequately upgraded using software downloads into "Flash" memory. Basic measurement performance factors cannot be changed by software. (For additional information see *"Can Performance Be Downloaded Into Field Test Instruments,"* by Masood Shariff, BiCSi 1994 Annual Conference.) This is not to say that the feature that allows the end-user to update the software is not a powerful product benefit. While hardware design cannot be changed, what is correctable via a software download includes changes to the standard limit values, software "bug" fixes, and feature enhancements.

End-connections and the two link models

TSB67 defines two models of a link: the Basic Link and the Channel. The definition of these links *excludes* the end-connectors. The end-connector, which is almost always an 8-pin modular jack (often referred to as an RJ-45 jack) for UTP cabling systems, is only half of the socket-plug pair used to establish the connection between the link and the end-user equipment. This connection and its performance are viewed as an integral part of the end-user equipment. Therefore, the link definition explicitly excludes the RJ-45 socket-plug pair at the ends of the link. This is because the performance of the equipment is verified with a plug inserted in the equipment jack.

The same reasoning holds for the field cable testers. When the tester is connected to the link, the performance of the connection is as much a function of the characteristics of the tester as it is a function of the plug at the end of the link. The standard requires that the effect of this connection is to be excluded. The 8-pin modular connection contributes an unpredictable amount of crosstalk, which can lead to a sizable error in the measurements (2 dB or more).

Near-end crosstalk, as the name properly indicates, is most prevalent near the signal source. It is almost always caused by point-sources of NEXT (such as connectors). Since transmissions originate at both ends of a Channel, it is important that NEXT measurements be made from both ends of the link. The ubiquitous RJ-45 end connection contributes significantly to the NEXT loss of a link. Some design precautions can be taken to limit this loss, but the connections remain an unpredictable, yet significant, factor of NEXT loss. This fact also establishes a significant challenge for field test equipment to measure NEXT with accuracy.

When testing the *Basic Link*, tester patch cords are used to connect the tester to the link under test. The tester design can limit the amount of uncertainty in NEXT (increase the measurement accuracy) by using a low NEXT connector in the instrument such as a DB-style connector (DB-9 or DB-15) or another special connection system for the instrument patch cords.

These special patch cord connections limit the accuracy of these instruments when measuring the performance of a *Channel* configuration. A Channel includes the end-user's patch cords, and its performance is measured using those patch cords. In almost all cases, those patch cords end in RJ-45 connectors to insert into the wiring concentrator (hub or MAU) at the one end, and the network interface card (NIC) in a network station at the other end. The most versatile test instrument, therefore, interfaces with the link under test using the RJ-45 connector while establishing a measurement technique to compensate for the inaccuracies of RJ-45 connections.

Fundamentally, field testers operate based on one of two different principles. The traditional *frequency domain* method is the swept-frequency test. The test frequency is set at a start frequency, the response measured, and then the test frequency is changed to a new value (possibly incremented from the start frequency) and the response is measured again. This continues until the stop frequency is reached. A second method, more recently developed, is a *time domain* method, where the response to test pulses is measured. These test pulses have a very high frequency content, so all frequencies are measured in parallel. A special-purpose digital signal processor (DSP) performs a Fourier Transformation to obtain the result as a function of frequency.

In the time domain response method, the response of the connector to the instrument can be estimated and subtracted out as part of the full link verification test suite. In simple terms, the impact of the local connector is "electronically" cut off. This allows a highly accurate measurement even if a modular (RJ-45) connection is used at the tester. To achieve a higher confidence in the accuracy of results, the local patch cord should be 1.5 meters in length or longer. A longer patch cord assures that just the local connector effects were removed. *All* test result data is available from individual tests, including the local connector effects.

The performance levels of testers can be summarized as shown in Table F-4.

Cable termination: common-mode vs differential-mode

There are two ways that manufacturers can terminate the wire pairs in a cable tester: common-mode and differential-mode. (See Figure F-22.) Common-mode terminations apply where all pairs are ultimately connected to a common instrument ground, where differential-mode terminations are left isolated from each other and ground. These terminations are made within the instrument itself and are not identifiable by looking at the outside of the cable tester.

Common-mode terminations provide greater immunity to phase imbalance between pairs of wires being tested. Ideally, the concept behind twisted-pairs is that, at any point along the twisted wires, the signal within one wire is exactly equal and opposite to the signal in the other wire. This provides a cancellation of the two signals' electromagnetic field, effectively eliminating any noise.

However, when cabling components (wire and connectors) are assembled into a link, some amplitude and phase imbalances will occur, though almost always at the connectors. The imbalance is where the signals in the twisted pair are not exactly equal in amplitude and opposite in phase at any single point along the two wires. The slightest shift in the amplitude and phase of these signals can cause some imbalance, which in turn causes EMI to be emitted, and also causes additional coupling mechanisms inside the link. The imbalance implies that a signal is developed between a wire pair carrying the signal and an adjacent, unrelated wire pair. This causes excess NEXT. Normally, the signal is between the two wires of a twisted wire pair only (called a differential signal). Common-mode terminations provide the damping of signals between wire pairs, and thereby reduce reflections. In the case of differential-mode terminations only, the common-mode signal path is left open, so a 100% reflection occurs for common-mode signals.

Every time a common-mode signal is reflected, it adds to excess NEXT. Common-mode terminations and attenuation in the link dampen these common-mode signals, but if there are no common-mode terminations, the dampening depends on the attenuation alone. Where the attenuation is low, the excess NEXT will show a resonance effect at frequencies with wavelengths that exactly match the length of the link. If the link is very short, the amplitude of the resonance gets higher because of less attenuation in the link. Thus, resonance will be most pronounced when the link is short. Also, because of the shorter wavelength, the problem becomes more accentuated at higher frequencies. The wavelength of 100 MHz is 3 meters.

Causes	Frequency Domain (Using Swept-Frequency)	Time Domain (Using Digital Signal Processing)
Basic Link	Accuracy Level II with low NEXT connector on the tester, requires a special patch cord. Accuracy Level I with standard modular (RJ-45) connector.	Accuracy Level II, no restrictions for the connector. Local patch cord 1 meter or longer.
Channel	Accuracy Level I, because of required modular (RJ-45) adapter.	Accuracy Level II, no restrictions for the connector. Local patch cord 1 meter or longer.

Table F-4. Field cable tester accuracy.

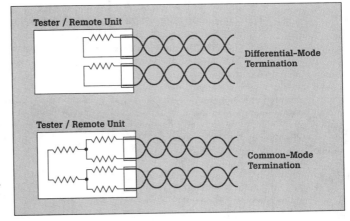

Figure F-22. Differential-mode and common-mode termination.

Resonance is described best by considering rubbing a wet finger around the top of a crystal glass. As you move your finger around the top of the glass at just the right speed, it will make a quiet rubbing/squeaking noise. This sound is transferred through the glass as a vibration, and a ringing tone is created by the crystal structure of the glass echoing and reinforcing other echoes of the vibrations made by your finger. After just a second or two the sound can get quite loud—this is equivalent to resonance. As soon as you stop rubbing your finger around the top of the glass, the sound quickly diminishes—this is equivalent to attenuation, because the vibration is dampened as it passes through the crystal. If you were to place your other hand around the glass while you rubbed the top, it would be the equivalent of the common-mode termination described in this section. It would prevent the sound from ever growing louder through resonance.

If the impedance discontinuity created by an imbalance in the cable or connection is the right distance from the signal source, it will create a resonance just like the crystal glass.

Figure F-23 shows the resonance effect as measured by a Network Analyzer. The graph shows results obtained using the same connectors for two tests. One test was made using differential-mode termination only, and the other using common-mode termination together. Note that the repetitive sharp peaks are virtually eliminated by using common-mode terminations. The two tests are compared to the TIA/EIA-568-A limit for NEXT.

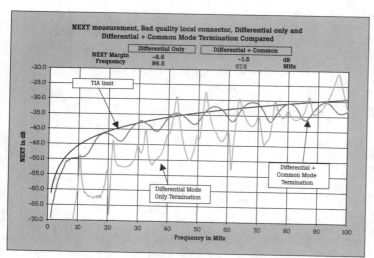

Figure F-23. *Network Analyzer test results using differential-mode and common-mode terminations.*

Common-mode terminations go a long way in minimizing the effects of these balance problems, where as differential-mode terminations will not diminish them at all.

Some cable testers that are currently available terminate the wire pairs in differential-mode, where others, such as the Fluke DSP-100, have common-mode terminations. It makes a considerable difference that they be terminated in a consistent fashion when comparing these testers to a Network Analyzer. To make a fair comparison between a field cable tester and a Network Analyzer as referenced in TSB67, accuracy verification tests require that both be terminated in the same manner. The Network Analyzer can be terminated in either mode by the user, while the field cable tester is manufactured with only one method of termination.

As network transmission speeds approach 100 MHz, noise immunity will become an increasing factor. To make the system less susceptible to imbalance of the signals in each twisted pair, common-mode terminations are used in all equipment—from NIC and hub connections to the cable testers. For complete and accurate testing, the cable termination in the field cable tester should be the same as the termination in the NIC and hub interfaces.

Importance of field tester accuracy

The field tester is the instrument used to provide a pass or fail verdict for each installed link tested. If the tester provides the "correct answer," all should be satisfied—even if the answer is a failing test result. The reason for a failure will need to be detected using the troubleshooting features of the tester. Once the defect has been located and corrective action has been taken, the link should pass and provide the desired quality of performance.

Problems arise if a field tester provides an incorrect answer. This situation will occur if the link is marginal to begin with, meaning that the test result is close to the limit (either over or under). Two cases should be considered: either the tester fails a good link (which is the more likely of the two possibilities, because most links are good) or the tester passes a bad link. Some troubleshooting may then pinpoint the potential defect or problem. Corrective action will then result in a higher-quality link.

The real problem arises when the tester passes a bad link–a link that does not meet all of the performance requirements. Since the tester gave it a "pass," everyone is happy and the job is considered complete. However, this link may start "acting up" some months later when a new "high-speed" network is installed. This is where the troubleshooting effort will cost a lot more than the simple cabling test. Network engineers will spend time analyzing what is happening, users will be disrupted, and eventually the bad cabling link will be identified. Table F-5 shows the probability that a tester will make a wrong decision based on its accuracy rating.

What should be tested

TSB67 contains specifications for the verification of installed UTP cabling links which consist of cables and connecting hardware specified in the TIA/EIA-568-A Standard. The primary field test parameters for such a UTP link are: Wiremap, Link Length, Attenuation, and Near-End Crosstalk (or NEXT).

In addition to the test parameters to be measured, TSB67 defines two model link configurations: the "*Channel*" and the "*Basic Link.*" Figure F-24 depicts the Channel. The important distinction is that the user patch cord must be used during the test, and the model of the *Channel* defines two transitions at each end, whereas the *Basic Link* defines one transition at each end of the link. The Channel is the link configuration, which is of interest to end-users and LAN system designers. Patch cords can make a significant difference, particularly because of a different mating of plugs and connectors (the cable of a patch cord rarely has much of an impact, unless it is severely damaged, and that is usually quite evident and detectable by a visual inspection). The end-user wants to verify the performance of the complete cabling link from wiring concentrator to the workstation, which must include the end-users' patch cables and not the instrumentation patch cables. Note that, at present, there are no standards available for patch cords. Standards committees are working on the issue, but it is turning into quite a challenge.

The quality of a new installation should always be tested using the Basic Link configuration. The Basic Link test is a few dB tighter than the Channel test, and provides some margin of performance when the test patch cord is replaced by a user patch cord. It also provides a better check on the quality of the installed components and the workmanship. Where possible, the Channel configuration should also be tested to ensure that the actual user patch cords are of acceptable quality.

Distance to test limit	Accuracy Level I (% incorrect) NEXT accuracy		Accuracy Level II (% incorrect) NEXT accuracy	
(dB)	4 dB	3 dB	2 dB	1 dB
1	30.9	25.2	15.9	2.3
2	15.9	9.1	2.3	0.0
3	6.7	2.3	0.1	0.0
4	2.3	0.4	0.0	0.0
5	0.6	0.0	0.0	0.0

Table F-5. *Level I and Level II field tester accuracy.*

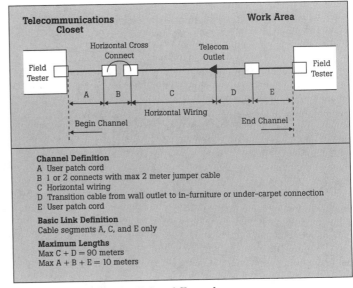

Channel Definition
A User patch cord
B 1 or 2 connects with max 2 meter jumper cable
C Horizontal wiring
D Transition cable from wall outlet to in-furniture or under-carpet connection
E User patch cord

Basic Link Definition
Cable segments A, C, and E only

Maximum Lengths
Max C + D = 90 meters
Max A + B + E = 10 meters

Figure F-24. *TSB67 Basic Link and Channel configurations.*

General Testing and Installation Issues

In the preceding statements, UTP links have been dominant in the discussion. There is still a lot of coax around in legacy networks, and occasionally coax or fiber will be installed for smaller, new networks, or to take advantage of the longer runs allowed. There are installation and maintenance issues that are different for coax and UTP. Below are several testing and troubleshooting issues for UTP and coax cable.

Twisted pair installation issues

- UTP cable used for medium- to high-speed networks requires a specified minimum number of twists per inch. The higher the speed, the greater the number of twists per inch. Flat, gray untwisted cable used for telephone systems (sometimes referred to as "silver-satin") should never be used for LAN applications. While the network may continue to operate after one or more of these links are installed, a quick look at the MAC-layer protocol is apt to show a noticeable increase in errors. Even if the network survives a small number of these links without a significant increase in errors, these links may yet be what pushes the network into failure when something else becomes marginal.

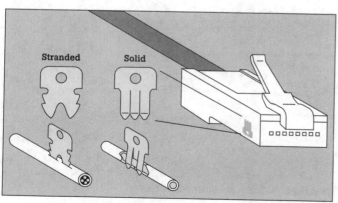

Figure F-25. Modular 8-pin (RJ-45) pin styles.

- Purchase and use only high-quality crimp tools for UTP. Poor-quality crimp tools often fail to press the pins evenly into the RJ-45—either by not pressing one end as firmly as the other, or by flexing in the center and not pressing the middle pins as firmly as the outside pins. The resulting problems tend to be intermittent, and are quite difficult to troubleshoot.

- When building your own UTP links, be particularly careful to purchase the correct connectors for the type of wire used. Stranded wire is always used for patch cables, and is almost always the connector type offered unless you specifically request solid wire connectors. In the short term, both will function adequately, but if the wrong connector is used, it will result in intermittent connections over time. Connectors for solid wire use a pin that straddles the wire, and a pressure fit to maintain the connection. For stranded wire, the pins are driven into the tight bundle of individual wires, where contact is again maintained by pressure. If a stranded wire connector is used for solid wire, the pin simply touches the top of the wire and will stop making contact after the link is flexed during normal use. (See Figure F-25.)

- It is somewhere between difficult and impossible to obtain good results when testing a UTP link that is still connected to a hub or MAU. The passive circuitry in the device interface distorts the signals used to test the link, and causes results to become marginally to wildly inaccurate. The test signals may also (briefly) confuse the port itself, though the port almost always recovers on its own after receiving a transmission of "normal" data. (An exception would be the Token Ring "Lobe" test, which requires a MAU loopback connection, and has no potentially adverse effect on the port.)

- Although it may work for slower-speed applications like telephone service, a single UTP link should never be used by two network stations, or two types of service unless your LAN has been specifically designed to be coexistent with the other service. Leave unused pairs idle if you want to avoid intermittent problems (like losing data every time the telephone rings). As the data transmission speed increases, the likelihood of problems increases (a 235 kHz LocalTalk connection is nearly immune to this problem, but a 80 MHz 100BASE-TX connection would be highly susceptible).

- No product is able to perform a link test on a UTP link without connecting a loopback device to the other end of the run. Part of the reason for this is that, in order to comply with the requirements of the Standards that govern link testing, a pass or fail judgment may not be given unless the suite of tests includes a "wire-map" test, and that cannot be made without the loopback device. Another reason is that the link must be terminated with a resistance value equal to the impedance of the link for other measurements to be made.

- If UTP cables are to be bound together, they should be bound loosely. There are a number of commercial fastening systems available that can be used to tidy-up a wiring closet or a cable bundle. Be sure not to over-tighten! When bundles of UTP cable are too tightly bound at intervals along the length of the link, it will change the electrical characteristics, causing network errors. You should always be able to slide a single cable in the bundle forward and backward through a fastening with little effort. If you must pull strongly (TIA/EIA-568-A paragraph 10.6.3.2 allows for a maximum of 25 pound feet of pulling tension), or if the cable cannot be moved at all, then your data is at risk. There have been instances where network problems disappeared when cable fastenings were cut to allow troubleshooting to begin.

- Handle LAN cable carefully during installation and later during use. If the cable is kinked severely, walked upon, or driven over, it will cause localized changes in the characteristic impedance, and may physically damage the insulation and wire. This abuse can result in point-source cable problems, usually NEXT failures.

- Be careful when specifying interconnecting hardware for UTP. Make sure that you use TIA/EIA-568-A pinouts for either the T568A or T568B specification throughout the *entire* network. If hardware made for both pinouts is used together, the color codes for the wire positions will be wrong, and the links will not work unless custom patch cables are used.

- If high-speed protocols will *ever* be used on the UTP cabling, it is vitally important to follow all of the installation guidelines for Category 5 cabling. This includes no sharp bends or kinks in the cable. Also, do not untwist the pairs more than absolutely necessary for any connection, and avoid routing cables near any sources of electrical noise, etc.

- Be sure to test UTP links for the frequency-dependent NEXT tests at both ends of a run. There is always a transmission source at both ends, and it is not uncommon to obtain different results at either end of the run. For the same reason, TSB67 requires both ends to be tested using the frequency-dependent tests. This will complete the link verification (or more loosely and incorrectly phrased, "certify" the link).

- Never mix cables with different characteristic impedances. Media filters can be used to adapt between new and old cable systems, but they introduce yet another potential failure point and should be avoided wherever possible.

- When untwisting wire pairs to install connectors or make connections at punch-down blocks, make the untwisted sections as short as possible. For compliance with Category 5 cabling standards, the untwisted section cannot exceed 13mm (about half an inch).

- Do not make sharp bends or kinks in the cable. The radius of bends in a cable should be larger than one inch, though TIA/EIA-568-A paragraph 10.6.3.2 permits four-pair UTP cable bend radii as tight as four times the diameter of the cable.

- Avoid installing long cable runs near ground planes, in metallic conduit, or near any other conducting surface. The result will be an additional 2–3% change in attenuation. High temperatures will also affect attenuation significantly.

Coax installation issues

- Coax requires a terminator at both ends of every run. The resistance value of the termination should be equal to the characteristic impedance of the cable–otherwise electrical "reflections" of the data will result. Sometimes the end of a coax run is attached directly to a piece of network equipment–which must then be configured to supply the required termination internally.

- Thin coax *may* be grounded at only one point along the run, and thick coax is *required* to be grounded at only one point along the run. Problems develop when a second ground connection point is present. The most common source of multiple ground points is when a thin coax "Tee" connector is rotated on the back of the PC and comes in contact with a grounded protective shield around the connector of another cable.

- A coax cable may be tested with or without the termination present at the other end. If the far termination is present and is the correct value for that cable, then you will not obtain a length measurement because the terminator is doing its job. If the far termination is faulty or not present, a length measurement will be possible. If there is a fault along the cable, then a distance-to-fault will be displayed whether or not the end of the cable is properly terminated.

- Never try to make a coax cable test from some point along the cable because you will receive signals from both directions down the cable, and the electrical characteristics will distort the results–possibly significantly. If you must test from a point along the run, disconnect the cable at that point and test each direction separately. (One exception is that dc resistance can be measured from any connection point. Along the cable you should see both terminators, and from either end you should see only one.)

- For the same reason that you never test from the middle of a coax run (see above), never attach an extra segment of coax–often called a stub–to a point along the run. This is because it will form a second path for the data. All station attachments to coax should be made directly to the "trunk." Adding stubs will cause severe reflections which will in turn corrupt any data transmitted.

- Few products are able to perform a length measurement test on a "live" network link. The TDR pulse is detected as a network error, the TDR pulse corrupts passing data, the passing data corrupts the TDR pulse, or data is detected as TDR errors. If your tester is unable to test a "live" link, try the test on an idle link (with all traffic removed). If that fails, either disconnect the link from all stations, or turn off all of the stations connected to the link while testing is performed.

- If multiple types of coax are used for a single run (RG–58, RG–59, RG–62, etc., these have different characteristic impedance–see the next item), the data transmitted will be partially reflected back toward the sender at each change of cable type. If the run is short enough, there will be no detectable effect from the user's perspective. When more cable is included to add more stations, the network will either operate intermittently or stop working altogether for no apparent reason. Since the network operated prior to the new additions, the old link will not be suspect.

- Never mix cables with different characteristic impedances.

- Important Note: The Ethernet Standard (IEEE 802.3) specifies that thin-coax installations be made with stranded coax. Stranded coax is harder to work with, and some installers may not want to use it (they may not tell you they are using solid core) so be sure to specify in bids and contracts that stranded coax be used for thin coax Ethernet installations.

New cabling—short-sighted or thrifty?

A common estimate is that 50% of the cost of a new network goes into the cable plant. It has also been said that cabling is a "once-in-a-decade" investment. It may seem like a great cost-cutting measure to install cable only to the places where it is currently required, to use Category 3 cable instead of Category 5, or to install only two pairs to each connection. Before you do so, consider how much more it will cost to rebuild the cable plant when you have outgrown your current network or must move to a media access protocol that requires four pairs of Category 5 wire.

The real cost for good-quality components, using four pairs instead of two, and running spare cables into spaces that may be needed in a year or two, is incremental compared to having a contractor come back again. Some companies are even having "dark" fiber optic cable pulled everywhere unshielded twisted pair (UTP) cable is installed, as a cost-savings measure, anticipating the time when the current network is unable to support the load. A well-designed and installed cable system can provide many years of service if the designers take into account the direction that leading-edge network solutions are headed.

Grounding and shielding cable

Although the primary purpose of requiring Screened UTP (ScTP) or Shielded Twisted Pair (STP) throughout most of Europe is to prevent network signals from leaking *out* of the cable, most people think of shielding as a way to prevent signals from leaking *into* the cable. The use of shielding is a good way to meet both requirements; however, there are some potential problems.

Restated: the fundamental purpose of a shield is to fully enclose a signal so no radiated field can enter the cable and disturb the signal lines, and equally important, so no field is radiated out of the cable, where it could interfere with other electronic devices. Note that is absolutely essential that shields *fully enclose* the signals in every regard. Extending a drain wire even a short distance past the shield of a cable to make a connection defeats the quality of the shield significantly. (See Figure F-26.) Proper installation requires mounting clamps that are located inside enclosed metal spaces, so that openings are absolutely minimal. Coaxial cabling systems and connecting hardware lend themselves easily towards this goal.

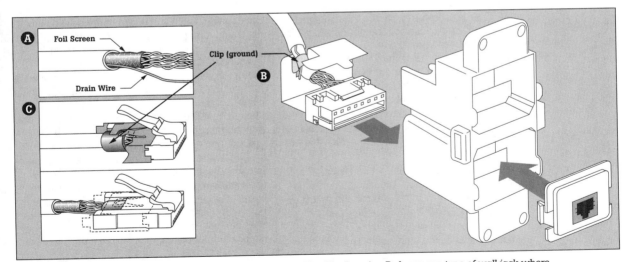

Figure F-26. *Drawing A shows the parts of a shielded UTP (ScTP) cable. Drawing B shows one type of wall jack where the shielding fully encloses the end of the cable, with an arrow indicating the point where the cable shield connects to the jack shield. Drawing C shows a cut-away of a correctly terminated, fully enclosed ScTP 8-pin modular plug (RJ-45), with an arrow indicating the point that the cable shield connects to the plug shield. Below that is an incorrectly terminated ScTP cable, where the cable shield does not enclose the wire pairs completely into the shield of the plug.*

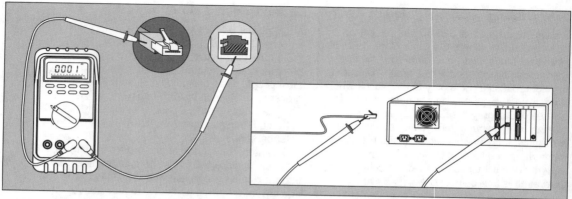

Figure F-27. Measuring a cable shield for ac voltage with a digital multimeter.

Generally speaking, a connection to ground is made for personal-safety reasons. To meet current safety requirements, all equipment must have a third wire safety connection to ground. The issue then becomes where (at what locations) connections have to be made between the earth ground (chassis) and the shield.

All earth ground connections eventually lead to a building ground location. Voltage potentials in the earth ground lead are caused by leakage currents in the various pieces of electrical equipment. The leakage current times the resistance of the ground wires cause voltage potentials, which easily can exceed several volts. Voltage potentials between buildings are generally very significant. Lightning is another important consideration when connecting buildings. For data communication between buildings, fiber optic connections are the only practical and safe solution.

You **do not** want to have a cable shield become a ground return path. This can be avoided in one of two ways:

1. Permit only a single connection between earth ground and the shield. Unfortunately, this is usually done only in coaxial cabling systems.

2. Make certain that there is no substantial voltage potential between the earth ground connections of the equipment and any connection to data communications systems.
   If there is no voltage, there will be no current, and therefore no problem. This is the solution that is followed for shielded twisted pair cabling systems (STP, ScTP).

In coaxial cable systems (10BASE2 and 10BASE5) the connection between earth ground and the shield is made at one location in the cable system. This is typically done at one end of the coax run. At all other locations there is isolation between tap connections and any earth ground source. For 10BASE2, protective plastic caps are often used to prevent accidental contact between the BNC "Tee" connector and the PC chassis.

When using shields with twisted pair cabling systems (ScTP, STP), one can verify the absence of ground loop potentials by testing for them after all non-LAN electrical equipment has been installed and is operational. Then activate the LAN equipment and measure the voltage potential between the shield of the other end and the chassis of the equipment to be connected. (See Figure 27.) If the voltage is less than 1 volt ac, one may be reasonably assured that there will be no ground loop effect.

If the voltage is substantially higher, you must locate the source of the leakage. This normally involves working with a qualified electrician to correct the problem that is creating the voltage potential. This is not always easy to do, and if not possible, you should convert the connection from copper to fiber optic cable.

FLUKE®

Appendix G — Switch Technology

What Is a Switch?

Unfortunately, there is no simple definition of a switch. Pared down to a basic, concise answer, a switch (depending on available features and current configuration) can act as 1) a repeater (OSI Layer 1 device), 2) a bridge (OSI Layer 2 device), 3) a router (OSI Layer 3 device), 4) or a combination of items 1 to 3. To further complicate the issue, these distinctions can be configured on a port-by-port basis, so that the answer changes depending on which path is taken through the switch.

The common description for a switch is that it creates private paths (direct connections) to the requested server or service on the network, without having to share bandwidth with other devices. Although it may seem simplistic, this description is relatively close to the truth. Figure G-1 below shows a symbolic representation of this description. Each station in Figure G-1 is having a conversation with only one other station. In practice, however, instead of connecting with another single device on the network, most stations will connect to one or more common servers or services.

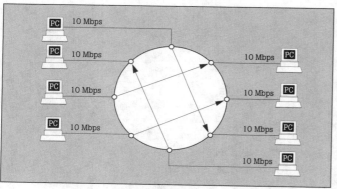

Figure G-1. *Functional diagram of a switch, showing four simultaneously switched conversations.*

The developing feature set offered by switches is creating a comparatively inexpensive solution to network congestion. Network congestion typically manifests itself to users with the following symptoms.

- Highly variable response times.
- Network time-outs or server disconnects.
- Inability to establish network connections.
- Slower application loading and/or running.

How do switches work?

Operationally, there are two common forwarding techniques used in switches, and two more techniques that are modifications of the first two. The names used to describe each of the techniques may vary. (For the purpose of clarity, examples used here will refer to Ethernet.)

The technique offering the lowest latency (delay) makes the forwarding decision as soon as the destination address has been received. While this technique is the fastest, there is invariably a tradeoff for performance: it will permit some of the MAC layer errors to propagate through to other physical network segments. This will be described as *cut-through*.

The best technique for blocking MAC layer errors is also the one with the greatest latency, because the entire frame is received and checked for errors before it is forwarded. This is known as *store-and-forward*.

A modification of the cut-through technique prevents a greater number of errors from being propagated, but also adds to latency. This third technique waits until at least 64 bytes of a frame has been received before forwarding to other physical network segments. Since most common Ethernet errors occur within the first 64 bytes, this effectively blocks nearly all common errors. This is known as *modified cut-through, adaptive cut-through,* and *fragment free.*

A fourth option, referred to here as *error sensing*, is available from the more expensive switches. That option is to change the forwarding technique dynamically, based on detected error levels.

Cut-through

A cut-through switch will make the forwarding decision after the destination MAC address has been read into the buffer. Because a cut-through switch starts forwarding before the complete frame is received, the packet can be forwarded with errors. However, the advantage is a low-latency time since the frame will be forwarded almost immediately. Besides, if a switch is being used to replace a shared-media hub, then the number of errors will be reduced from the level forwarded by the shared-media hub by some amount (the physical network will experience a gain in performance even though some errors are still forwarded). (See Figure G-2.)

Store-and-forward

A store-and-forward switch will read the entire frame into a buffer before forwarding the frame to the destination port. This has an advantage in that error frames will not be forwarded since the switch will check the frame prior to forwarding. The drawback, however, is that the latency is proportional to the length of the frame. This could result in a performance problem if store-and-forward switches are connected in series.

This is the same technique used by a standard bridge for forwarding. (See Figure G-3.)

Modified cut-through

A modified cut-through switch (sometimes called adaptive cut-through or fragment free) attempts to offer a compromise between the store-and-forward and cut-through technologies. This switch will buffer the incoming packet until the first 64 bytes are received. This means that the switch effectively filters out collision fragments and the majority of error packets, since a bad frame can usually be detected within the first 64 bytes. In effect, this type of switch acts as a cut-through switch for frames larger than 64 bytes and as a store-and-forward switch for 64-byte frames. (See Figure G-4.)

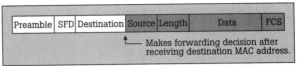

Figure G-2. *Diagram of where the forwarding decision is made using a **cut-through** technique.*

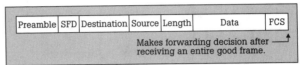

Figure G-3. *Diagram of where the forwarding decision is made using a **store-and-forward** technique.*

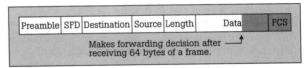

Figure G-4. *Diagram of where the forwarding decision is made using a **modified cut-through** technique.*

Error sensing

At some level of detected errors, the switch port can change techniques from *cut-through* to *store-and-forward* dynamically. When local conditions improve and the error level drops back into an acceptable range, the port will resume using the cut-through technique. This configuration offers what is perhaps the best compromise of performance versus speed.

Switch functions

In addition to switching data paths, switches are designed to handle other tasks as well. Usually they can perform repeater functions, bridge functions, and the more expensive switches even offer built-in router functions.

A quick description of how each level of switch operation (in relation to the OSI 7-Layer model) is implemented in a network follows.

Repeater functions

(See Figure G-5.) Repeaters indiscriminately amplify and retransmit everything observed on one port to all other ports. That is to say, not just good traffic is forwarded. Repeaters will attempt to forward everything, even if it does not remotely resemble the expected traffic for that media access protocol.

It is not uncommon for one port of an Ethernet repeater to detect noise from any number of sources (fluorescent lights, electrical power lines, radio transmitters, etc.) and to create a signal to send to all other ports. This sounds like the description of a failed device, but it is the correct thing for a repeater to do. Because of the CSMA/CD technology used in Ethernet, all stations connected within a collision domain *must* be informed that there is a signal present somewhere within the collision domain. By forwarding the signal to all parts of the collision domain, a repeater will prevent collided data from reaching a destination station without the source station becoming aware of the problem. This will be accomplished by either causing a collision or by simply occupying the available bandwidth for a time and preventing any station from sending data. If the sending station becomes aware that a problem has occurred during its transmission, the Ethernet protocol will usually be able to handle retransmission attempts. These attempts will continue until the data gets through, without incurring the delay associated with notifying higher layers of the protocol stack that problems are being encountered.

Bridge functions

(See Figure G-6.) Bridges are often used to block traffic that is local to one physical network segment (both stations involved in the conversation are attached to the same physical network segment—the same port on the bridge) from being sent to all other physical segments. If the two stations are not on the same physical network segment, the bridges will prevent most errors from being forwarded to other physical network segments. A notable exception is that broadcast traffic is not blocked by a bridge.

By monitoring which MAC addresses are detected in the source address field of frames, bridges build and maintain a "bridge forwarding table." When a frame is detected on one port, the bridge checks the table to see if the destination MAC address is known to reside on the same port. If the destination address is found to be on the same port, the bridge will ignore the frame, but if *not* found to be on the same port, it will either forward the frame to the port where the station is known to be connected, or to all other ports when the destination MAC address is unknown. Only "good" frames are forwarded.

Ethernet networks often suffer from throughput problems when average traffic loads approach the generally accepted maximum average capacity level of 40%. The first solution to excessive traffic is to segment LANs into smaller sub-LANs by installing bridges. If relatively little inter-segment traffic must traverse the bridge, this solution works well—though broadcast traffic can become a problem because it is always forwarded to all bridged segments. However, substantial inter-segment traffic can overload some bridges and cause network delays. To prevent this, the network administrator should limit inter-segment traffic by carefully considering which nodes should attach to each segment. The process involves an investment of time and may need to be repeated regularly on extremely dynamic networks.

Router functions

(See Figure G-7.) Unlike bridges, routers make forwarding decisions based on the OSI Layer 3 address (IP, IPX, etc.). Having to decode more of the frame in order to reach a decision point introduces added delay to the network, but routers greatly limit the amount of traffic that is forwarded to other parts of the network. As a general rule, bridges forward to *all* ports when an address is *not* known, and routers forward *only* when a destination network *is* known.

Using routers to segment networks solves one problem and creates others. Routers are excellent general-purpose internetwork firewalls. They are very useful where the division of networks into logical groups (logical subnetting) must occur. Because routers operate at OSI Layer 3, they can effectively distinguish between, and separate traffic from, different logical networks. For example, Internet Protocol (IP) traffic can be separated from DECnet and other kinds of traffic. The network administrator needs to take into account that routers are far more expensive than bridges on a per-port basis. Further, they are often unnecessary in situations where complex logical subnetting and exotic wide-area communications are not required.

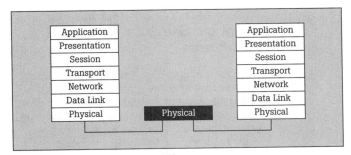

Figure G-5. *Where a repeater fits in the OSI basic reference model.*

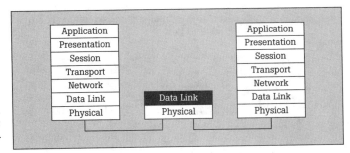

Figure G-6. *Where a bridge fits in the OSI basic reference model.*

What Problems are Encountered in Switched Environments?

Generally, the problems found in a switched environment are identical to those experienced in a shared media environment. Issues that should be considered are:

- How busy is each segment (port)?
- How do you identify and track the source of errors?
- What is the source of a broadcast storm?
- Are bridge forwarding tables corrupted?
- What stations are attached to specific segments?
- How do you determine where to start looking for a reported problem?

Typically, it's not the switch that causes the problem, but the inability to "see" inside it.

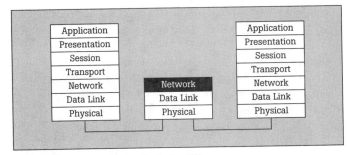

Figure G-7. *Where a router fits in the OSI basic reference model.*

How Do You Find Which Port or Switch Has a Problem?

If you have fully implemented and maintained a network management system, you can use the SNMP management features of a switch to send traps whenever utilization or errors exceed a set amount, then use a network management or network monitoring tool to discover what is happening locally.

The alternative is to wait for user complaints. In most networks, this second option will be the more common solution. Once a user complains, you can start the troubleshooting process from his connection point.

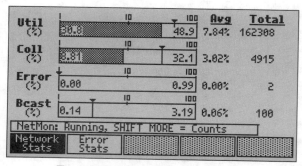

Figure G-8. Fluke LANMeter **Network Stats** test results screen.

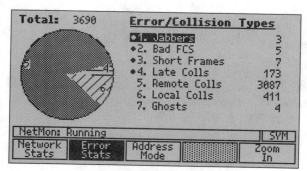

Figure G-9. Fluke LANMeter **Error Stats** test results screens.

Proactive efforts to prevent problems from affecting users include regularly interrogating each switch with SNMP, and monitoring the quality of traffic on each switch port—just as any other segment would be monitored on a regular basis.

Using the Enterprise LANMeter and SwitchWizard to troubleshoot switched environments

The SwitchWizard option for the Fluke Enterprise LANMeter test tool allows you to monitor and troubleshoot switched environments by utilizing the SNMP agents embedded as a standard feature in most switches. The SwitchWizard option is able to interrogate SNMP agents using standards-based MIBs (MIB II, RMON, etc.), and present the information in an easy-to-understand manner.

Test the local connection for errors

Connect an Enterprise LANMeter test tool to the network and run the Network Monitor, **Network Stats** test. This will monitor the local physical segment for utilization levels and check for any errors. **Network Stats** and **Error Stats** (which run simultaneously) allow the MAC layer to be verified for proper operation. (See Figures G-8 and G-9.) If any errors are detected, they should be corrected before attempting to diagnose higher-layer problems. For best results, enable the traffic generator to add a small amount of traffic to the local segment in the background while monitoring.

Identify the local switches and manageable devices

Run the Internet TCP/IP, **IP Auto Config** test to obtain a valid IP address for the segment, then run the **Segment Discovery** test. (See Figure G-10.) The attached segment will be analyzed, and all critical network attributes will be catalogued. With the SwitchWizard option installed, **Segment Discovery** will identify bridges and switches and will identify problems, as well as search for IP Routers, subnet information, IP Servers (including DHCP, BOOTP and DNS servers), SNMP agents, and local hosts. (See Figure G-11.)

Use SNMP to diagnose the local switch

When the *Switches/Bridges* category is selected and the *Zoom In* softkey is pressed, the SwitchWizard option will display the IP address and the device type, and will automatically resolve the name if a DNS server is discovered during the test. Additionally, SwitchWizard will inform you if the switch is using the spanning tree protocol and also report the designated port for that segment.

By selecting the IP address of the switch and running **MultiPort Stats**, you can quickly and easily "see" what is occurring at each port of the switch. (See Figure G-12.) The test displays utilization and error information for up to eight ports simultaneously, while it monitors all other ports on the switch in the background.

With the SwitchWizard option, information can be sorted by port number, average utilization or average error rates. The *Find Port* feature also allows you to enter a MAC or IP address, and SwitchWizard will automatically find and display the port to which the device is attached. This test will display information on any type of switch port—10BASE-T, Token Ring, Serial Links, Fast Ethernet, even FDDI—therefore minimizing the need to purchase additional interfaces for existing analyzers.

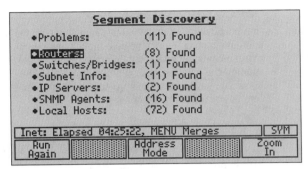

Figure G-10. *Fluke Enterprise LANMeter* **Segment Discovery** *test results summary screen.*

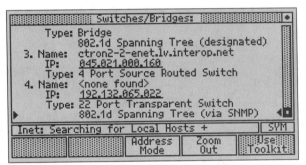

Figure G-11. *Fluke Enterprise LANMeter* **Segment Discovery** *test results, "zoomed" on the Switches/ Bridges screen.*

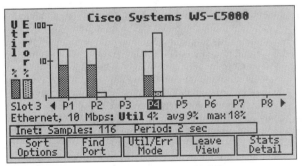

Figure G-12. *Fluke Enterprise LANMeter* **MultiPort Stats** *test results screen.*

Identify the port(s) experiencing problems

If a particular port on the switch appears to have high utilization or error rates, simply press the **Stats Detail** softkey to obtain additional information on the selected port. (See Figure G-13.) The SwitchWizard option will provide detailed information including utilization, error rates and broadcast levels.

If the problem is errors, simply press the **Interface Errors** softkey to obtain detailed information on the error types occurring at the switch port. (See Figure G-14.)

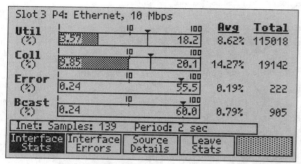

Figure G-13. *Fluke Enterprise LANMeter **MultiPort Stats** test results, "zoomed" on **Stats Detail, Interface Stats** for a selected port.*

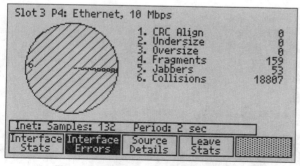

Figure G-14. *Fluke Enterprise LANMeter **MultiPort Stats** test results, "zoomed" on **Stats Detail, Interface Errors** for a selected port.*

Identify the source of any detected problems

Once you have discovered the errors, it is quite easy to determine which devices are attached to the specific switch port by pressing the **Port Details** softkey. (See Figure G-15.) This feature will display the list of MAC addresses attached to the port, together with their associated IP addresses and DNS names (if available).

If the switch vendor supports standards-based MIBs or RMON, the information outlined above is available for any type of interface, including:

- 802.3 10BASE-T
- 802.5 Token Ring
- 802.3 100BASE-TX
- 802.3 100BASE-FX
- 802.12 (VG)
- ANSI X3T9.5 FDDI
- ATM

Are there other ways to diagnose switched environments?

The single biggest problem in any switched environment is the inability to "see" inside a switch (such as traffic and error levels for each port). Consequently, troubleshooting a switched environment involves many new techniques in order to obtain the same level of information found in a shared-media environment. In a switched-environment network, diagnostic tools must be combined with features of the switch itself to provide similar information to shared-media LAN analysis.

Using network management systems

Network management can be used to check all segments and ports that lie between the two devices, including the local ports for each. Network management systems make use of the embedded SNMP agents within the switched hub. Most switched hubs implement standards-based MIBs (MIB I/II), the manufacturer's private MIB, and RMON. Some of the simple information available from a network management platform would include:

- Port utilization for each port connection between the problem station and the desired network resource.

- Error rates for each of the same ports.
- Error types (if RMON, or the correct transmission MIB is available).
- Error sources (if RMON is available).
- Broadcast traffic rates and sources.

In the real world, network management systems are often not fully implemented and maintained. When this is the case, they are of little use in troubleshooting network problems. Even when they are fully implemented and maintained, the sheer quantity of information available can slow down or impede the troubleshooting process. If network management is not available on your network, then some of the features of the switch itself will not be available to aid in troubleshooting.

To attach a troubleshooting tool to a switched hub involves more planning than just connecting to a shared-media hub. Simply connecting a traditional monitoring tool like a protocol analyzer to a switched hub port provides little or no benefit. The only traffic the analyzer is likely to see is broadcast traffic since switches, by design, only forward traffic to a specific destination port. There are, however, a number of techniques available to allow access to a switched hub. Unfortunately, none are ideal for troubleshooting.

Three basic techniques can be used to gain visibility into switched environments.

Adding a shared-media hub

Using a shared media hub involves a strategic placement of the monitoring tool. In many networks, most traffic will be received or transmitted by a shared resource such as a file server. Adding a shared-media hub between the switch port and the file server allows an analyzer to be connected to the same segment as the file server, as shown in Figure G-16.

This technique enables the analyzer to see all the traffic to and from the file server, which enables the network support staff to diagnose problems such as the inability to log on to a specific server.

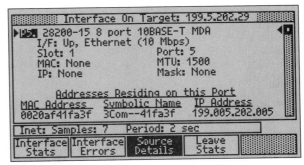

Figure G-15. Fluke Enterprise LANMeter **MultiPort Statistics** test results, "zoomed" on **Stats Detail, Port Details** for a selected port.

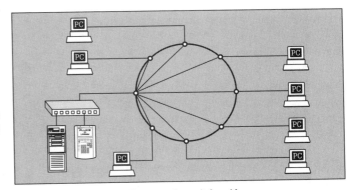

Figure G-16. Functional diagram of a switch, with a shared-media hub being used to monitor all traffic to and from a file server.

This approach is impractical in most situations, particularly where there are multiple servers attached to switched hubs, and where there is a possibility of multiple switched hubs. Where do you locate the shared-media hub? On all shared resources? If you choose to move a shared-media hub around as needed, are you prepared to interrupt the network long enough to install the hub? This delay is often long enough to cause dropped connections. Additionally, shared resources may be connected via a Fast Ethernet, FDDI or other technology port that your monitoring tool may not support.

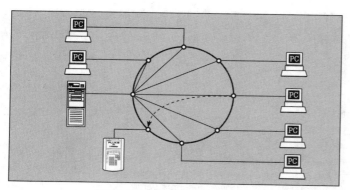

Figure G-17. *Functional diagram of a switch, with a monitoring tool being used in a **port tap** configuration.*

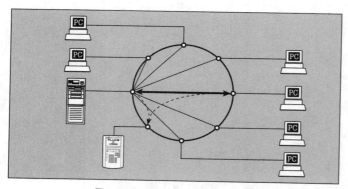

Figure G-18. *Functional diagram of a switch, with a monitoring tool being used in a **circuit tap** configuration.*

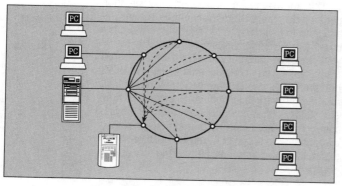

Figure G-19. *Functional diagram of a switch, with a monitoring tool being used in a **switch tap** configuration.*

Port aliasing

Also called port mirroring, this technique is provided by most vendors to allow a monitoring tool to be connected to a designated monitor port on the switched hub.

The implementation of this technique varies between vendors. There are, however, three common implementations. Note that with most switch vendors, the forwarding technique employed by the switch will also be used to filter data sent to the monitor port. This means that for most switches, most of the errors are filtered by the switch, and do not appear on the monitor port. Thus, for troubleshooting purposes, port aliasing can be quite ineffective because the problem is concealed by the switch itself.

Port tap

This implementation forwards all the traffic received or transmitted from a specified port to the actual destination ports and also to the monitor port. (See Figure G-17.)

Circuit tap

All traffic exchanged between two ports is forwarded to the monitor port by this implementation. (See Figure G-18.)

Switch tap

Using this implementation, all the traffic is forwarded from *any* port to the monitor port. (See Figure G-19.) The major disadvantage of the switch tap is that the monitor port can easily become overloaded and, consequently, drop frames.

In most cases, switch vendors support one or more of the above techniques. However, a switch that supports Fast Ethernet or FDDI interfaces, in addition to 10BASE-T ports, will generally not allow the high-speed ports to be mirrored to a 10-Mbps switch port.

In addition, all the above implementations must be configured either from a console or a Telnet session. This involves bringing a PC or terminal along with the monitoring tool so that the switch can be reconfigured as required for troubleshooting.

When are Switches Appropriate?

Several topics are discussed in this section as a starting point to determine whether your network would benefit from a switch. Until you have identified specific characteristics and areas of your LAN where you need improved performance, it will be difficult to supply a switch vendor with the information necessary to help you select the right features for your network. It is important to note that in some situations the addition of a switch could actually decrease performance.

Why use a switch?

Ethernet suffers performance decreases when average traffic loads approach or exceed 40%, or when sustained peak loads exceed around 60%. It is difficult to pinpoint the exact load level where performance will begin to degrade, because so many variables affect performance. The numbers mentioned above are intended only as guidelines. The number of stations transmitting and the number of small frames transmitted at any given time are two of the factors that will have a great influence on performance. A high number of large frames will provide the greatest throughput, simply because the medium is occupied longer with valid data. When many small frames are present, you lose the greatest amount of time to collisions and idle time (during the backoff period, and during the interframe gap). (See Figure G-20.)

Two good reasons to install Token Ring switches are 1) to reduce the number of stations on each ring, and 2) to protect other rings when beaconing or other debilitating problems occur on one ring. However, simply connecting each ring station to an individual switch port will reduce performance on source routed networks. You can also use switches with translational bridge capabilities to join Ethernet and Token Ring segments.

What kind of switch should be used?

To obtain the best performance at the least cost, first identify the category of switch that is right for your application. (See Figure G-21.)

One important aspect of switch technology is parallel networking—in this case, the ability to run simultaneous separate conversations (see Figure G-1 for an extreme example of how this could look). Parallel networking combines the benefit of circuit switching (moving information over dedicated dynamically-created physical connections) and packet switching (moving information units belonging to potentially diverse logical circuits in an orderly fashion over a communications channel).

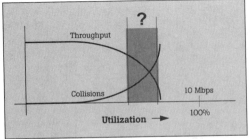

Figure G-20. Ethernet performance chart showing sharp reduction in throughput due to collisions.

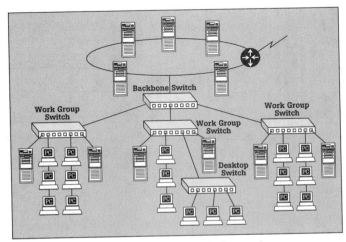

Figure G-21. Functional diagram of a switched network design.

The increase of throughput is directly proportional to the number of LAN segments that can be created by joining LAN segments on the opposite sides of a switch. An "n" port switch can create a maximum of "n/2" LAN segments because each LAN segment is made up of (at a minimum) any two ports on the switch. The number of nodes or hosts on each segment is limited, generally, only by configuration rules and the bandwidth demand of each node.

Switch architecture is usually flexible because several hosts can share a segment (switch port) or a single host can have a dedicated segment to itself. To optimize throughput opportunities, servers can be provided with a dedicated segment that may be 10BASE-T, Token Ring, or high-speed connections like Fast Ethernet or FDDI.

The alternative, and lower-cost solution, is to divide your network so there are fewer users per segment and then dedicate bandwidth to shared devices such as servers. Although routers can be used to perform this segmentation task, keep in mind that they are more expensive, more complex to setup and administer, and typically slower than switches.

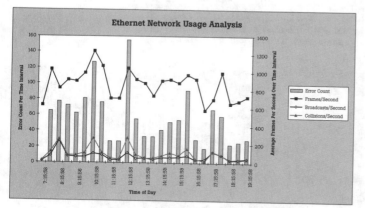

Figure G-22. *Partial Fluke* **HealthScan** *PC Software test results plotted from a LANMeter datalog file.*

How to decide if a switch would help

To increase network performance, switches are often a better choice than routers. The major benefit is that switching can be used with your existing installed base of NIC's, hubs and routers without redesigning the network significantly.

However, be aware that the introduction of switched technology into your network, despite the obvious advantages, is not a panacea for network performance problems. You need to be absolutely sure where the bottlenecks in your network reside before you begin to add switches. Also, remember that most switches are nothing more than fast, multiport bridges that experience many of the same problems that plague traditional bridged networks.

As already discussed, the increased demand for bandwidth may be caused by a number of factors. As a first step, check segment utilization and error rates, as well as the amount of broadcast traffic. The problem of too much broadcast traffic will not be resolved by a switch (bridges forward all broadcasts). Two options for performing this test exist: 1) use a monitoring tool to view performance "live" as a quick check (see Figure G-8), or 2) use statistical analysis to view performance over a longer time period as shown in Figure G-22.

If high utilization is caused by retransmissions due to errors, determine the types and sources of the detected errors. For Ethernet, if the majority of the errors are the result of various types of collisions, then a switch may reduce contention for the available bandwidth. (See Figure G-23.) In the case of both Ethernet and Token Ring, if utilization is high but errors are low, a switch may be of benefit by making more bandwidth available to each station.

When considering the addition of switches, it is essential to know the sources of high traffic. This information makes it easy to decide which users will benefit from a dedicated switch port. It is quite likely that a small percentage of the network users are consuming the majority of the available bandwidth. When this is the case, a single switch connecting those users and the network resources they are requesting may be enough to improve performance of the entire network. (See Figure G-24.)

It is sometimes beneficial to know which protocols are used most heavily, as well as the stations using those protocols. A higher–performance switch can isolate some protocols through routing features, so that those frames reach only the appropriate segments of your network.

A network baseline report (see Chapter 1) should be prepared for the network segment that you are examining. Armed with this information, you can determine whether increased network performance can be achieved by adding switches.

The optimum design would be for each device to have a dedicated path connected directly to each service required by the device. Since this is not realistic, compromise is called for. Careful implementation of switched technology can improve network performance. However, simply replacing existing shared–media hubs with switched–hubs will not generally result in significantly improved performance. To obtain the greatest benefit, some network redesign will be necessary.

Purchasing considerations

In order to decide which switch will provide the greatest benefit for your network, it is necessary to understand several additional concepts. Each vendor's equipment offers different performance for each of these parameters, and you will have to decide which is more important for your network when making performance trade–off decisions.

Latency

Switch latency is the time delay from the point when the switch starts receiving the packet to when it forwards the frame to the destination port. The major influence affecting latency is the forwarding technique used by the switch. For example, a cut–through switch has a fixed latency, usually about 40 microseconds, since it is designed to forward the packet after receiving the destination MAC address. The latency of a store-and-forward switch is dependent on the size of the frame since it must receive the complete frame before making the forwarding decision. To illustrate, a 1000-byte frame on a 10BASE-T network will have a minimum store-and-forward latency of 800 microseconds (1000 bytes = 8000 bits at 0.1 microseconds per bit).

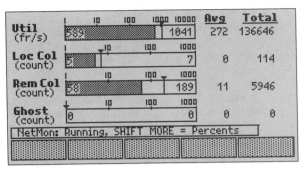

Figure G-23. Fluke LANMeter **Collision Analysis** test results.

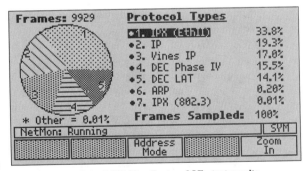

Figure G-24. Fluke LANMeter **IP Matrix** test results.

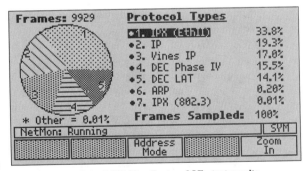

Figure G-25. Fluke LANMeter **Protocol Mix** test results.

Single and Multiple-MAC

A Single-MAC switch will store and support only one MAC address on each individual port. Single-MAC switches are primarily designed to allow connection of a single user or device to each switch port. This arrangement is most common for inexpensive switches that are designed to directly support individual end-users (desktop switch). A Multiple-MAC switch will allow connection of a number of MAC addresses to a single port (workgroup switch). For instance, a particular switch port may be connected to a shared media hub supporting multiple end-users. The actual number of MAC addresses that may be supported

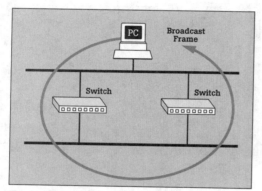

Figure G-26. *Functional diagram of a network with parallel bridged paths.*

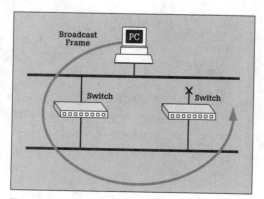

Figure G-27. *Functional diagram of a network with parallel bridged paths where spanning tree has blocked a path.*

by the switch varies from vendor to vendor, and often port-by-port on all but the most expensive switches. It is extremely important to be aware of the address limitations of the switch. If the number of MAC addresses exceeds the amount of storage available in the bridge forwarding database in the switch, it should forward any frame with an unknown address to all switch ports but might simply discard the frame.

Spanning tree

Ethernet does not normally permit two segments to be connected through more than one interconnect path. Segments or subnets connected by more than one path typically result in a "bridging loop." Since switches are essentially multiport bridges, they are exposed to the same types of problems as bridged networks, including bridging loops.

Figure G-26 shows how a bridging loop occurs when a broadcast frame is transmitted on one segment, bridged to another segment, and finally returned to the original segment via a different path. On returning to the first segment, the frame will be forwarded through the loop again and again. This situation is sometimes described as a broadcast storm, where the same broadcast frames circle endlessly and consume all available bandwidth.

Spanning tree protocol (usually IEEE 802.1d) allows bridging devices on the network to communicate with each other, and the spanning tree algorithm negotiates the optimum path as the forwarding path. All other paths are then blocked as shown in Figure G-27.

Additionally, the spanning tree algorithm monitors path failures and automatically opens an alternative path in order to recover from a path failure. Bridging loops may be inserted accidentally or through carelessness when a redundant backup path was intended. If the switch does not support the spanning tree protocol, great care should be taken to avoid bridging loops.

Management

Managing a switched network is challenging because a switch is in fact a multiport bridge, and that means managing the equivalent of a large distributed LAN. There are basically two methods available at this time. The most common method is where the internal switch management software gathers statistics on each frame forwarded by the switch and makes these statistics available through an SNMP management agent. This method allows the switch to be interrogated using SNMP from anywhere on the network and report statistics based on MIB I/II or RMON standards. The second method is known as port aliasing or "mirroring," where the switch forwards traffic seen on a particular port, or ports, to a specific designated "monitor port." Unfortunately, there are no standards related to port aliasing and the implementation is vendor-specific at this time.

Use of older traditional external monitoring tools (such as RMON probes, hardware or software protocol analyzers, or other handheld monitoring tools) is either ineffective or very difficult to implement in a switched environment. It is nearly impossible to gain a sense of what is taking place on a switched segment when you can only "see" the conversation passing through a selected port.

Full duplex

Full-duplex Ethernet performance significantly exceeds the performance of switched Ethernet. Full duplex requires a connection where both the switch and the host allow for simultaneous transmission and reception on each pair of the cable. This means that (under ideal circumstances), a full-duplex port can sustain 100% utilization on each channel, effectively producing a theoretical maximum of 200% utilization with no possibility of collisions. Unfortunately, full-duplex transmission is an expensive alternative, since the switch requires a full-duplex port and the connected device also requires an NIC card capable of supporting full-duplex technology.

Virtual LANs

A Virtual LAN, often called VLAN, may be considered a separate logical network or simply a collection of hosts in the same broadcast domain. This capability simplifies moves, additions, and changes to network configurations because it allows ports on the switch to be grouped into logical networks where unicast, broadcast and multicast packets are forwarded only to those stations contained in a Virtual LAN description table. Each Virtual LAN contains its own bridge MIB information and supports its own implementation of the spanning tree protocol. Unfortunately, at the time of this writing, there are no standards governing Virtual LANs and vendors have a unique methods of implementation, which may lead to interoperability problems when using equipment from different vendors.

Types of switches

Most LAN switch vendors provide a full complement of products that address the requirements of desktop, workgroup or segment, and backbone switching applications. However, each application has its own unique requirements and each vendor has optimized the different types of switch for these specific environments. The following information is designed to provide an insight into the requirements of each application:

	Backbone	Workgroup	Desktop
Price per port	Moderate/high	Moderate/low	Low
Port count	Scaleable (usually via cardslots)	Scaleable/fixed	Fixed
High-speed port count	Scaleable (FDDI, Fast Ethernet or ATM)	Expandable (Fast Ethernet)	Fixed
Packaging	Modular	Stackable	Fixed configuration
MAC addresses per port	High (usually greater than 1024)	Medium (usually greater than 512)	Low (often single MAC per port on all but one port)
Inter-networking	Full bridging, broadcast and packet filtering, spanning tree support, translational bridging and IP fragmentation for FDDI, Layer 3 routing capability	Full bridging, spanning tree support, translational bridging	Simple bridging
Fault tolerance	Redundant power supplies Hot swappable modules	Redundant power supply (possibly)	None
Management	Configuration management, SNMP MIB I/II or RMON capability	Configuration management, status monitoring	Status monitoring
Other	Virtual LAN support Aggregate performance Congestion tolerance	Virtual LAN support, congestion tolerance	Stackable, Virtual LANs

Appendix H — Glossary

Appendix H — Glossary of LAN Terms

10BASE2 An IEEE Standard for Thin Coax Ethernet networks—10 Mbps transmission, Baseband signaling, 185 meters per coax segment. Also known as Thinlan, Thinnet and Cheapernet. 10BASE2 is specified as part of the IEEE 802.3 and standard.

10BASE5 An IEEE standard for Thick Coax Ethernet networks—10 Mbps transmission, Baseband signaling, maximum 500 meters per segment. Also known as Thicknet.

10BASE-T An IEEE Standard for unshielded twisted pair Ethernet networks—10 Mbps transmission, Baseband signaling, requiring two pairs of Category 3, 4, or 5 unshielded twisted pair cable. Maximum allowable cable length is 100 meters.

100BASE-T4 An IEEE standard for Ethernet networks—100 Mbps transmission, Baseband signaling, requiring four pairs of Category 3, 4, or 5 unshielded twisted pair cable. Maximum allowable cable length is 100 meters.

100BASE-TX An IEEE standard for Ethernet networks—100 Mbps transmission, Baseband signaling, requiring two pairs of Category 5 unshielded twisted pair cable. Maximum allowable cable length is 100 meters.

802.12 A media access networking protocol that was developed by an industry consortium, and was commonly known as 100BASE-VG, 100-VG (AnyLAN), and other similar names. Upon adoption by the IEEE organization all references to "VG" were dropped, and a descriptive title replaced the short name.

Alignment error A frame received from the medium does not pass a test to ensure that the frame ends on a proper octet-boundary (there are no extra or missing bits necessary to form an 8-bit character out of the very last part of the message).

Abort delimiter A signal sent by a Token Ring station indicating that the message it was sending was terminated partway through the transmission, and is known to be incomplete. The station will then increment the soft error counter for Abort Delimiter Transmitted, and send a soft error report within two seconds.

Active monitor A single network interface card (NIC) on the ring that initiates the transmission of tokens and provides error recovery services on the ring. Any active NIC can become the active monitor when the current active monitor fails, or because of the claim token process.

Address Resolution Protocol (ARP) A mechanism whereby a station using the TCP/IP protocol is able to learn the MAC address of another station when it knows only the IP address. The ARP protocol is one of the TCP/IP protocols, and resides at the network layer. When a station knows the IP (Layer 3) address of another station it needs to communicate with, the first station will send a broadcast ARP frame on the local segment in order to learn which MAC (Layer 2) address should be used as the MAC layer destination address for messages intended for the known IP address. This local MAC address could be the destination station, or it could be the MAC address of a router.

Anomaly An impedance discontinuity causing an undesired signal reflection on a transmission cable.

AppleTalk A network protocol developed by Apple Computer. Included in AppleTalk are specifications for LocalTalk, EtherTalk and TokenTalk. Because of the very slow transfer rate of 250 kbps, LocalTalk is able to operate on unshielded, untwisted wire with little or no interference from a normal business environment. EtherTalk and TokenTalk permit connections to Ethernet and Token Ring, respectively.

ARCNET (Attached Resource Computer Network) A token bus local area network standard developed by Datapoint Corporation. ARCNET is typically configured in a star topology running on RG62 coax, twisted pair, or fiber optic cable with a basic signaling rate of 2.5 Mbps, and using active or passive hubs. A recent modification to the protocol now supports 20 Mbps signaling.

ATM (Asynchronous Transfer Mode) A data transfer technique based on a switching technology, similar to the public telephone network. (It contrasts with Ethernet and Token Ring, whose shared-media approach is similar to a party phone line.) In ATM, fixed length units of data (53 octets each) are transmitted at high rates of speed. The information sent over ATM can be a mix of voice, video and data. ATM promises very high transmission speeds (155 and 622 Mbps products are available), and is capable of handling voice, data, and video in LANs and WANs. ATM can be used "to the desktop," but is most common in backbone and WAN applications.

Attenuation A reduction in the strength of a signal; the opposite of gain. As attenuation increases, signal power decreases.

Attenuation-to-Crosstalk Ratio (ACR) The ratio of worst-case received signal level to noise level, measured at the receiver input (expressed in decibels). The ACR measurement may be expressed as NEXT (dB)-Attenuation (dB). The ACR measurement does not include noise intruding into the cable from external sources, (justifiably) assuming external noise to be insignificant. Higher ACR ratios provide better channel performance. When ACR equals zero, the desired signal is equal in strength to the noise, and cannot be decoded or recovered. See also Signal-to-Noise Ratio.

AUI (Attachment Unit Interface) A cable with a DB15 shell connector at either end used to connect a transceiver (Medium Attachment Unit) to a station adapter card—typically in a 10BASE5 environment.

Backbone A backbone is a central distribution and connection point for a segmented or campus style network. The individual segments are attached as "ribs" to the backbone, and through the backbone may access all other segments of the network. Many high-speed network concentrators or "stackable" hubs offer very high-speed backplanes, which can be implemented as "collapsed backbones," where the logical backbone of the network is entirely contained inside that device.

Balun An impedance-matching device that connects a balanced line (such as a twisted-pair cable) to an unbalanced line (such as a coaxial cable).

Bandwidth A measure of the information capacity of a transmission medium. The measurement is expressed in hertz (Hz) and describes the difference between the highest and lowest frequencies that the medium will pass.

Baseband A method of transmitting where the entire bandwidth of a medium is used to carry a single digital signal. See also broadband.

Basic Link A cable test configuration specified by EIA/TIA-568-A, TSB67, which includes two patch cables and up to 90 meters of solid-core twisted pair cable. The 90-meter segment may have one transition point along the way, such as a patch panel. See also channel.

Baud rate The switching speed of a signal. In low-speed transmissions the rate is measured in bits per second (bps). In higher-speed transmissions the expression of baud rate may not accurately represent the number of bits per second transmitted due to a variety of data compression techniques employed.

Beacon A MAC layer error frame transmitted by the NIC that detects a problem with the token claiming process or a station that detects a signal loss in an 802.5 Token Ring network. A beacon frame on the network indicates a serious problem such as a broken cable. A ring starts beaconing after normal error recovery methods, such as ring purge and monitor contention process, have failed.

Beaconing The condition of a ring that has one or more active stations transmitting beacon frames to indicate a failed segment of an 802.5 Token Ring network. Beacon frames are sent to all stations on a local ring, and indicate a hard failure of the network. The Token Ring protocol is able to recover from some types of hard failures through the beaconing process. Beaconing is always considered to be a serious network problem.

BNC A coaxial cable connector, used with thin coax (10BASE2) Ethernet networks.

Bridge A network device that connects two separately functional networks together at the OSI Data Link layer. A switch is a multi-port bridge, typically with additional router-like functionality. Bridges are used to form a single logical network to centralize network administration. See also repeater, router and gateway.

Bridging loop A condition in which parallel paths have been established between bridged network segments, and where the bridging protocol is not preventing messages from using the parallel paths to circle endlessly between the attached segments.

Broadband A method of transmitting where the bandwidth of a medium is shared by multiple signals. This transmission scheme is often used to transmit voice, data and video signals over a single medium. When a medium is used for broadband communications, each channel is separated by using different frequencies. Cable TV is an example of broadband communications. See also baseband.

Broadcast address The special protocol-specific address that means all stations on the logical segment. Frequently this is an address of all 1's.

Broadcast storm A condition in which most or all of the network traffic is made up of broadcast messages, and where normal network traffic is slowed or stopped as a result.

Brouter Offers the functionality of both a bridge and a router. Brouters can route one or more protocols, and bridge all other traffic. Brouter is a term created for marketing purposes to indicate product functionality at both the Data Link and Network layer.

Burst error A Token Ring soft error indicating that the reporting station failed to see any signal transitions for at least five half-bit times.

Burst mode protocol A method of increasing network throughput while still performing error checking at the Transport layer, developed by Novell for their NetWare network operating system. When burst mode is enabled, a software acknowledgment is required only after large blocks of data have been sent, instead of after each frame. However, if a failure is detected, the entire large block must be resent.

Bus topology A physical network design in which every device on the network segment is capable of (nearly) simultaneously receiving a signal transmitted by any other station on the segment. Bus topologies utilizing thin coaxial cable are often installed at smaller sites where the majority of stations are close together in groups, or where cost is a significant concern. See also ring topology and star topology.

Carrier Sense Multiple Access (CSMA) A network access method in which simultaneous station transmissions resulting in collisions are possible. When a collision occurs it can be resolved by several methods, including collision avoidance (CSMA/CA) and collision detection (CSMA/CD). CSMA/CD is defined by IEEE standard 803.3, and is most commonly referred to as Ethernet.

Channel A cable test configuration specified by TIA/EIA-568-A, TSB67, which includes all cables and connectors between the connection to the NIC card in a station and the associated hub or MAU port. This link can be up to 100 meters long, including up to 90 meters of solid core twisted pair wire with one transition point (such as a patch panel), and up to 10 meters of patch cables that are usually stranded twisted pair cable. See also basic link.

Characteristic impedance The total opposition (resistance and reactance) to the flow of ac current that a transmission line would have if it were infinitely long. In general, the greater the impedance, the shorter the distance current can be sent down a cable without regenerating the signal. This property depends on the physical characteristics of a cable that are determined at the time of manufacture. Manufacturing variations can cause slight differences in characteristic impedance for the same cable type.

Checksum A method of error checking that is implemented by most network protocols. Some portion of the message (always including the data cell) is passed through a complicated mathematical algorithm in order to obtain a unique number that represents a good message. The number is often appended to the end of the message. The receiving station uses the same process to obtain a checksum, which is then compared with the checksum included in the message by the sending station. If the two numbers match then the message is believed to be uncorrupted. If the numbers are different the message is discarded and an error generated.

Claim token A Token Ring frame that initiates an election process for a new active monitor station. Claim tokening can result from expired timers, or from any other condition that causes any station to suspect a problem with the current active monitor.

Client-Server A computing system in which processing is distributed among "clients" on the network that request information from "server(s)" that store data, let clients share data, coordinate printing operations, etc. Clients may communicate only with the server, and not directly with other clients. This restriction can be mitigated by running an application on the server that establishes a communications session individually with all of the clients, and routes requests between clients. To the clients that are thus communicating, the conversation appears to be direct. Security is usually a commonly implemented feature of Client-Server network operating systems. See also peer-to-peer.

Coaxial cable A type of cable in which the single inner conductor is surrounded by a tubular outer conductor, which acts as a shield. Coaxial cables typically have a wide bandwidth. Two types of coaxial cable are used with Ethernet networks, known as "thick" and "thin" for their respective diameters.

Collision The result of two stations simultaneously attempting to transmit data on a shared network transmission medium (such as Ethernet).

Collision domain A single CSMA/CD network segment. In 802.3 Ethernet, any station either on the same physical segment or separated by a repeater is within the same collision domain. Bridges and routers separate collision domains, while switches either partially or fully separate collision domains depending on how they are configured.

Collision fragment The measured signal on an Ethernet segment that results from a collision. This signal is almost always shorter than 64 octets, and does not pass a checksum test for corrupted data. See also runt packet.

Common-mode termination A type of cable termination where a pair of wires is terminated by a resistance matching the cable impedance, *and* by a similar termination between all pairs and signal ground. Common-mode terminated cables are less likely to allow disruption of network communications. See also differential-mode termination.

Community String A password used with the SNMP protocol. SNMP community strings are used for both *read only* and *read/write* privileges. A community string is case sensitive, and may include some punctuation characters. See also SNMP.

Concentrator A type of signal distribution center used in star topology networks. Concentrators typically have high port densities and card slots that accept several types of multi-port modules. The modules connect on a common backplane that causes all of the modules installed in the concentrator to appear as a single repeated connection away from each other. More advanced modules offer switching, bridging and routing capabilities. See also hub.

Controlled Access Unit (CAU) A network component that ties several lobe attachment modules (LAMs) into a Token Ring network. Each LAM allows multiple stations to connect to a Token Ring. The ring-in (RI) and ring-out (RO) ports of the CAU may be adapted to either copper or fiber optic cable. A CAU may also be used without any LAM units as a fiber optic-to-copper converter, or a repeater on the network.

Copper Data Distributed Interface (CDDI) A variation of FDDI proposed by Crescendo Communications that permits data to be transmitted at 100 Mbps across a copper cable connection. CDDI has been superseded by the adoption of 802.3u "Fast Ethernet" by the IEEE, and is encountered now only in legacy networks.

CRC (Cyclic Redundancy Checksum) See Checksum and Frame Check Sequence.

Crossed pair A wiring error in twisted pair cabling where a pair on one connector of the cable is wired to a different pair on the other end of the cable.

Crosstalk The introduction of unwanted signals from a nearby communication pair. Cables with multiple pairs are particularly susceptible to crosstalk. "Crosstalk" is often used as a verbal abbreviation for near-end crosstalk (NEXT).

Data Link Layer (DLL) The Open Systems Interconnection (OSI) standard defines the data link layer as layer 2 of the OSI 7-Layer basic reference model. Very generally stated, the data link layer breaks message sections into individual data bits for the physical layer (layer 1) to transmit across a network cable. At the receiving end, the data link layer reassembles the data bits back into a message section and verifies that it was not corrupted during the transfer. Additional services are provided to establish, maintain and release communications between the data link layers in other stations of the same local network. The data link layer is divided into the Logical Link Control (LLC) sub-layer, which interfaces with layer 3, and the Media Access Control (MAC) sub-layer, which interfaces with layer 1.

dB The abbreviation for decibel. A logarithmic unit of measure expressing the amplitude ratio between two signals.

DB-9 connector A modular connector used for shielded twisted-pair (STP) wiring. The DB-9 connector is assembled with 4 of 9 possible conductors used to accommodate 2 pairs of wires, and is a common connector used in Token Ring installations.

DC continuity A resistance measurement often used to verify end-to-end continuity of a cable or wire pair, and to determine the resistance value of the cable termination.

DELNI An industry adopted term indicating a multi-port transceiver, also known as a fan-out, and generally limited to AUI connections in Ethernet. Originally, this was a product introduced by Digital Equipment Corporation as the DEC Local Network Interconnect (DELNI).

Differential-mode termination A type of cable termination where a pair of wires is terminated by a resistance matching the cable impedance, but there is no termination resistance between that pair and any adjacent pairs. For low-frequency signals this is often acceptable, but for a high-frequency environment (whether due to high-speed network protocols, or due to transmission towers nearby), this allows large voltages to exist between one pair and an adjacent pair. See also common-mode termination.

DIX (Digital/Intel/Xerox) The early 1980s consortium of manufacturers that promoted the *Ethernet Version 1* and *Ethernet Version 2* variations of a CSMA/CD media access protocol. This DIX "standard" was then submitted to the IEEE, where after some modifications it was released as IEEE Standard 802.3. The DIX version did not include specifications for UTP or Fiber Optic cable.

Downstream The direction of data flow on a Token Ring network. Downstream is the opposite of upstream and represents the unidirectional transfer of data from one station to the next around the ring. Data flows from the *Ring In* to the *Ring Out* connections on a MAU, usually physically from left to right. On some 16 Mbps Token Rings a feature called *dual counter-rotating tokens* has been enabled, and data flows in both directions on a cable.

Drop cable A network cable used to attach a station to the network. This cable is attached between a station and a transceiver, hub or MAU. On Token Ring it is also known as a lobe cable. See also patch cable.

Ethernet A local area network protocol using Carrier Sense Multiple Access with Collision Detection (CSMA/CD). Ethernet is used as the underlying transport vehicle by several upper-level protocols, including Novell, TCP/IP and XNS. Ethernet is defined by the IEEE standard 802.3, and allows for signaling at 10 Mbps over several different cable mediums. See also fast Ethernet.

Fast Ethernet A 100 Mbps upgrade/revision to the IEEE 802.3 standard, specifically 802.3u-1995. For many parameters, it is simply a more rapid copy of the original Ethernet standard. However, due to the encoding and compression of data to achieve the higher throughput, several significant aspects of the physical signaling were changed.

Fault domain A fault domain defines the boundaries of an isolating soft error on a Token Ring network. The fault domain limits the problem to two stations, their connecting cables, and any equipment (a MAU, for example) between the two stations. The two stations involved are the station reporting the error and its Nearest Active Upstream Neighbor (NAUN).

Fiber optic cable A transmission medium that uses glass or plastic fibers, rather than copper wire, to transport signals. Signals are imposed on the fiber via pulses of light from a laser or light-emitting diode (LED). Fiber optic cable has a high bandwidth and is often selected because of its immunity to electromagnetic noise, high-speed transmission rates, and its ability to transmit relatively long distances between signal regeneration devices. Fiber optic cable is also often selected as the transmission medium for broadband applications.

Fiber optic Data Distributed Interface (FDDI) The ANSI X3T9.5 networking standard that permits data to be transmitted at 100 Mbps across a fiber optic or copper cable.

Frame A frame is a unit of data transmission. "Frame" often refers to a unit of data at layer 2 in the OSI 7-Layer model, though may be used at other layers. In Token Ring, a frame is a token that has been modified by a station to include data of some sort.

Frame Check Sequence (FCS) A field transmitted in many network protocols that encodes error checking information. The number placed in the FCS field is usually calculated based on a complicated mathematical algorithm, and represents a number unique to the pattern of data in that message. See also checksum.

Frame copy A Token Ring error that is reported by any ring station that believes that its MAC address may be in use by another ring station, creating a duplicate address problem.

Framing error An Ethernet error indicating that a frame had some number of extra bits (less than an additional octet), or that the frame was larger than the maximum (1518 octets) allowed. See also alignment error.

Frequency error A Token Ring soft error indicating that the reporting station measured an input signal clocked at the wrong frequency (usually only slightly different than the speed of the ring—not the other possible ring speed).

Ghost A new term coined by Fluke to mean energy (noise) detected on the cable that bears similarities to a real frame, but does not include a valid start frame delimiter. To qualify for this category of error, the event must be a minimum 72 octets. Ghosts are a strong indication of a physical problem on the local segment.

Gateway A network device that connects two separately functional networks together that have totally dissimilar protocols. Gateways operate up through the application layer (layer 7) of the OSI 7-Layer basic reference model. See also bridge, repeater and router.

Hard error A serious hardware or cable problem on the network that often requires manual intervention prior to resuming reliable operation.

Hermaphroditic connector A loopback or self-shorting connector typically used with Type 1 (STP) Token Ring cable.

Heterogeneous network A network assembled from a variety of cable types, brands and models of interface cards, media access protocols, transport protocols, and network operating systems. This type of network is typically found in a WAN environment, or an existing installed network. Most new networks tend to be implemented with very little variation of hardware and software (homogeneous), but quickly grow into heterogeneous networks. See also homogeneous network.

Homogeneous network A single-protocol, single-network operating system, a simple network often assembled with only one brand or model of interface card. The network may or may not be bridged or routed into a WAN environment. Homogeneous networks are rarely encountered, but tend to be the easiest to manage because the number of potential conflicts is reduced. See also heterogeneous network.

Hops The count of logical segments traveled, or hops, by a network message to reach its destination. Usually "hop" indicates that a message has crossed a routed connection, but may also indicate crossing a bridged or repeated connection.

Host A term often used to describe any device using the TCP/IP protocol (i.e., PC, workstation, server, printer, router, bridge, etc.).

Hub A network device used to connect other network devices in a star topology. Hubs are usually multi-port repeaters, but the term has become generalized and may indicate other types of equipment. The latest model hubs may offer "stackable" or common-backplane features that allow several physically independent hubs to be joined as one logical unit, and appear to the network as a single repeated connection. See also concentrator and MAU.

Impedance See characteristic impedance.

Interframe spacing The amount of idle time between frames required by the 802.3 Ethernet standard. The interframe spacing, or interframe gap, is 9.6 microseconds for 10 Mbps Ethernet.

Internal error A Token Ring error reported by any ring station that detects a recoverable problem with itself.

Internet An association of organizations including most universities, many businesses, and US government institutions such as ARPAnet, MILnet and NSFnet, that use TCP/IP protocols to form a single virtual network.

IP (Internet Protocol) A layer 3 protocol developed by a consortium of educational and research facilities as part of the US Government Advanced Research Projects Agency Network (ARPAnet) protocol commonly known as TCP/IP. For more detailed information on the current form of IP and TCP/IP, check the current Request For Comment (RFC) documents available online, and from most major university libraries.

IPX (Internetwork Packet Exchange) A layer 3 protocol developed by Novell for their NetWare network operating system.

Isolating error A type of soft error in Token Ring where the station addresses identified in the fault domain of a reported error limits the scope of the failure to those stations and the cable path between them. See also fault domain, non-isolating error.

Jam signal A physical layer signal sent on 802.3 Ethernet networks to reinforce or exaggerate a collision, so that other stations have enough time to detect the presence of the collision and act appropriately. A jam signal is at least 32 bits in duration, and is composed of any combination of binary data with the single exception that it may not form a valid checksum for data already transmitted prior to the collision.

Jabber A network fault condition described in the 802.3 Ethernet standard where one station is continuously transmitting data (longer than 20 milliseconds). Network protocols, such as Ethernet, specify maximum packet lengths that any one station may transmit before other stations are allowed to access the network. Jabber occurs when an Ethernet station has transmitted for an illegally long time. A jabber frame may have a valid or invalid FCS checksum, but is usually the result of noise or failed hardware. See also long frame.

Late collision An Ethernet collision that takes place on the local segment *after* 64 bytes of a frame have been received. Late collisions are usually detected only on coax networks, because the 10BASE-T monitoring station would have to be transmitting at the same time in order to detect a late collision. Late collisions may also be inferred by detecting the presence of a "jam" signal at the end of a frame that is larger than 64 bytes.

Latency The amount of delay time introduced (by a network component, such as cable, NIC cards, bridges, and routers) when forwarding a message. The duration of time measured from when the signal enters the component until it leaves again is the amount of propagation delay or latency introduced by that component.

Line error A Token Ring error reported by any ring station that detects an FCS checksum failure, or some type of protocol code violation in a received frame.

Layer One of seven levels in the Open Systems Interconnection (OSI) basic reference model. See also Open Systems Interconnection.

Link pulse A single bit test pulse that is transmitted not less frequently than between 25 and 150 milliseconds during idle periods on 10BASE-T link segments to verify link integrity.

Link segment The point-to-point full-duplex medium connection between two and only two medium dependent interfaces (MDIs). A link segment is usually the cable system used to attach a network device (i.e. workstation, printer, server, etc.) to a hub, MAU or concentrator.

Lobe cable A network cable used to attach a station to the network. This cable is attached between a station and a transceiver, hub or MAU. The lobe cable can be several cable segments connected together. On Ethernet it is also known as a drop cable. See also patch cable.

Local Area Network (LAN) A physical network technology used over short distances (up to a few thousand meters) to connect many workstations and network devices using a media access protocol such as Token Ring, or Ethernet. See also Wide Area Network (WAN).

Local collision An Ethernet collision that either creates an over-voltage state that is detected by the interface circuits in an NIC card on coax networks, or the NIC detects the presence of an inbound signal on the RX pair while transmitting on the TX pair. The simultaneous state of receiving and transmitting constitutes a local collision for 10BASE-T networks. Full Duplex Ethernet cannot have local collisions because "full duplex" means that both TX and RX are normally active at the same time.

Lobe Attachment Module (LAM) A network component that allows multiple stations to connect to a Token Ring. A LAM is connected into a controlled access unit (CAU) in order to join the local Token Ring. LAM units are available to receive either Type 1 or Type 3 cable connections.

Logical Link Control (LLC) **Layer** The OSI Data Link sub-layer protocol that allows for information to be sent and received with, or without, establishing a link to the LLC layer of another station. If no link is established the LLC layer does not perform error recovery or flow control. The LLC layer is associated with the upper-half of layer 2 of the OSI 7-Layer basic reference model. See also MAC layer.

Long frame A message that is illegally long, per the rules of the protocol. A long frame in Ethernet is longer than 1518 octets. Typically, a long frame will have a valid FCS checksum, and will be only slightly longer than allowed. See also jabber.

Lost frame A Token Ring error reported by any station that does see a transmitted frame return to it before a timer expires.

Medium Access Control (MAC) **Layer** The OSI Data Link sub-layer protocol that controls and mediates access to the network. It allows for, but operates independently of, the physical characteristics of the medium in enabling the exchange of data. The MAC layer is associated with the lower half of layer 2 of the OSI 7-Layer basic reference model. See also LLC layer.

MAU See Multi-Station Access Unit and Medium Attachment Unit.

Manufacturer prefix The first half (first three octets) of a MAC address. Manufacturers of network components obtain unique blocks of addresses to hard-code into their products. The prefix of the address is thus predefined in blocks, while the remainder of the address uniquely identifies the device. Lists of the issued prefixes are not published except by permission of the manufacturer.

Margin The distance between a measured test result and the limit imposed by the networking standard. In cable testing the margin headroom is the most important factor, and indicates the worst margin result detected during a twisted-pair cable test. Margin is usually used in relation to NEXT test results.

Medium A physical carrier of an energy signal. Common network medium examples include unshielded twisted pair (UTP), screened UTP (ScTP), shielded twisted pair (STP), coaxial, and fiber optic cable.

Medium Attachment Unit (MAU) Also known as a transceiver, a MAU is used to connect a device to the IEEE 802.3 transmission medium (cable), and is common in 10BASE5 environments. The MAU contains a small amount of circuitry to interface directly with the coax cable, while the majority of the circuitry and all of the software remains with the adapter card in the device. An AUI cable is used to connect the station to the MAU.

MTU (Maximum Transmission Unit) A configuration parameter used for all network interconnect devices (bridges, routers, etc.) and many network operating systems. The MTU parameter establishes the largest frame size that should be transmitted onto the medium, or the largest frame size that will pass through a LAN or WAN path. If larger frame sizes are encountered they will either be fragmented according to the rules of the protocol, or discarded. An error may or may not be generated when an over-large frame is discarded. WAN paths frequently have smaller MTU sizes than LAN protocols. Also, different LAN protocols almost always have different frame sizes (the largest Ethernet frame is 1,518 octets (including the header), while Token Ring frame sizes can reach 4,500 octets or 18,000 octets, depending on ring speed).

Multi-Station Access Unit (MAU or MSAU) A wiring concentrator for lobes on a Token Ring network that provides the means for attaching devices to the ring. Devices are physically attached to the MSAU with individual point-to-point cable connections, creating a star topology network. A MAU uses electromechanical relays to physically connect or remove stations from a ring. A given MAU may be passive or active. An active MAU is aware of the behavior of stations connected to it, and will disconnect a station that is disrupting the flow of data on a ring.

NAUN (Nearest Active Upstream Neighbor) The active station that is directly upstream from a given station. Within a Token Ring network data is described as flowing in a downstream direction; therefore, a particular station's NAUN is the station transmitting to it. Perhaps more accurately, NAUN indicates the Nearest *Addressable* Upstream Neighbor because some monitoring devices are able to observe data on the ring without actually participating in the process.

NEXT (Near-end Crosstalk) Signal leakage from one twisted pair to a neighboring twisted pair, measured at the same end of the cable as the disturbing signal source. The amount of signal that crosses over from one pair to the other pair is measured on the idle pair, and represented as a NEXT test result.

NetWare Link Services Protocol (NLSP) Also sometimes referred to as NetWare Link State Protocol, it is a link-state protocol used to supply routing information to all neighboring routers. NLSP was developed by Novell.

NIC Network Interface Card The printed circuit assembly that provides an interface between a network device and the network. The NIC plugs into a network station and connects that station to the network through the network cable.

Node Any active device on a network may be described as a node, or discrete connection point. Other terms include; station, workstation and device.

Non-isolating error A type of soft error in Token Ring where, due to the specific nature of the particular error type, the scope of the failure may not be limited to the station addresses identified in the fault domain and the cable path between them. See also fault domain, isolating error.

NVP Nominal Velocity of Propagation The speed of signal propagation through a cable, expressed as a percentage of the speed of light in a vacuum. Typically, the speed of the electrical signal in a cable is between 60% and 80% of the speed of light.

Octet A term indicating exactly eight binary bits as a group or unit. A less precise term for *octet* is *byte*.

Open A break in the continuity of a circuit, which prevents signal transmission.

Open Systems Interconnection (OSI) A theoretical 7-Layer basic reference model used for defining, specifying and referencing communications protocols published by the International Organization for Standardization (ISO) as the Open Systems Interconnection (OSI) model. The OSI model describes network operations in terms of seven functional layers, and describes the specific tasks or functions that must be performed by, or available, at each of those layers. For more information see ISO 7498:1984 [10].

Layer 7. Application	Provides interface with network users.
Layer 6. Presentation	Performs format and code conversion.
Layer 5. Session	Manages connections for application programs.
Layer 4. Transport	Ensures error-free, end-to-end delivery.
Layer 3. Network	Handles internetwork addressing and routing.
Layer 2. Data Link	Performs local addressing and error detection.
Layer 1. Physical	Includes physical signaling and interfaces.

Packet A group of bits in a defined format, containing a data message that is sent over a network. Packet is usually used to describe a network message unit at OSI layer 3.

Patch cable A network cable used to attach one network distribution device to another, such as between hubs and MAUs or between ports on patch panels. Other cables known as drop cables or lobe cables are used to connect stations to the network. See also drop cable and lobe cable.

Peer-to-Peer A relationship between two processes that use common procedures to send or receive messages. A peer-to-peer computing system allows each station to communicate directly with each other station, with equal access to the resources of all stations. Thus, station one could read or write a file on a storage device in station two without the operator at station two intervening. Peer-to-peer networks are often installed where network security is not as significant an issue as sharing of resources such as storage devices and printers. Security may be implemented on a peer-to-peer network if the operating system allows for that feature. See also client-server.

Phantom drive A DC voltage level applied by a Token Ring station that will cause a relay in a MAU to change states and connect the station to the network.

Plenum cable Cable which has been certified for installation in air ducts and open spaces over suspended ceilings without conduit. Plenum cable is fire-resistant and does not emit toxic fumes until exposed to a very high heat.

Preamble The binary timing information that precedes an Ethernet message at the physical layer, and allows the receiving stations to synchronize their clock circuits on the incoming message so the data can be retrieved without error.

Propagation delay The amount of signal delay caused by the medium. See also latency and (NVP).

Protocol A specific set of rules, procedures or conventions that control the format and timing of data communications that stations must follow to exchange information on a network. The three fundamental categories that protocols fall into are bit-, byte- and character-oriented.

Protocol analyzer A complicated test device that allows network support staff to view and manipulate the entire contents of a signal retrieved from the network medium. Recent software improvements have reduced the amount of technical knowledge required of the operator by including databases of common patterns that are used to post-process the signal and suggest potential problems or solutions.

Purge A Token Ring frame sent by the active monitor station that causes all other ring stations to stop transmitting, reset certain timers and parameters to default values, and then wait for a new token to be originated before resuming normal operations. Purge frames are the primary mechanism used by the active monitor to restore proper ring operation.

Range error An Ethernet error where the length field inside the frame described a different number of octets than what was actually counted by the receiving station. This error can also happen when the length field indicates a frame so small that the frame would not meet the Ethernet minimum-size requirements.

Receiver congestion A Token Ring error reported by any ring station that receives a frame addressed to itself, but has no room in its buffer to store the frame. The frame is then discarded, and within two seconds the station will report how many times this happened over the reporting period.

Remote collision An Ethernet collision where the *local collision* characteristics are not met, but the frame is shorter than the minimum legal frame size, and the FCS checksum fails. See also collision fragment and local collision.

Repeater A signal regeneration device that is used to extend the length of a network. Repeaters operate at the physical layer (layer 1) of the OSI 7-layer model. Repeaters forward all messages transmitted on the local segment. Repeaters are often used to connect small numbers of stations to a network from slightly distant sites. See also bridge, router and gateway.

Report soft error frame A MAC frame that is transmitted when an intermittent, or soft, error is detected. The report soft error frame contains information about the error(s) on the ring, and is sent only every two seconds. Each frame contains a count of the quantity of the soft error(s) being reported for that reporting interval.

Return loss A measure of the effect of mismatches in impedance at all locations along the cable link. The primary impact of increases in return loss is increased signal jitter.

Reversed pair A wiring error in twisted-pair cabling where the pins on a pair are reversed between connectors on each end of the cable (pin 1 is connected to pin 2 at the other end, and pin 2 is connected to pin 1 at the other end, for instance).

Ring See Token Ring and ring topology.

Ring topology A physical network layout structure in which each station is connected to the next station to form a complete loop. Networks are not commonly configured as true ring topologies because of the inconvenience of routing cables, but are more frequently configured as star topologies. Token Ring is an example of a network protocol that may be wired as a ring topology. See also bus topology and star topology.

RJ-45 connector An 8-pin modular connector used for network cable systems. The RJ-45 connector has eight conductors to accommodate four pairs of wires and has become the dominant connector used in twisted pair network installations. Other uses of the RJ-45 connector include connecting sophisticated telephone desk units to wall jacks through untwisted wire. Untwisted wire should never be used with networking equipment.

Router A network device that connects two separately functional networks together that have similar or different protocols. Routers operate up through the network (layer 3) layer of the OSI seven-layer protocol standard. Routers are often used to isolate traffic on a network where the conversation is between two stations on the same segment, forwarding only those messages that are intended for stations more distant than the local segment. See also bridge, repeater and gateway.

Routing protocols There are two basic types of routing information protocol algorithm: link-state and distance-vector. Link-state routing protocols send updates only when the network topology changes, unlike distance-vector routing protocols, which send periodic updates (usually every 30, 60 or 90 seconds). By not sending routing information updates unless there is new information, the adverse impact on a local link is reduced. This reduction of overhead traffic is particularly important in WAN environments where telecommunications links are relatively slow. Examples of link-state routing protocols include NetWare Link Services Protocol (NLSP) and Open Shortest Path First (OSPF). An example of a distance-vector routing protocol is Routing Information Protocol (RIP).

Runt An Ethernet frame that is shorter than the valid minimum packet length, usually caused by a collision. The term is imprecise, and may indicate a collision, collision fragments, a short frame with a valid FCS checksum, or a short frame with an invalid FCS checksum.

Screened UTP (ScTP) Foil screened UTP has been written as either (ScTP) or (FTP) for some time, though the ScTP designation has recently gained in popularity. The 100 twisted-pair cable has a foil screen around the inside of the outer jacket, but the individual pairs are not screened.

Segment A physical or logical portion of a network. An example of a logical segment is the cable, connectors, hubs, repeaters, etc., attaching together some number of network devices on a CSMA/CD LAN. A CSMA/CD segment is also known as a collision domain, and would not cross any bridges or routers, but would include everything up to any bridge or router connections.

Shielded Twisted Pair (STP) Cable that is both twisted by pairs and shielded. This eliminates crosstalk to a greater degree than UTP cable and minimizes crosstalk at high transmission rates. The 150 twisted-pair cable has a shield around the inside of the outer jacket, and around each of the individual twisted pairs.

Short frame An Ethernet frame that is shorter than the legal size of 64 octets, but with a valid FCS checksum indicating that, except for being too short, it is a good frame.

Signal-to-Noise Ratio (SNR) The ratio of worst-case received signal level to noise level, measured at the receiver input (expressed in decibels). The SNR may be expressed as NEXT(dB)-Attenuation(dB). The SNR measurement includes noise intruding into the cable from external sources. The Higher SNR ratios provide better channel performance. See also Attenuation-to-Crosstalk Ratio.

SNMP (Simple Network Management Protocol) Part of the TCP/IP protocol suite, SNMP is governed by the RFC process instead of a formal standard (see the Operation section of Appendix D). Other than proprietary protocols, SNMP is the only common method of managing network devices remotely. Virtually all network interconnect (switches, bridges, routers, etc.) and WAN devices offer SNMP management support capabilities. SNMP data is obtained by issuing queries and commands from a network management console (or similar device) to an SNMP agent. An agent is the SNMP monitoring process running on a network device that makes available certain information about the device. In order to access the agent, an SNMP Read Only or Read/Write *community string* (password) must be known. In addition to the community string, a variety of other security features are available. In addition to direct access of the agent, a network management platform may be used to configure an agent to send unsolicited *traps* back to the management platform when specific events occur. A trap is simply a report sent by an agent whenever a predetermined event is detected, usually when a selected threshold is exceeded or when an error is detected. A typical SNMP query appears as a string of integers separated by periods, along with one of four commands. The four basic commands are GET, GET NEXT, SET and REPLY.

Soft error An intermittent error on a Token Ring network that interferes with the normal flow of messages on the local ring.

Split pair The error of using one wire from each of two different twisted pairs to transmit or receive. The cable may have correct pin-to-pin continuity between ends but, because the transmission circuit is split between two twisted pairs, this error cancels the crosstalk elimination characteristics of using twisted pair wiring and produces crosstalk. Use a single twisted pair for transmit and another twisted pair for receive to minimize crosstalk.

SQE (Signal Quality Error) Also referred to as heartbeat, is a signal sent by transceivers after a frame is transmitted in order to verify the connection, and is also used by the transceiver to notify the station that a collision was detected. The SQE is primarily used in 10BASE5 environments as a test signal to reassure the station that the transceiver is still operating properly. Some older network devices will not operate properly unless SQE is enabled; almost all new devices do not require SQE. SQE should always be disabled when a transceiver is connected to a repeater (including a 10BASE-T hub), or if it is not required.

Star topology A physical network layout structure in which a cable from each individual station is brought to a central connection point such as a HUB or MAU. The star topology is becoming the most commonly installed network topology because of the ease of maintenance and reduced impact to other users in the event of a cable failure. Most network protocols may be configured as star topologies, including ARCNET, Ethernet and Token Ring. See also bus topology and ring topology.

Start Frame Delimiter (SFD) A binary pattern at the end of eight octets of timing information in an Ethernet frame that tells the receiving station that the timing information is over, and all subsequent signal represents an actual frame. The pattern is two 1's after a long string of alternating one, zero, one, zero, etc. The one octet SFD field is 10101011 in binary.

Subnet The process of dividing a TCP/IP address range into smaller address blocks, or the network portion of a TCP/IP address block with all of the host bits set to zero.

Subnet mask A 32-bit string of 1's and 0's that is logical ANDed with a TCP/IP address in order to learn which part is the network address, and which part is the host address. A subnet mask is usually represented in dotted-decimal notation (255.255.255.0, for example).

Symbolic name A symbolic name is the arbitrary name label used to associate an address with a user or network resource to make it easier for network maintenance staff to identify (JOES_PC vs C003E8000008, for example).

TCP/IP A popular protocol developed for the US Government Defense Department by a consortium of colleges and research institutions. TCP/IP is actually a suite of protocols, and is governed by a consensus process using Request For Comment (RFC) documents rather than an official standards organization. TCP/IP can be operated over a variety of media access protocols, such as Ethernet and Token Ring.

TDR (Time Domain Reflectometry) A technique for measuring cable lengths by timing the duration between when a test pulse is issued and when the reflected pulse from an impedance discontinuity on the cable (such as an open at the end of the cable) returns to the measuring point.

TDX (Time Domain Crosstalk) A new technique pioneered by Fluke for isolating the location of a near-end crosstalk problem along the length of a twisted pair cable. The screen display is similar to a standard TDR test, except that the faults shown are related to crosstalk instead of shorts, opens and other impedance discontinuities.

Terminator A resistor connected to the end of a coax cable which is intended to match the characteristic impedance of the cable. Signals are dissipated in the terminator, eliminating reflections. Twisted-pair cables are typically terminated inside of the network device as a part of the circuitry design.

TIA/EIA-568-A The Electronic Industries Association/Telecommunications Industry Association's Commercial Building Telecommunications Wiring Standard (Revision A). Specifies maximum cable lengths, installation practices, and performance specifications for generic building wiring.

Token A frame that gives a station permission to transmit on a Token Ring network. A token consists of information that identifies it as the token and that tells the receiving station that it is ready to be made into a frame.

Token error A Token Ring error reported by the station performing the job of active monitor. Token errors are reported when several conditions are true, such as when a timer expires indicating that it has been too long since a token was last seen, or when an illegal code violation is detected in the start delimiter of a token or frame.

Token Ring A network arranged in ring or star topology and which uses token passing to control access. Token Ring has been defined to operate at 4 or 16 Mbps per the IEEE 802.5 standard.

Token Ring protocol A network protocol based on collision avoidance. Collision avoidance is accomplished by passing permission, in the form of an electronic token, to a station prior to allowing it to transmit onto the network. Token Ring may be used as the underlying transport vehicle by several upper-level protocols, including Novell and TCP/IP.

Topology The organization of network components. The topology of Token Ring network components is in a ring or star. Adding or removing a Token Ring station changes the topology, because it introduces or removes another cable on a star topology.

Transposed pair A wiring error in twisted-pair cabling where a twisted pair is connected to a completely different set of pins at both ends (instead of pin 1 to pin 1, and pin 2 to pin 2, the cable is incorrectly wired pin 1 to pin 8, and pin 2 to pin 7, for example).

Trap An unsolicited report sent by an SNMP agent to an SNMP management platform based on a predetermined event. Reported events include when thresholds are exceeded or when errors are detected. See also SNMP.

TSB67 Part of the EIA/TIA-568-A standard. TSB67 describes the requirements for field testing an installed Category 3, 4 or 5 twisted pair network cable.

Twisted pair A pair of wires that are twisted together to minimize crosstalk. Crosstalk is minimized by canceling the magnetic fields generated in each of the two twisted wires. Twisted-pair cable (UTP, ScTP or STP) is typically made up of several twisted pairs of wires within a surrounding protective sheath. The cable may or may not be shielded.

Unshielded Twisted Pair (UTP) Cable that is twisted by pairs but not shielded. This minimizes crosstalk by canceling the magnetic fields generated in each of the twisted wires, but only when a pair of wires are twisted together and used for transmit or receive.

Upstream Upstream is in the opposite direction to that of the data flow on a Token Ring network. See also downstream.

Virtual LAN A logical network segment established using switches that may cross WAN and routed connections transparently to the user. VLAN segments may be established based on selected switch ports, or based on OSI layer 2 or 3 addresses.

VINES (VIrtual NEtworking System) A network operating system customized for enterprise networking offered by Banyan Systems Inc.

Wide Area Network (WAN) Two or more local area networks (LANs) that are connected by microwave, satellite, telephone or other long-distance signal transmission technique.

Wiremap A cable test used to determine whether each pin has connectivity with the appropriate pin at the other end of the cable. A wiremap test is also required to test for split pairs.

Notes

FLUKE ®

Appendix I — Index

Appendix I — Index